It Is Union and Liberty

It Is Union and Liberty

Alabama Coal Miners and the UMW

Edited by Edwin L. Brown and Colin J. Davis

THE UNIVERSITY OF ALABAMA PRESS

Tuscaloosa and London

Copyright © 1999
The University of Alabama Press
Tuscaloosa, Alabama 35487-0380
All rights reserved
Manufactured in the United States of America
1 2 3 4 5 6 7 . 05 04 03 02 01 00 99

Cover design by Gary Gore

∞
The paper on which this book is printed meets the minimum requirements of
American National Standard for Information Science–Permanence of Paper for
Printed Library Materials, ANSI Z39.48-1984.

Library of Congress Cataloging-in-Publication Data

It is union and liberty : Alabama coal miners and the UMW /
edited by Edwin L. Brown and Colin J. Davis.
p. cm.
Includes bibliographical references and index.
ISBN 0-8173-0999-3 (alk. paper)
ISBN 0-8173-1000-2 (pbk. : alk. paper)
1. United Mine Workers of America History. 2. Trade-unions—Coal
miners—Alabama—History. 3. Coal miners—Alabama—History. I.
Brown, Edwin L. II. Davis, Colin J. (Colin John), 1954–
HD6515.M616 U554 1999
331.88'122'109761—dc21
99-6205

British Library Cataloguing-in-Publication Data available

If you work at a non-union mine, you are required to disclaim any connection with any labor organization; you must work for wages and under conditions fixed by the company. In fact, you must do anything that the "boss" requires of you. He can dock you, he can fine you, he can lay you off, or he can fire you out, and you have no appeal. . . . It is union and liberty, or it is individualism and slavery.

—*Birmingham Labor Advocate,* October 28, 1899

Contents

Acknowledgments   ix

Introduction   1
Edwin L. Brown and Colin J. Davis

1. The Early Years: Alabama Miners Organize,
    1878–1908   11
    Daniel Letwin

2. Having It Their Way: Alabama Coal Operators and the Search
    for Docile Labor, 1908–1921   38
    Brian M. Kelly

3. Rising from the Ashes: Alabama Coal Miners,
    1921–1941   62
    Peter Alexander

4. Alabama Coal Miners in War and Peace,
    1942–1975   84
    Glenn Feldman

5. Wildcats, Caravans, and Dynamite: Alabama Miners and the
    1977–1978 Coal Strike   111
    Robert H. Woodrum

    Appendix: Officers of the United Mine Workers of America
    District 20, 1898–1998   131

    Notes   133

    Bibliography   165

    Contributors   179

    Index   181

Acknowledgments

The editors wish to express their appreciation and indebtedness to Alison Schmied, who spent hours correcting our errors, and Charmagne Sturgis in the preparation of the manuscript. Each of the editors and authors also expresses thanks to the officers (especially John Stewart, Wilburn Lollar, and Gary Pickett), members, and retirees of the United Mine Workers of America District 20.

The editors are also grateful to Nicole Mitchell and Mindy Wilson at the University of Alabama Press for their guidance and support throughout this project. Thanks are also due to the copy editor, Jonathan Lawrence.

The following have given permission for inclusion of extracts from their works named, and for the use of photographs; this permission is gratefully acknowledged:

The University of North Carolina Press. Materials from Chapters 3, 4, and 5 of *The Challenge of Interracial Unionism: Alabama Coal Miners, 1878–1921,* by Daniel Letwin. Copyright © 1997.

Photographs from the Birmingham Public Library Photographic Archives, General Collection.

Photographs by Lewis Hine from the University of Maryland Baltimore County, Bafford Collection.

Photographs by Arthur Rothstein from the Library of Congress, Farm Security Administration.

Photographs were also supplied by Bonnie Groves, director of the Alabama Mining Museum, and Dennis K. Hall, director of public relations, Jim Walter Resources, Inc.

It Is Union and Liberty

Introduction

Edwin L. Brown and Colin J. Davis

The year 1998 marks the centennial in Alabama of District 20 of the United Mine Workers of America (UMW). The miners' history is a rich tradition of combativeness and sacrifice. From the first, Alabama coal miners saw the union as the vehicle that could best effect progress in their living and working conditions. The history of the men and women who dug Alabama's coal is one of struggle and defeat, yet also one of remarkable victories. An extraordinary line of leaders, black and white, mostly native-born, played a major part in the politics of the union, and by the twentieth century theirs would be the most influential voice in Alabama's labor movement. It was a voice that consistently called for progressive reform, including elimination of child labor, abolition of the convict lease and county fee system, free public education and textbooks, and the right of all workers, regardless of race, to organize.

In a state where racial segregation was the norm, the UMW stood as a beacon of interracial organization. Challenged by coal operators and political elites (who were often one and the same), Alabama miners were at the center of the fight for economic justice, offering a radical alternative to the prevailing racial animus that gripped the South following the Civil War. *It Is Union and Liberty* surveys the history of Alabama's working coal miners through a chronological narrative that details their lived experience.

Until the 1950s, most Alabama coal miners lived in company towns in four-room clapboard houses. One turn-of-the-century observer, after traveling throughout the district, reported living conditions "among the worst he had ever seen."[1] Pay was in company scrip (called "clacker" in Alabama),

Progressive photographer Lewis Hine documented child labor in Alabama's coalfields in a 1912 trip through the state. The boy pictured here was a greaser. Lewis Hine Collection, University of Maryland Baltimore County Library.

and the tools that miners were required to furnish as a condition of employment, the blasting powder they needed to expose and remove the coal, and even everyday necessities like cornmeal, flour, syrup, white meat, and beans ("Esau" to the miners) were all purchased at the company commissary ("pluck me's"), often at inflated prices. The company controlled and disciplined its workforce through the blacklist, yellow-dog contracts, indebtedness, the convict lease, and finally through security officers (called "whipping bosses" or "shack rousters" by the miners). John Drain, a retired miner, remembered his Irish-immigrant father being hired as a whipping boss based solely on his reputation as a brutal, no-holds-barred fighter in the saloons of Cullman County.[2] The coal operators left little to chance.

Hardship, while part and parcel of everyday life in the coal camps, steeled the miners' will to improve the lot of all workers. Thomas Duke Park, Birmingham and Jefferson County's first public-health officer, de-

The Thomas Works Company Store. Such stores were often called "pluck me's" by the miners. No date. General Collection, Birmingham Public Library Archives.

scribed the resolve of union miners and their families when confronted by heavily armed police forces and militia during the pivotal strike of 1908:

The militia is passing . . . as I write, coming and going to the scene of the strike in various parts of the county. This present strike has exemplified many things. It shows how the forces of government always come in the end to hold up the house of have, to uphold property. Deputy sheriffs using their guns to kill rather than defend themselves precipitated the present disorder and of course the militia is called out . . . to suppress disorder originated by our bloodthirsty constabulary. . . . For the union man to endeavor to dissuade a non-union man is considered a terrible offense by this gentry here.[3]

District 20 president J. R. Kennamer knew the 1908 strike was a key moment for the UMW in Alabama, representing the confrontation as a "life or death" struggle for better conditions of employment.[4]

It Is Union and Liberty has five integrated essays that capture this and other key moments in the UMW's history. The authors are engaged in pri-

Interior of the Imperial Coal and Coke Company Commissary, circa 1935. Photograph courtesy of the Alabama Mining Museum, Dora, Alabama.

mary research on Alabama coal miners, and each represents the cutting edge of the new social and political history being written today. Their work shares a consistent theme on the permanence of class in determining power in the state of Alabama. Race, while vital to any understanding of southern labor history, was not the sole factor in working people's lives. As these authors show, Alabama miners, black and native white, had much in common, and they knew it. The earliest District 20 contract proposals demanded equal pay for equal work, regardless of color. Birmingham's weekly trade union press, the *Labor Advocate,* reporting on the 1900 UMW convention (just a year before Jim Crow legislation passed the Alabama legislature), noted that black and white miners not only met together but sang together. A black miner, Charles Farley, it reported, gained the convention floor and led a "rousing" sing-a-long to the tune of the old gospel song "We Are Marching to Canaan":

Who is there among us,
The true and the tried
Who'll stand by his fellows,
Who's on the Lord's side?[5]

Biracial meetings were risky undertakings in an environment that separated the races by custom and legal stricture.

The UMW's history stands as a counter to much of the contemporary orthodoxy that characterizes the trade union movement in the South as exclusionary and racially fragmented. Other scholars, notably Eric Arnesen in his work on New Orleans longshoremen at the turn of the century, and Michael Honey in his book on Memphis workers discuss similar experiences with racial solidarity in the South. On the political level, Robin Kelley's work on Alabama Communists did much the same.[6]

All of this is not to say that race was not an important factor, for the authors all agree that it was. In the end, however, scant research has been done on the influence of race or class upon Alabama workers, save Philip Taft's institutional history of Alabama organized labor and recent work by Robert J. Norrell and Henry McKiven about steelworkers in the Birmingham district.[7] Two recent edited collections by Robert Zieger have incorporated new approaches to labor history in the South and have addressed notions of southern exceptionalism. These two outstanding collections build on earlier works by Gary Fink and Merl Reed.[8] With the exception of Robert Ward and William Rogers's survey of the 1894 strike, the history of Alabama coal miners has yet to be written.[9]

The publication of these essays comes at an exciting time in U.S. labor history. The subdiscipline has actively engaged the twin themes of race and labor. According to Eric Arnesen, "the study of race and labor has become an academic growth industry."[10] Playing a substantial role in this "growth industry" was Herbert Hill's critique of American trade unions as "white job trusts." Hill's critique of Herbert Gutman's study of black UMW officials during the Gilded Age as mythicizing cross-racial alliances has galvanized labor historians to look more closely at the twin issues of race and labor.[11] The authors in this collection represent this increasing attention. This collection clearly makes the case that the issue is far more ambiguous than Hill suggests. True, the UMW did not push for social equality, but on the critical issue of equal pay the union maintained its ground that there should be no disparity between the races. Just as vital, the membership was open to all coal miners regardless of race.

These authors also highlight that Alabama coal miners shared much with their counterparts throughout the United States. Scholars have described southern workers as peculiarly romantic and hedonistic, and as separate from the American labor experience. W. J. Cash, writing a half century ago, characterized southern workers as noteworthy for their "simple childlike psychology and curious romantic-hedonistic heritage," unable to sustain the concerted effort required of organization, frequently powerless, and motivated by base emotion rooted in virulent racism.[12] Moreover, industrial workers especially did not fit the idyllic stereotype and mythology of the rural South. Their lives, when examined at all, remained on the periphery of the regional experience. *It Is Union and Liberty* provides an antidote to that view and arrives at a most exciting time as the notions of race and ethnicity, social construction, class, and group interdependence have captured the attention of social, political, and labor historians.[13]

In the first chapter, Daniel Letwin introduces the reader to the formative years of the coal industry in Alabama and the emergence of an organized and militant labor force. During the late nineteenth century, miners' grievances revolved principally around issues of pay (determined by tonnage at the tipple) and working conditions. A series of strikes, beginning in 1888 and culminating in 1908 with the defeat of the UMW, reveals the lengths to which the operators would go to defeat the union. As will be echoed throughout this volume, the miners confronted powerful opponents willing to use every weapon, including violence, to subdue them. Armed private police (sometimes paid for with state revenues), compliant state and local authorities, and the convict lease—established in 1866 to control and discipline freedmen—all circumscribed the UMW's efforts at reform. Another consistent theme noted by all the authors of this volume was the attempt by coal operators to use race to divide the workforce.

Letwin sets the stage by detailing how Alabama miners created a defensive organization primarily to counter the enormous power of the coal operators and their political allies. The union's successes were few, modest, and always fleeting. The Greenback Party of the 1870s, followed by the immensely popular Knights of Labor (two communities in Birmingham, Trevellick and Powderly, bear the names of the founders of the order) and finally the United Mine Workers, created a rich tradition of defense of the rights of all working people in Alabama. Although the UMW faced devastating defeats in the early years, and utter ruin in 1908, the operators could not erase the miners' memory of the union.

Chapter 2, by Brian Kelly, sketches the reemergence of District 20 as a dynamic and powerful voice for coal miners a decade after the 1908 defeat. Kelly's essay discusses the employers' determined efforts to eliminate any vestiges of the miner's union. Indeed, the union, which had swelled to 20,000 during the 1908 strike, counted fewer than 700 members at the strike's end. Again the operators used raw force, followed by an insidious exploitation of race to alienate the miners from the wider community. The union held out for two months, aided, in part, by small farmers. Once the governor intervened on the side of the coal operators, the union could not sustain the strike. Unable to change or influence their working conditions, Alabama miners left the state in droves, mostly for the mines of the Midwest.

Ironically, the operators' victory in 1908 left the Birmingham district woefully lacking in skilled workers. The well-publicized poor working and living conditions ensured that immigrant workers thought twice about coming to the state's mines, and those who did come seldom stayed. Management learned that the use of force had the unintended effect of inhibiting their ability to recruit and maintain a skilled workforce. The largest companies increasingly set up elaborate welfare schemes to build stable and reliable employees. But even the paternalistic trappings of welfare capitalism did not guarantee worker compliance, and when given the choice during the World War I years, miners opted again for the UMW. The union's gains once again proved transitory, however, and by 1921 management had recovered the upper hand and withdrawn recognition.

Peter Alexander picks up the narrative in chapter 3 by examining the decade of the 1920s and then the reemergence of the union during the New Deal. His essay describes a workforce suffering continual bouts of unemployment and deprivation. These were bleak years for Alabama coal miners, but miners and their families proved tenacious and utilized remarkable strategies to survive, including cultivation of gardens, fishing, hunting, and simple pilferage to supplement their meager income. It was, for most miners and their families, a hand-to-mouth existence. By the end of the decade, coal operators confidently pronounced the end of the UMW in Alabama. The 1930s, however, witnessed a remarkable turn in the fortunes of Alabama miners as a vigorous union movement was reborn. Nurturing the union were the sympathetic federal government's labor policies of Franklin Delano Roosevelt, which encouraged collective bargaining. The miners remembered the UMW and were eager to organize, with thousands of miners attending mass meetings to reestablish the union. The rank and file turned a deaf ear to the clamor for racial division and again called for organization of all coal miners with equal pay for equal work. Alexander discusses the emergence of a dynamic union leadership that built a permanent institution that could survive economic vagaries and political attack.

In chapter 4, Glenn Feldman details the rapid changes of the UMW between 1942 and 1975. Between 1933 and 1941 the union had remarkable success, tripling wages and cutting the average workday in half. Now it sought to consolidate these gains. During the World War II years the UMW experienced a previously unknown phenomenon of union protection and advance, and, most important, regular work. Coal miners' attention increasingly turned to the day-to-day demands of work and the excesses of managerial control. Issues such as safety and health, as well as the living conditions in the coal camps, where there had been little improvement, took center stage. Job protection, including defined job classifications, became primary bargaining objectives. Labor-management battles continued to frame much of the union's attention, but throughout the 1950s and 1960s the politics of race dominated Alabama. Yet even following the extreme racial polarization that gripped Alabama after *Brown v. Board of Education* and the Montgomery bus boycott, the miners' union still insisted on biracial unionism.

Economically, the coal industry was flourishing. Government spending on massive coal generating power plants ensured continuous employment and enabled the UMW to negotiate significant improvements in wages and working conditions. But not all was well. By the 1960s the industry was undergoing rapid improvements in productivity through mechanization and strip mining. These improvements proved a double-edged sword for union miners, for while wages improved, jobs were being lost. Additionally, internal political discord pitted the rank and file against its leadership. From the mid-1960s to the late 1970s, union miners resorted to scores of wildcat strikes to resolve grievances. At the national and local level, union politics increasingly divided the membership.

In the final chapter, Robert Woodrum concentrates his study on the 1977–78 strike, the largest in the history of the UMW. Coal production during the strike in the United States was brought to a virtual standstill. Alabama miners voted to strike, convinced they would succeed. In the end, however, it proved to be a fight for their very survival. The union in 1976 was coming out of five years of internal political conflict, which had left it weakened and vulnerable before the national negotiations with the Bituminous Coal Operators Association scheduled for the summer of 1977. The operators confidently predicted strong contract language ending wildcat strikes, and even stronger language on working rules. Both sides underestimated the other, though, and negotiations reached an impasse almost before they had begun. The 1977–78 strike embodied a hostile, opportunistic management against a union membership determined not to give ground, whatever the sacrifice. As Woodrum shows, the tenacity of the rank and file won the day.

The operators' weapons in 1977–78 were not much different from those of their predecessors of 1894 or 1908. This time, however, the union had four decades of experience and leadership to fall back on. Despite the state police, federal government, company spies, and private police forces allied against them, the miners prevailed. It was an immense struggle, one in which many miners had to go back to the subsistence living their parents knew in the 1920s and 1930s to make ends meet. Nevertheless, the union met and won its biggest challenge since the 1932 strike.

The period after the 1977–78 strike saw both advance and setback for union miners. Technology, strip mines, global competition, and environmental regulation all cost jobs in Alabama's mines. The UMW still negotiates contracts that are the envy of most workers, and most coal in the state continues to be union coal. The mine workforce has also been changing.

Women are no longer an uncommon or unwelcome sight in Alabama's mines, overcoming a social taboo that existed for generations. Strikes in other parts of the country, especially the 1990 Pittston strike in Virginia, saw carloads of Alabama miners stand in solidarity with their union brothers and sisters as they had in the 1960s and 1970s.

It Is Union and Liberty conveys to the reader the struggles, against enormous odds, that Alabama coal miners fought over the last one hundred years. Although experiencing repeated defeat, the miners learned from their setbacks and girded themselves for future fights. But the book is more than just a litany of heroic actions; rather, it hopes to portray the world that these miners, both black and white, made. Through their determination, persistence, and sacrifice, union miners answered Charles Farley's question of a century ago, "Who is there among us . . . who'll stand by his fellows?"[14] Their actions improved the working conditions of all Alabama workers.

1

The Early Years: Alabama Miners Organize, 1878–1908

Daniel Letwin

Birmingham, Alabama, lies at the southern tip of Appalachia, at the heart of an extraordinary concentration of coal and iron. Along its southeast edge looms Red Mountain, a hundred-mile-long ridge of hills rich in hematite. Sandwiching the city are three coalfields, the Cahaba and Coosa fields to the south and east, and—by far the largest—the Warrior field, extending seventy miles long and sixty-five miles wide to the north and west. Birmingham was established in 1871 at the initiative of financiers and railroad investors eager to develop the coal and iron deposits of northern and central Alabama. The extracting of coal in antebellum Alabama was a modest, primitive enterprise. The absence of adequate railroad links, regional markets, capital, and knowledge about local geology prevented the rise of a coal and iron center in Alabama to rival those of Pennsylvania and Ohio.[1]

By the 1870s, however, Alabama's coalfields were ripe for development. Although the depression of the mid-1870s momentarily derailed the takeoff forecast by Birmingham's founders, by the end of the decade large-scale production was under way. Beginning at the nearby Pratt mines and expanding across much of Jefferson, Walker, Bibb, and Tuscaloosa Counties, the surge of coal (along with iron) production during the late nineteenth century placed the Birmingham district onto the industrial forefront of the New South. In 1870 the Alabama mineral region produced a modest 13,000 tons of coal, while a mere thirty years later it yielded a whopping 8.4 million tons.[2] The population of Jefferson County, where Birmingham was situated, likewise soared, from 12,345 in 1870, to 23,272 in 1880, to 88,501 in 1890, to 140,420 in 1900.[3]

As drifts, slopes, and shafts took the place of small-scale surface mining, so the scattering of local citizens engaged in the gathering of coal was replaced by a convergence of wage laborers from far and wide. The labor force of the coalfields was racially mixed from the start. In the early years, whites made up a modest majority of the miners; over the 1880s and 1890s, however, African Americans comprised a growing proportion of the workforce, and by the turn of the century they were in the majority.[4] Both blacks and whites worked as skilled pick miners, generally in the same mines, although seldom side by side in the same "rooms." Blacks figured predominantly, but not exclusively, among the laborers who worked under the supervision of skilled miners, either black or white.[5] At many mines, convicts leased from the state or the counties, overwhelmingly black, were used as cheap and controllable labor.[6]

Observers were struck by the diversity of the mine labor force. A traveler captured it vividly in 1893: "The fellow clad in stripes in the county prison camp at Coalburg, the diminutive Hungarian slav, or Slavisch, as locally known, the industrious German or Frenchman, the native Afro-American in the majority, the honest Scotchman with his twang, all are here in one and the same mine. The native Alabamian of the mountains and experienced and raw material from every section of the United States are likewise on hand in no contemptible numbers."[7] This variety of social backgrounds, and especially the mix of black and white, would intensify the challenge, and the drama, of miners' organization throughout the late nineteenth and early twentieth centuries.

Despite their social diversity, there was much that the miners experienced in common. Like other mineral regions around the country, the Alabama coalfields witnessed chronic tensions between the miners and the operators. Living conditions in the coal camps—the company store, rent levels, wages, the weighing and screening of coal, the hours and conditions of work, the subcontracting of unskilled labor, the leasing of convicts, the operators' power to fire, dock, and otherwise penalize the miners, the miners' right to unionize and to receive contractual recognition—all provoked rancorous and at times bloody conflict.[8] Alabama miners particularly detested the sweeping power wielded by many coal and iron operators. In 1890 a Carbon Hill miner complained bitterly that the operators "assume the power to buy

Flat Top prison mine and camp in west Jefferson County. Convict lease was finally
abolished in 1927 following the public outcry over the torture death of a seventeen-
year-old convict. No date. General Collection, Birmingham Public Library Archives.

and sell alike. They dictate to us when we shall work, how we shall work,
how long we shall work, how much work shall be done, and the amount of
pay they shall pay for the labor performed. Labor has no rights."[9]

Miners responded to meager pay, harsh conditions, and overbearing employers in varied ways. Many acted individually, moving from mine to mine,
alternating between mining and farming, shifting among different occupations around the district, or balancing mining with other activities, such as
hunting, fishing, gardening, and varied forms of leisure.[10] Even prisoners
forced to work underground found ways to confront their dehumanizing
circumstances—whether through labor strikes or hunger strikes, physical
resistance or flight. Such desperate lines of response usually ended in defeat,
but each succeeded now and then in placing a check on the company's
power.[11]

But it was through organization that the miners aired their aspirations
most visibly. The first stirrings of a labor movement in the mineral belt arose
at the very dawn of coal and iron production, under the standard of the

Convicts (dressed in white) often worked alongside regular miners as pictured here at the Banner mine, circa 1912. General Collection, Birmingham Public Library Archives.

Greenback-Labor Party.[12] Throughout 1878 and 1879, Greenback-Labor clubs proliferated across the Birmingham coal district. Through regular meetings, contributions to the *National Labor Tribune,* and participation in political campaigns, the Greenback-Labor Party gave Alabama's early miners a collective voice. Their grievances ranged from the swelling power of finance and industrial capital throughout the nation, to the corrupt hegemony of Redeemer governments around the South, to the immediate issues of low pay, unsafe mine conditions, and, most heatedly, the leasing of convicts to the mines. While Greenbackism enjoyed wide appeal among the miners in statewide elections of the late 1870s and early 1880s, it faded as an active movement in the coal belt by the end of 1880. In its wake, however, the loyalties of Greenback miners now flowed to another, more broadly structured movement, the Knights of Labor.

Drawing on the Greenbackers' moral critique of Gilded Age America and the Redeemed South, the Knights of Labor first set down roots in Ala-

bama in 1879.[13] Birmingham rapidly emerged as one of the hubs of southern Knighthood, claiming dozens of local assemblies and nearly four thousand members during the peak years of 1886–87. The Alabama Knights
emphasized the coal district in its legislative agenda. More significant still, it
extended miners' activism into the workplace itself. Throughout the 1880s,
the coalfields witnessed a series of skirmishes between miners and operators,
chiefly strikes or lockouts. While these were mostly isolated, short-lived affairs, the Knights provided a moral vocabulary, an organizational vehicle,
and a network of support to embolden miners, as one Knight exhorted, "to
resist the tyranny imposed . . . by the selfish and greedy, who think that the
employer ought to have it all and the poor, hard-working miners nothing."[14]
Increasingly, however, the Knights' role in these efforts wavered between
active involvement and aloofness, reflecting the order's uneasiness over
conflict with employers, especially strikes. By the end of the decade the
Knights of Labor was in decline around the Birmingham district, as it was
throughout the nation.

Neither the Greenbackers nor the Knights achieved a lasting presence in
the Alabama coalfields (although two local communities, Trevellick and
Powderly, bear the names of the founders of the Knights). Each succumbed
to the power of the operators, internal divisions over strategy, the regional
opposition to organized labor, and their group's decline nationally. But these
early movements shared meanings that cannot be measured in concrete
achievements. First, at the dawn of the Birmingham district they challenged
the notion (widespread at the time, and since) that southern labor was in-
different to organized labor. Second, they established that, even in the late-
nineteenth-century South, a racially mixed workforce was not always inca-
pable of labor solidarity.

Of course, any effort by southern workers to organize across the color
line was charged with drama. The prevailing culture of the region was
scarcely hospitable to labor movements of any sort, let alone interracial ones.
Although white and black miners experienced common conditions and
often had close contact underground, their lives outside the mines were
sharply divided by the color line that spread through all parts of the New
South. In mining communities across the district, blacks and whites lived in
separate sections, sent their children to separate schools, worshiped in sepa-

rate churches, and fraternized in separate lodges, athletic clubs, sewing circles, and brass bands. Black and white inhabitants did interact on the margins of daily life, on terms that ranged from amicable to hostile, and at times even violent.[15] Consider an 1891 episode at the mining camp of Cardiff, involving no less a bastion of American culture than baseball. A game in progress between the "white nine" of Cardiff and the "negro nine" of nearby Brookside, the *Birmingham Age-Herald* reported, came to an abrupt halt when a young white man named John Harden appeared with a Winchester rifle, announced that the white team "would not play with the negroes that day," and ran the black players out of town. An integrated game between racially defined teams; a festive atmosphere dashed by an act of sour intolerance—here were captured both the extent and the limits of interaction between blacks and whites in the mining communities.[16]

The shared concerns of black and white miners underscored the imperative of organizing across the color line. The Jim Crow attitudes and distrust between the races that permeated the region—and the mining towns themselves—highlighted the obstacles to interracial unionism. From the outset, local Greenbackers and Knights of Labor faced a crossroads familiar in American labor history. One path for white unionists was to exclude African Americans, or to banish them to the periphery of the organization. The alternative was to organize all workers in the trade, regardless of race.

In the Alabama coalfields, both the Greenbackers and the Knights chose the path of interracialism. Both campaigns sought out—indeed, were built by—miners of each race, as networks of black and white Greenback clubs and Knights local assemblies cropped up around the district.[17] Within each movement blacks and whites shared leadership roles by organizing local bodies, recruiting members, negotiating with the operators, delivering speeches, and reporting of current struggles to local or national organs.[18] And each group fervently advocated fraternity between black and white miners. One white Greenback organizer urged miners of his race to "drop our prejudice and bigotry," describing these as "the lever that's keeping labor in bondage to capital." The Knights of Labor, the *Birmingham Negro American* observed, "are doing a noble work . . . in trying to elevate and protect the rights of the working classes. It also relegates the color line."[19] Such depictions should not be exaggerated. Each movement went only so far in confronting the dominant assumptions of white supremacy. None wholly eliminated racial strains or hierarchies within their ranks, or overcame stubborn veins of antipathy among the miners to interracialism. And to the extent that white Greenbackers and Knights did challenge these assumptions, their motivations flowed at least as much from the practical perils of labor disunity as from qualms about racial injustice. Still, through their egalitarian rhetoric and their very existence as racially mixed enterprises, these associations stood as a conspicuous exception to the culture of white supremacy. There is no sign that racial tensions within them contributed to the decline of either organization.

However short-lived, the impassioned campaigns of the Greenback-Labor Party and the Knights of Labor signaled that Alabama's coal miners were prepared to organize—even across the color line—to attain higher wages, better working and living conditions, and greater dignity and independence at the mines. In the 1890s a new, more lasting organization would emerge to build upon that promise.

In January 1890, about one hundred delegates from miners' groups around the country convened in Columbus, Ohio, to establish a new organization, the United Mine Workers of America, charged in its preamble with "educating all mine workers in America to realize the necessity of unity of action and purpose, in demanding and securing by lawful means the just fruits of our toil." At its founding, the UMW represented an estimated seventeen thousand miners, divided into twenty-one districts.[20] That April a gathering of miners in Birmingham founded District 20 of the UMW.[21]

An air of expectancy greeted the launching of District 20, as organizers set about building locals across the coal belt. But through the year the operators, led by the Tennessee Coal, Iron, and Railroad Company (TCI), declined either to recognize the union or to entertain any of its demands.[22] In late November the union called a strike, and the response was immediate. By the end of December the strike had spread to all the major companies— the Tennessee, the DeBardeleben, the Sloss, the Cahaba, the Virginia and Alabama, and the Mary Lee—involving fifteen to twenty thousand miners in such key coal towns as Pratt Mines, Blue Creek, Blocton, Coalburg, Cardiff, Brookside, Carbon Hill, Warrior, Henry Ellen, Cordova, Corona, and Brookwood. The mineral district had never seen a strike of this scale.[23] But by mid-January the union—unable to overcome mass evictions, strikebreakers, repression by armed guards, and a hostile press—conceded defeat. The effect of the miners' loss was most vividly illustrated at Warrior, where returning strikers were made to sign "iron-clad" contracts curtailing their right to raise demands, and conceding the company broad powers over hiring and firing, discipline, and the organization of work.[24]

The tactics used by the operators to defeat the strike were familiar to veterans of the coalfields. At Blue Creek, however, the flamboyant Henry F. DeBardeleben of the DeBardeleben Coal and Iron Company introduced a new inflammatory element, with repercussions that would extend well beyond the strike—the company began systematically to recruit African Americans from outside the district to work as strikebreakers. Before long, the other major operators followed suit.

The introduction of black strikebreakers tested as never before the miners' capacity to withstand the divisive potential of race. Certainly that potential was very real. On New Year's Day at the Blue Creek town of Adger, a group of white miners' wives reportedly "got rampant when they saw the colored folks sandwiched among them," and confronted them with frying pans, tongs, tin pans, "and everything else imaginable," causing the frightened blacklegs to take refuge in the mines. The women then unfurled a banner depicting a black miner, the word "scab" inscribed underneath. There were reports of strikers shooting and otherwise intimidating the newly arrived black strikebreakers.[25] The UMW worked hard to preserve unity between black and white miners. "We have no fight to make on the negro," declared national organizer Patrick McBryde. The union pledged material support to strikers of each race, and implored them to curb their hostility toward black strikebreakers. The strategy paid off, as large numbers of black miners rallied to the union's call. The union-affiliated *Alabama Sentinel* regularly described spirited meetings of black and white strikers.[26]

Reminiscent of the Greenback-Labor Party and the Knights of Labor, the interracialism of the UMW was hardly absolute. While white unionists denounced employer manipulation of race, they also succumbed to the values of white supremacy themselves by charging their adversaries with betraying it. Even the pro-labor, racially moderate *Sentinel* pointedly asked how many Birmingham merchants wished to see the coalfields filled with "negroes, dagos and Hungarians?"[27] These ambiguous racial dynamics would become a recurrent theme of miners' struggles in the decades ahead.

If the effects of DeBardeleben's strategy were mixed, the outcome of the strike was not. The Alabama miners' largest strike to date, and their first under the banner of the UMW, had suffered a sharp defeat. For the next several years, despite periodic efforts to revive organization, collective action was scarcely in evidence. Not even a dramatic uprising by Tennessee miners against the convict lease during 1891 and 1892 could reawaken labor activism in the Birmingham mineral belt.[28]

In 1893 the Birmingham district was rocked by one of the harshest economic panics in American history. As work at the mines grew scarce, talk of wage reductions filled the air. So too did resentment over the continued use of convict labor in the midst of widespread distress. That fall, unionists conducted an organizing drive throughout the mineral district, the first of any consequence in three years, under a newly formed United Mine Workers of Alabama. The union retained the District 20 structure, although it did not formally reaffiliate with the national organization. The atmosphere of a labor crusade with Populist overtones was once again palpable. One miner described a series of "great revival meetings" conducted across the district by a "celebrated Georgian evangelist" who lambasted the large manufacturers as "mean, contemptible creatures" for reducing their workers' wages. "Soulless sinners, you are going to hell at express speed!" the preacher would thunder.[29]

As the depression stretched into 1894, hardship grew around the district and miners began streaming out of the state. In early spring the operators proposed a 22.5 percent wage reduction. Accusing them of seeking the "virtual enslavement of the miners and the turning of our nineteenth century civilization back into its barbaric past," the union declared a district-wide strike. Again, the response was impressive. On April 14 some 6,000 miners came out. Morale was bolstered a week later by the launching of a massive strike called by the national UMW in response to wage cuts ranging from 10 to 30 percent. Before long nearly 200,000 bituminous miners around the country had answered the call. The breadth of solidarity in the Birmingham district was demonstrated on April 23 when 4,000–5,000 strikers, evenly composed of blacks and whites, marched through the city, carrying banners of the various coal towns. By the end of the month 9,000 miners were out.[30]

Henry F. DeBardeleben, now a vice president of TCI, took charge of the operators' campaign with his usual flair. Extra convicts, along with new mining machinery, were brought in to replace the miners; strikers were evicted from company housing; whole mines were leased out by the furnace operators to contractors; the pro-company press, most prominently the *Birmingham Age-Herald,* embarked on ritual denunciation of the strikers as misguided and lawless. But the centerpiece of the operators' strategy was the renewed importation of black strikebreakers. Pioneered in 1890, the tactic came as no surprise now, but this time DeBardeleben pursued it with a boldness only hinted at four years earlier. Early in the strike he pronounced Blue Creek a potential "Eden" for black workers, a place where black miners could establish "their own churches, schools and societies, and conduct their social affairs in a manner to suit themselves. . . . This can be a colored man's colony." His offer was also a challenge: "Colored miners, come along. . . . You can . . . prove whether there is intelligence enough among colored people to manage their social and domestic affairs by themselves."[31]

The coalfields seethed over the influx of black strikebreakers. "Our enterprising city can now boast of a flourishing *slave trade* in our midst," one striker wrote. Pinkertons employed by Governor Thomas G. Jones reported mounting agitation among white strikers. "That is about all their conversation," detective "J.H.F." wrote the governor. And much of their anger was expressed in terms of race. Notably, racial slurs by white miners were reserved for the black strikebreakers, described as "niggers," "coons," or "DeBard's pets"; such slurs were seldom directed toward black strikers. Indeed, observers were struck by the camaraderie that persisted among black and white strikers. At the miners' saloons where they plied their trade so assiduously, the Pinkertons would find miners of both races drinking, smoking, and discussing the latest developments together.[32] In late May an estimated three hundred Pratt City strikers, black and white, descended on the mayor's office to protest the arrest of a black striker charged with shooting into the home of a black labor agent. In Blossburg, one detective observed a "large procession" of wives and children, "both white and black." At the head was

Armed company guards at the TCI mines during the 1894 strike. Erskine Ramsay Collection, Birmingham Public Library Archives.

a banner reading "No blacklegs." Throughout the conflict, black miners remained widely committed to the strike. "We, the colored miners of Alabama, are with our white brothers," read a sign at a mass rally.[33]

As production resumed and prospects for the strike dimmed, the union showed no sign of giving in. In the mining communities, feelings intensified. The first serious violence occurred on May 6, when two hundred Horse Creek strikers marched on Price's Mines and dynamited the operations. Mass evictions at Coalburg, Blossburg, Brookside, and Blue Creek provoked heated battles. Rumors flew that the strikers were preparing to seize the Pratt City stockades and dispatch the convicts from the district, in the recent manner of the Tennessee miners. Over the course of May 16, Chat Holman, a black labor agent for TCI, was fired upon, arrested and jailed for carrying a concealed weapon, and threatened with lynching. Matters came to a head on the night of the twentieth, when Walter Glover, a black strikebreaker, was shot to death through the front door of his home. Local sympathies were suggested when the two men charged with the murder, one white and one black, were acquitted despite strong evidence of guilt. Less indulgent, Governor Jones ordered Alabama's Second Regiment to nearby Ensley, where they soon conducted wholesale arrests of Pratt City strikers.[34]

In mid-June the national strike wound down to an ambiguous conclusion, and the Alabama miners were fully on their own. Over the summer, as blacklegs continued to pour in, hardship spread. The presence of raw young troops from the Black Belt and southern Alabama, armed with Gatling guns and arresting strikers, stirred high indignation in the mining communities; military excursions here and there in response to false alarms only heightened the tensions. As strikers' desperation grew, railroad trestles became the targets of fires and dynamiting, and several incidents left strikebreakers and company guards dead. Despite disclaimers by the union leadership, public opinion swung sharply against the strikers.

Union miners placed their final hopes in that August's gubernatorial election, which pitted the Populist-leaning Reuben F. Kolb against Governor Jones's anointed successor, William C. Oates. The Kolbites championed the strike and lambasted the use of convicts, the importation of strikebreakers, and the deployment of troops. The elections became the talk of the coal district. Kolb drew the support of a clear majority of miners—black and white—who clung to the hope that a Populist would turn the tide in their struggle. Opponents of the strike lined up behind Oates. Many miners shared a common Populist concern that the state Democratic machine would find ways to deny a genuine Kolb victory. "If Kolb is elected we ought to put him in if we have to take up arms to do it," a striker confided, unknowingly, to a Pinkerton.[35]

On election day Oates narrowly carried Jefferson County, but all the major mining towns backed Kolb. Evidence of strong Kolbite support from both white and black miners suggested how far interracial unity had progressed in the coalfields, spilling beyond collective labor action into the arena of politics as well. But statewide, amid charges of fraud, Oates prevailed. Prospects for the strikers now looked dimmer than ever.

In mid-August, as the strike approached its fifth month, TCI and the union reached a settlement under which the miners' base wage would be a dismal 37.5 cents per ton (to rise when iron prices rose). It was a doleful outcome. The largest miners' walkout yet in the district had failed to keep down production, attain an adequate wage, or gain union recognition. Ultimately, a daunting array of obstacles—inexhaustible reserves of convicts and strikebreakers, a hostile governor, a depressed economy, and an ambivalent public—had again conspired to thwart the miners' chances.

The strikers returned to a dreary situation. As the depression dragged on through the mid-1890s, employment remained sporadic; miners sometimes worked only one or two days a week. Some operators took measures to increase the pool of consumers at the company store, or to dilute the militancy of the "old-timers" with more docile "green-hands."[36] A statement by union officials in early 1895 conveyed the many ways the operators now flexed their muscles:

Since the late strike last summer certain Companies in Alabama have been subjecting their employees to treatment fitting only for slaves; by depriving them of the right to meet in public under penalty of discharge; by refusing them the right to have checkweighmen on the tipples and dumps; by docking cars of coal for small quantities of slate; by discharging men for not dealing in Company Stores and "pluck-mes"; by forcing employees to sign agreements or "iron-clads" under threats of discharge; by keeping up a systematic method of blacklisting . . . by lengthening the already long hours of work from 7 A.M. to 5 P.M. to 6 A.M. to 6 P.M.; and other outrages too numerous to mention.[37]

Even amid these demoralizing circumstances, embers of unionism remained in localities across the mining district. But as the depression extended into 1896 and 1897, the great majority of Alabama miners remained unorganized. Anemic markets for coal and iron, continued use of convicts, overrecruitment of labor, and the weakness of organized labor nationwide combined to discourage a renewal of miners' unionism. Still, the tradition of collective militancy retained a palpable if rickety presence in the form of District 20, and through the voices of the *Birmingham Labor Advocate* and the *United Mine Workers Journal.* Local victories here and there through the mid-1890s kept that tradition alive. All in all, unionism neither blossomed nor vanished during the mid-1890s.

In July 1897, as the nation's worst depression yet approached its fifth year, 3,000 TCI and Sloss company miners struck to stave off wage reductions to an abysmal minimum of 37.5 cents per ton. Their strike failed to last the month, and its failure marked a low point for the miners.[38] For many, however, the defeat served as a prod for revitalizing unionism. Hopes were raised that fall, when 150,000 miners in the midwestern Central Competitive Fields won a three-month strike, resulting in the national UMW's first interstate contract. The unexpected triumph galvanized the American labor movement. The UMW looked southward, recognizing that the unorganized coalfields of central and southern Appalachia subverted the interests of miners everywhere.[39] Both locally and within the national union, the time seemed ripe to revive organization in Alabama. On September 25, delegates from the key mining towns gathered in Birmingham to launch the new campaign. The convention voted to reaffiliate with the national union and elected two members, A. H. Gentry (white) and C. M. Coker (black), to organize locals.[40]

In the months that followed, the union gradually reestablished itself across the district. Prospects were brightened in early 1898 by an accelerated demand for coal and iron following the outbreak of war with Spain. The organizing drive culminated in May, when delegates from the eight major mining centers, chiefly those of TCI and the Sloss company, convened in Birmingham to reestablish District 20 of the national UMW. The shout "An advance in July!" greeted speeches by District 20's English-born president William R. Fairley, African-American vice president S. P. Cheatham, and other officials as they toured the district. The advance materialized at the end of June, when the Tennessee and Sloss companies raised the base mining wage from 37.5 cents to 40 cents per ton.[41]

Most notably, they signed these contracts with District 20, inaugurating broad-based union recognition for the first time in the Alabama coalfields. For the next six years the key operators negotiated annual contracts with the UMW and dealt regularly with the miners' local union pit committees and officials. In doing so they followed the lead of their counterparts to the north, who, amid the renewed prosperity, were pursuing stable relations with "conservative, responsible" unions. The years surrounding the turn of the century indeed saw a startling increase in union recognition throughout

America; between 1897 and 1904 the American Federation of Labor swelled from 447,000 to more than 2 million members, the national UMW from 9,700 to 251,000.[42]

Recognition both reflected and bolstered the miners' power. In the months after the first union contract, organizers continued to build locals around the coal belt. At the time of District 20's founding in May 1898 it claimed more than 1,000 members. By the end of the year it had organized 15 locals with 2,300 members, and by 1903 there were 95 locals and 14,000 members. The hub of District 20 was Pratt City's Local 664, which by 1900 numbered nearly 1,500 members, making it the largest UMW local in the country.[43]

This surge of organization was part of a broader revival of unionism in and around Birmingham. By 1899 the district had 10,000 union members, including iron and steel workers, coke workers, iron ore miners, printers, machinists, blacksmiths, railway workers, clerks, carpenters, bricklayers, tailors, stonecutters, cigar makers, team drivers, powdermakers, and musicians, as well as coal miners. At the turn of the century, District 20 had links with a revitalized Birmingham Trades Council and two newly established statewide organizations, the Alabama State Federation of Labor and the Union Labor League. A branch of the Socialist Party was active within and beyond the coalfields, and periodic visits by Eugene Debs drew large crowds.[44]

District 20 pressed the usual range of issues regarding working and living conditions. Even at the union's height, some of its goals—abolition of the convict lease, an eight-hour day, organization of the entire district—proved beyond reach. But in many ways District 20 achieved impressive gains. The pay scale rose from a minimum of 37.5 cents per ton in 1897 to upwards of 55 cents two years later.[45] Under union contracts the weighing and assessing of coal was systematized, and monitored by miners' checkweighmen. So too was the disciplining of miners, as the union imposed a check upon the company's power to fire or dock its labor. Pressures to patronize the company store were widely curtailed. Union contracts ratified a custom that entitled miners to take temporary leave from their work. (A miner could remain away for up to three days without losing his job, or even having his room underground reassigned.) Upon the death of a miner at work, production was suspended from that moment until his funeral; likewise, work would cease for the funeral of a miner's wife. Labor subcontracting (where a skilled miner hired a helper) was eliminated at large operations around the district. Subcontracting, as Fairley stated, should be abolished because "every man should have an equal share of the wealth that he produces." Where subcontracting was found to persist, a union committee would order it discontinued in favor of a more egalitarian "buddie" arrangement.[46]

Corrupt practices in the distribution of cars and rooms underground were also scaled back. In 1899 the men at Blocton No. 3 mine forced the resignation of a mine boss who sold rooms to the highest bidder. One "Enos" recounted the episode in verse:

> There was a boss at No. 3
> Who with his men couldn't agree,
> And so the Blocton miners struck
> And said this boss must light a shuck!
> This smart boss was on the move
> To try his innocence to prove,
> But all his efforts came to naught
> When men turned up whose room [they] had bought;
> They to the truth did firmly stick,
> And this poor boss turned quite sick.
> Then to the office straight he went
> And in his resignation sent.
> It was accepted and there will be
> No more rooms sold at No. 3
> A better chance we now will stand,
> For our new boss is a very fine man.[47]

Dramatically, then, the UMW enhanced the miners' livelihood and sense of independence. One miner made the point by describing the unappealing alternative: "If you work at a non-union mine, you are required to disclaim any connection with any labor organization; you must work for wages and under conditions fixed by the company. In fact, you must do anything that the 'boss' requires of you. He can dock you, he can fine you, he can lay you off, or he can fire you out, and you have no appeal. . . . It is union and liberty, or it is individualism and slavery."[48]

The years surrounding the turn of the century were by and large a time of stable relations between District 20 and the operators. Labor conflict, however, had by no means vanished, even at places governed by UMW contracts. Local skirmishes punctuated the era of recognition, over a variety of demands: a wage increase for day laborers, the eradication of subcontracting, the reversal of a contested firing, and the elimination of deductions for schools and doctors. In 1902 more than four thousand TCI miners walked off for the right to have members' donations for striking anthracite miners in Pennsylvania deducted by the company.[49]

In a number of ways, large and small, the local union became a part of the social atmosphere of the mining towns. "We have the I.O.O.F. [Odd Fellows], the K. of P. [Knights of Pythias], the Red Men and the Masons, and the U.M.W. of A.," reported a resident of Brookwood. At Republic, the Odd Fellows met regularly at the local UMW hall. When Cardiff won the Alabama championship football cup in 1898, District 20 president Fairley and national UMW Executive Board member Fred Dilcher were on hand to address the celebration. Miners gathered on the monthly payday "holiday" at the local union hall. Union locals served as soliciting agents for the miners' hospital in Birmingham.[50]

The turn of the century not only brought union recognition to the Alabama coalfields—it also saw the spread of legal segregation and disfranchisement around the state and region. Jim Crow cast its shadow across the coalfields as well. "While white and colored miners worked in the same mines, and maybe in adjoining rooms," black UMW national organizer Richard Davis reported from the district, "they will not ride even on a worktrain with their dirty mining clothes together. . . . Oh, no, the line is drawn."[51] To survive in such a setting, the miners' union had to find some way to resist, or at least to deflect, the divisive pressures of Jim Crow without perishing in a frontal assault on that hardening "way of life."

Reflecting the demography of the coal belt, District 20 was made up of approximately equal numbers of black and white miners. Their collaboration flowed naturally from shared work experiences, but facing common conditions did not in itself ensure interracial empathy. More than ever, labor interracialism had to become an ongoing project. From the outset, black and white organizers toured the coalfields. Union gatherings often brought together black and white miners, and these were typically addressed by speak-

ers of each race. Black miners had a significant presence among the delegates
to district and national conventions.[52] They figured prominently as well
among union officials. According to custom, District 20's vice president was
always black, and African Americans had a place on all major committees.[53]

As in the early 1890s, union leaders stressed how racial division played
into the operators' hands. At a Walker County miners' rally in 1900, Henry
C. West of the local union committee called on black and white miners to
"shake hands over the pick and shovel or these companies will have us just
where they want us and both the white man and negro will toil for their
victuals and their clothes and not much of that." Appeals to black miners
were sometimes cast in the language of racial uplift. Black District 20 vice
president Benjamin L. Greer argued in 1904 that, in sticking with the union, blacks would enhance their self-respect, not to mention their standing
in the eyes of whites. Thus he grafted the tone of Booker T. Washington
onto a union clarion call that would have mortified the Wizard of Tuskegee.
Whites were urged to accept African Americans in the union, if only for
self-protection.[54]

In challenging the color line, District 20 went beyond rhetoric. On its
insistence, annual contracts decreed that (in the words of the 1901 agreement) "no discrimination is to be made in the distribution of work against
the colored miners, but all competent colored men are to have an equal
chance at all work." The UMW contested Jim Crow above ground as well.
In 1901, at the insistence of black members, District 20 petitioned the Birmingham Trades Council to repeal the color bar from its constitution and
to "open wide their doors to colored organized labor of the district." Within
a few days, the BTC complied.[55] When the merchants who owned the Birmingham hall where District 20 customarily met objected to the presence
of African Americans at its 1901 convention, the UMW took umbrage.
"The Negro could not be eliminated," national organizer William Kirkpa-
trick told the merchants. "He is a member of our organization and when we
are told that we can not use the hall because of this fact then we are insulted
as an organization." When the union threatened a commercial boycott of
Birmingham, the merchants apologized. To gauge how sharply District 20's
stand tacked against regional currents, consider the actions of another con-

vention of the moment: just weeks before, the state of Alabama had ratified its revised disfranchisement constitution.[56]

However striking its racial policies may have been, District 20 was in its own ways constrained, and influenced, by the surrounding racial order. The conflicting imperatives of labor unity and white supremacy produced an interracialism that was highly qualified, often cramped, at times sharply circumscribed. Never fully submerging race, the union forged what might best be called a collaboration between the races, at once accommodating and testing the boundaries of segregation.

The union's structure reflected this ambiguous approach. While several locals were racially mixed, the typical mining camp had one for each race. However cordial in tone, however much rooted in the broader patterns of the miners' lives, the color line remained clearly drawn in their union. Black and white members adjourned from common district conventions to attend separate banquets; they marched in the same Labor Day parade, but retired to separate parks. Union positions, filled annually by election, were allotted according to a carefully constructed formula. The presidency was reserved for white members; the vice presidency, for blacks; the secretary-treasurer's position, for whites. The various committees usually comprised a modest majority of whites. District convention delegations were likewise apportioned by racial quotas.[57] As for the disfranchising of African Americans then gathering steam, the UMW had little to say.

For many years following the dual defeats of the coal strike and the Kolb campaign in 1894, the miners' union steered clear of politics—above all, racially charged politics. The limits of interracialism remained evident in the union press as well. Sprinkled amid frequent praise of black union miners were the derogatory images of African Americans all too familiar in the Jim Crow South. Race was not the only lens through which white miners regarded black miners—it was, however, always there. Ultimately, the racial approach of District 20 involved a brew of tensions, strategic and ideological: the union brought black and white miners into common association, but never contemplated wiping out the color line entirely; it asserted their shared concerns, but avoided an all-encompassing equality; it advanced black material conditions, but deemphasized black political rights; it hon-

ored black unionists, but remained open to the notion of black inferiority.[58]
Within these limits, the interracial miners' union achieved a fragile stability
from 1898 through the first few years of the new century.

Cracks in this era of relatively good feelings became visible in 1903,
when, for the first time in five years of union recognition, annual negotiations broke down. Only the intervention of a board of arbitration, grudg-
ingly agreed to by the operators, averted a district-wide strike.[59] The following year brought many signs that the peace would not last long. Renewed
efforts to organize locals at the Walker County towns of Cordova and Horse
Creek met with the raw resistance—marked by mass firings and armed
guards—long associated with that area. Because of court injunctions pro-
hibiting union meetings, Blue Creek miners on strike against the reintro-
duction of subcontracting held meetings in the guise of religious services at
a nearby church.[60] That spring, the use of heavy-handed measures against
unionists—firings, arrests, violence, suppression of meetings, importation of
cheap immigrant labor—provoked bitter strikes at the Pratt Coal Company
mines at Mineral Springs and Arcadia, the Little Warrior Coal Company
mines at Littleton, and the TCI mines at Blocton. When a popular union
miner was fatally shot by a mine boss during the Blocton strike, between
fifteen hundred and two thousand people attended his funeral.[61]

Conflicts such as these were not unknown during the previous five years,
but the new developments portended larger struggles ahead. At the end of
1902 the economy had entered a downturn that would last for the better
part of two years. The slowdown coincided with, and encouraged, mounting hostility to the labor movement among employers nationally. In 1903
the National Association of Manufacturers launched a concerted open-shop
drive to reverse the foothold unions had attained in recent years. Supported
by a flood of bills and injunctions restricting the right of unions to picket,
boycott, or conduct sympathy strikes, the open-shop drive placed unions
drastically on the defensive. In September 1903 the Alabama legislature
passed a draconian anti-boycott bill. Potential repercussions for the
coalfields arose shortly, when a Blue Creek striker was arrested for violating
the law.[62]

In this ominous climate, by the summer of 1904 many regarded the
approaching contract negotiations uneasily. The apprehension proved war-

ranted. From the start it was evident that the major operators had cooled to collective bargaining. While the smaller commercial companies were willing to renew the union contract, furnace operators showed little inclination to negotiate. The real issue, TCI chairman Don H. Bacon told his stockholders, came down to who would run the mines: "The authority of your representatives over the property in their charge, as to the manner in which the work should be done, as to what should constitute a fair day's work, and as to who should be employed, had to be restored and maintained." If it took a major showdown to restore the open shop and thus enable the company once again "to fully control its own operations, untrammeled by union restrictions," Bacon added, it would be worth it. By the end of June the furnace operators had succeeded in provoking a strike; while the commercial operators signed extensions of the current union contract, nine thousand miners for the furnace companies walked out.[63]

Soon the familiar features of a district-wide coal strike fell into place. From the start the operators had at their disposal convict miners, whom they shuffled around to maximize production. By mid-August trainloads of strikebreakers, mostly black, were arriving regularly from Tennessee, Virginia, West Virginia, and Kentucky. Beginning at Blue Creek and spreading through such mining towns as Dolomite, Coalburg, Sayreton, Blocton, Brookside, and Blossburg, production gradually picked up. Meanwhile, the operators moved to evict strikers from company houses in order to make room for their replacements, and evicted miners found themselves arrested for trespassing on company property. As the courts brushed aside legal challenges to the evictions, tent colonies arose to shelter the families of strikers. Union leaders toiled to keep the strike alive, distributing relief and mobilizing rallies across the district, but by the end of August pessimism was mounting and an air of violence descended on the district. Clashes among union miners, blacklegs, and deputies erupted at Dolomite, Graves mines, Brookside, and Adamsville. A series of federal and state injunctions in September imposed draconian restraints on union organizers, and soon deputies deployed to monitor union meetings and arrest those who challenged strikebreakers. By winter, union membership had sunk to barely 3,000, down from more than 10,500 a year earlier. Those who remained settled in for a long fight to the finish, bolstered by weekly provisions of food and supplies.

And so it went for another year and a half. The union fought on with grim tenacity, with cooperation between black and white strikers remaining firm. A relatively small number returned to work at non-union mines. The tedium of protracted idleness was alleviated by social gatherings and animated mass meetings. In July 1905 more than six thousand people attended a union barbecue at Blocton, featuring ball games, dancing, a parade, music, and speeches. The national UMW, eager to keep the southernmost stretch of Appalachia in the fold, poured more than half a million dollars into the strike.[64] Time, however, was on the operators' side, and in August 1906 District 20 voted by a margin of over two to one to discontinue the twenty-six-month-old strike.[65]

In the aftermath of the union's defeat, the situation looked grim. Many who had struck were now blacklisted. Thousands pursued work in other trades or left the district altogether. The mines were now worked largely by newcomers, many freshly arrived from other lands, who had come as blacklegs. The economic panic of 1907 sent iron and steel prices plummeting, further dampening the miners' outlook. The acquisition that year of TCI by U.S. Steel introduced a corporate presence as staunchly anti-union as it was powerful. District 20 nonetheless retained a foothold in the coalfields. From 1905 through 1907, membership hovered between 3,500 and 4,000. Many worked for those companies—the commercial operators or Alabama Consolidated—who continued to negotiate union contracts.[66]

District 20's last stand began with a campaign to defend these contracts. As 1908 approached, Alabama Consolidated announced a 17.5 percent cut in miners' wages, effective January 1, well before the contract's expiration. Incensed, the miners walked off. In June, as the strike entered its sixth month, the commercial operators demanded a similar reduction as a condition for renewing the union contract.[67]

The national UMW decided the time had come to call all Alabama miners out on a do-or-die strike for recognition. On July 6 approximately four thousand miners, primarily at the commercial mines, answered the call. By the second day, the strike had spread to the major furnace companies. Unionists scrambled across the district, reviving dormant locals, speaking from street corners, organizing rallies, mobilizing picket lines, and setting up union commissaries. As the strike entered its second week, the union claimed more than eight thousand new members.[68]

The presence of deputy sheriffs and company guards brandishing pistols and rifles stirred predictable resentment in the mining communities. The intruders broke up meetings, closed churches, evicted and arrested townsfolk, prevented them from moving about freely, subjected them to abusive language, and forced them to return to work. The sheriffs and guards were also prepared to use their weapons, and over the weeks a number of strikers were killed or wounded. Trains carrying new strikebreakers became the targets of armed attack. These actions inspired heated denunciations of labor violence, obligatory disclaimers from the union, and finally a proclamation by the governor announcing the deployment of troops to quell "disorder and lawlessness."[69]

A charged atmosphere greeted the first arrival of troops. "The train was the most unusual that ever steamed out of Birmingham," the *Birmingham News* observed. "The gondola car at the head of the train presented a very formidable appearance, with the fringe of gun barrels bordering the side." By July more than five hundred troops, mostly young white men from the Black Belt, patrolled the strike district. "Everywhere," the *United Mine Workers Journal* reported, "one sees guns and hears the tramp of the soldiers." Strikers initially made a show of embracing the troops as their protectors, but soon the troops themselves were arresting strikers in large numbers. "It seems," one striker concluded, "that they are just as bad as the company guard." "We haven't any governor!" another cried at a mass meeting as W. R. Fairley recounted the excesses of the troops. "I rather differ with my friend," Fairley replied. "I think we have too much governor!"[70]

By August, union membership had grown to eighteen thousand, embracing the vast majority of miners. Affirming the importance it attached to the battle, the national union dispatched Vice President John P. White to assume command, along with more than two dozen national organizers; it would ultimately pour over $400,000 into the strike.

Once again the sight of black strikebreakers failed to drive a wedge between black and white strikers. Miners of each race attended the same meetings, spoke from the same platforms, and inhabited the same tent colonies (although divided into black and white sections). Black strikers at Adamsville confronted black strikebreakers; white strikers at Republic rallied behind the prosecution of a white deputy sheriff who had killed a black striker. If the union spent little time trumpeting its interracial stand, neither did the stresses of the conflict trigger visible racial tensions. Race in fact did not figure much in public discussion during the first month of the district-wide strike.

That would soon change. Starting in mid-August, a series of anti-union voices—newspapers, political figures, and operators themselves—raised a drumbeat of inflammatory allegations that the union was encouraging social equality between the races. The Alabama Coal Operators Association (ACOA) spoke of bands of armed strikers, black and white, roving the district. A *Birmingham Age-Herald* headline blared, "The Social Equality Horror." Opponents of the union took pains to accentuate the sexual dimensions of social equality. The *Birmingham News,* generally less strident in its anti-unionism, added that the strikers' tent colonies (despite their biracial layout) had engendered "the too intimate association of whites and blacks in the camps, developing by degrees racial familiarity, if not equality, [and inflaming] the public mind." Former Birmingham mayor Frank Evans wrote ominously of "pluralism in the sex of devils" afoot in the strike district. Intimacy between blacks and whites, "in the very presence of gentle white women and innocent little children," recalled the "terrible days of Reconstruction." (Evans was quietly paid $500 by the ACOA "for services rendered as newspaper correspondent" during the strike.) The ACOA also paid *Age-Herald* editor Edward W. Barrett $3,000 "for the assistance rendered by that paper."[71] And there was the inevitable specter of interracial rape. Evans reported that white women had been subjected to "criminal assault by Negroes" in the strike district. Governor Braxton Comer warned that the presence of five to ten thousand blacks in a state of vagrancy at the tent colonies was a circumstance "too dangerous to contemplate," nothing less than a threat "to the integrity of our civilization."[72]

To amplify the sexual side of interracialism, opponents broadened their concern to include women. Evans highlighted efforts "to organize the women of both races . . . into female unions known as the 'Woman's Auxiliary.'" Perhaps the most inflammatory language came from the pen of society columnist Dolly Dalrymple, who took time from her usual cheery fare to voice her outrage: "White women and black women meeting on the basis of 'Social equality' indeed! White men holding umbrellas over black speakers! Black men addressing white men as 'brother'!" Good taste prevented her from describing relations between blacks and whites across the gender line; only vague allusions would do. Social equality in the coalfields was "an unspeakable crime," the very thought of which "caused the women to shudder. . . . It is monstrous!" Never had interracial unionism in the district encountered such fevered race-baiting.[73]

The union strained to refute the charges. UMW advocate Duncan McDonald accused opponents of devoting "their entire time in lying about 'social equality,' 'women's auxiliaries,' and other base falsehoods in order to cover up the real issue." The UMW, Vice President White insisted, "did not go to Dixie Land to preach the doctrine of social equality; neither did we practice it." The miners' cause, he bristled, was merely "an industrial one."[74] In fact, the UMW was never a purely bread-and-butter movement. The range of concerns the union addressed—from mine safety to company stores, wages to housing—inevitably engaged the wider community. Never did the union emerge more fully as a community institution than during strikes. The mass evictions of miners' families, the provocative intrusion of troops and company guards, the vital roles of both women and men in confronting strikebreakers and sustaining livelihood and morale—these developments turned labor battles into broad-based social struggles. The UMW's expansive presence in the mining community bolstered the strikers, but it also left outsiders more receptive to the insinuation that its racial practices amounted to "social equality."[75]

Ultimately, the union's disclaimers about social equality won the strikers little protection. Within the volatile climate of 1908, racial demagoguery readily inflamed public opinion. "The scene has been shifted," a committee of union officials grimly informed national vice president White. "You are no longer dealing with the industrial question, but with the racial problem." Governor Comer seized the moment to deal the strikers a series of crippling blows. In late August he prohibited the union from holding public meetings. He then ordered the tent colonies, now swelled to accommodate seventy thousand people, cut down by the militia. Soon, in a manner both somber and dramatic, the job was done. At Republic, an observer reported, troops marched upon the makeshift settlement, and "with their swords and bayonets cut the ropes, slashed the canvas and reduced all to a complete wreck." Comer cited unsanitary conditions—a charge the union vehemently denied—but amid mounting hysteria over the collaboration of black and white miners (and their families), avowed concerns about hygiene were not easy to separate from the assault on interracialism. The governor himself offered an earthier explanation, in private, to District 20 leader J. R. Kennamer: "You know what it means to have eight or nine thousand niggers idle in the State of Alabama, and I am not going to stand for it."[76]

Whatever the pretext, the effect was devastating. "The militia is . . . tearing down our tents at Republic and other places, and piling them up with the people's furniture in heaps," one striker wrote. As the troops went about trashing their camp, strikers conducted a prayer meeting along the nearby railroad tracks. Thousands scrambled to recover their worldly possessions, while Comer summoned the union leaders and issued an ultimatum: call off the strike, or he would convene a special session of the legislature to enact a vagrancy law under which every striker could be arrested; in essence, they would be returned to the mines as convicts. More quietly, union officials received warning that if the strike persisted, "blood would flow in the streets of Birmingham" and eight of the most prominent leaders "would swing." On August 31 the UMW announced the strike over, effective the following day.[77]

For the second time in three years, a district-wide strike had come up empty. The 1908 defeat was far more conclusive, and the miners knew it. With the coalfields now entirely open shop, the *Birmingham Labor Advocate* brooded, "the miners are . . . the same as serfs. . . . [They] will have to dig coal at whatever price and under any condition." The bleak prediction was soon borne out, as working and living conditions deteriorated markedly. Word came from the mining camps of stringent new work rules conferring greater power to the companies, a return to extensive dockage of pay, increased pressures to patronize the company store, severe restriction on local movement, checkweighmen now chosen by the company, and so forth. The coalfields were reportedly riddled with detectives, and miners with union ties were discharged en masse. Hundreds of miners, demoralized and unable to obtain work, departed the district in the months that followed. "Good-bye," one wrote the *United Mine Workers Journal;* "may we meet above, where we won't be bothered with governors."[78]

The mass departure of miners, and the distress of those who remained, nearly wiped out the union. Within a few months, membership had plummeted to 762.[79] In early 1909, William Leach of Cordova recalled wistfully how local miners had defied the rough regime of Walker County and joined the strike: "The Empire local met every day, 351 strong—open air exercises, with prayer—and that good old song was sung at every meeting, 'We Will Overcome Some Day.'" Leach recalled the scene for inspiration. "Dear Brothers, let us not drop that old song, but still sing it. If we stick together we will overcome some day, for that old tyrant governor soon will step down and out."[80] But the union would languish well beyond Comer's departure in 1911. Few could have imagined in the gloomy aftermath of 1908 that, within a decade, the UMW would reemerge in Alabama, stronger than ever.

2

Having It Their Way: Alabama Coal Operators and the Search for Docile Labor, 1908–1921

Brian M. Kelly

Between the staggering defeat of the UMW in 1908 and the equally devastating outcome of the 1920 strike, Alabama operators set out to reconstruct district labor relations in such a way as to permanently rid themselves of union agitation. The 1908 strike shattered District 20 of the United Mine Workers of America. From a high of nearly 20,000 members at the peak of the strike, only 278 remained a year later. UMW influence was reduced to a skeletal organization at several small mines in the Birmingham district, and the Alabama Coal Operators Association (ACOA), formed in the final days of the strike, would attempt over the next several years to dislodge the union from these few remaining footholds. One of the operators' first actions after the termination of the strike was to contract with the Austin-Robbins detective agency to "keep a close watch and try to prevent further organization of unions." For several months following the strike, agents' duties included preparing reports of "the number of loyal [union] men in each camp," but by early 1909 the ACOA acknowledged that since it was "not known that any organizers were [left] in the district," there was "really very little [detective] work to be done."[1]

Observers from all sides recognized that the outcome of the strike had fundamentally shifted the balance of power in the coalfields. The *Birmingham Labor Advocate,* a newspaper not usually prone to exaggerating the weaknesses of organized labor, noted that the miners' defeat had left district labor relations "a one-sided affair." "The operators are organized," editors admitted, "while labor is not." John Fitch, an industrial correspondent for the nationally distributed *Survey* magazine, confirmed several years later that area operators had "had things their own way," and that their authority was "exercised with a heavy hand by every company in the district." Federal investigators reported in 1910 that the outcome of the strike had left the Alabama mines "peculiarly under the control of the employers," and a national UMW delegation sent south to survey prospects for reorganization several years later spelled out just how this "control" affected miners in their daily lives. Organizers found an atmosphere of "fear bordering on terror," where "if it becomes known that [miners] have met or talked with our representatives they are immediately discharged." By all accounts, their triumph over the UMW had placed the operators firmly in the saddle.[2]

Although using labor unrest against the UMW never completely disappeared from the operators' attempts to garner public sympathy, the ACOA acknowledged in its more candid, internal discussions that their rout of the UMW had left them in undisputed command. Their 1909 annual report boasted that the Birmingham district coalfields had been "singularly free from labor troubles since the end of the strike,"[3] as did nearly every other report between 1908 and 1917. Coal operators found much to celebrate in the aftermath of the 1908 strike, but they also expressed a growing concern that they had perhaps overplayed their hand: skilled miners, disproportionately white, were leaving the district in droves and seeking employment in the more heavily unionized northern fields, aggravating the perennial problems associated with labor supply.

One observer precisely described the Alabama's operators' dilemma as one of "capital seeking labor supply."[4] Ideally, area employers preferred to have at their disposal a large labor reserve which embodied in equal measure the qualities of skill and docility: like their counterparts elsewhere in the South, Birmingham operators wanted an efficient, non-union workforce willing to labor for paltry wages. With their rout of the UMW, the operators had clipped the wings of labor militancy for the foreseeable future, but the cost of this industrial peace was high. Lacking realistic, short-term prospects for reversing the setback in Alabama, skilled miners voted with their feet and headed north, raising the fear among employers that the resulting shortage would rob them of the fruits of their hard-won victory over the UMW.

Both the operators and their adversaries in the labor movement seem to have recognized the potential disaster that this portended for the Alabama coal industry. UMW supporters reported that the men brought in to break the strike were bankrupting the operators by their inefficiency. "All I want is for the union to remain dead in Alabama about twelve months longer," a UMW supporter from Searles quipped sarcastically, "and the company will *make* the men organize." Less than a month after the strike ended, the operators themselves expressed their concern that the exodus of skilled miners was taking its toll on the labor supply, a complaint that won them little sympathy from organized labor. The "mines will be worked by the riff-raff shipped in to take [the strikers'] places," editors at the *Labor Advocate* predicted. "[The operators] have sown the wind and will reap the whirlwind."[5]

From the earliest days of the district's industrial development in the 1870s to its emergence as the New South's industrial powerhouse before the turn of the century, Birmingham's promoters had loudly trumpeted the district's remarkable abundance of natural resources. The close proximity of all the elements for steelmaking, one observer predicted, favored the district with "an advantage that could not be overcome." At one of the many blast furnaces dotting the city's horizon, a visitor to the district calculated, "it would be quite possible for a sharpshooter to stand on the water-tower and with a rifle send a bullet into the mines out of which the ore was dug. With a revolver he could put the men in the limestone quarries in danger; and with a peashooter he could annoy the workers at the coke ovens." The most significant advantage enjoyed by district operators over their competitors in the northern fields was not their easy access to mineral abundance, but rather the low cost of native labor. Indeed, in their attempts to lure northern capital southward, industrial leaders throughout the New South stressed the cheapness of local labor, along with southern workers' alleged "disposition against organizing unions," as the most attractive aspects of doing business in the region.[6]

The linchpin of their low-wage regime was the employers' large reserve of relatively defenseless black laborers, who were so desperate to leave behind the brutality and monotony of Black Belt agriculture that they could be employed at wages below those demanded by experienced industrial workers of either race. The obvious disparity in power between planters and their (mostly) black tenants, the web of legal restrictions by which planters kept black labor chained to the cotton economy, and the arsenal of terror

Dogs, goats, and mules pulled wagons in Alabama's mines well into the 1940s. The animals were often looked on with affection and were the subject of story and song. George Korson collected one laconic song in his *Minstrels of the Mine Patch* (Grafton Press, 1927) titled "My Sweetheart's a Mule": "My sweetheart's a mule in the mines, / I drive her without any lines, / On the bumpers I sit and tobacco I spit / All over my sweetheart's behind." Photograph courtesy of the Alabama Mining Museum, Dora, Alabama.

Man, wagon, and goat working a "dogtrot" mine in Tuscaloosa County. No date. Photograph by Dennis K. Hall, courtesy of Jim Walter Resources, Inc.

(including deployment of the Klan) that landowners had at their disposal all militated against black workers' open protest against their exploitation. In this respect, the regime that the operators constructed in the coalfields borrowed heavily from the example set by planters in the Cotton Belt. Indeed, downstate planters had figured prominently in the ranks of the district's early operators, and the management methods they had grown accustomed to in their dealings with agricultural labor were imported wholesale into their treatment of mine labor.

Black miners were not the only ones to pay the price for Jim Crow, however. In an industrial setting, the degradation of black labor under the racial caste system threatened the livelihood of workers of both races: not only could blacks be employed at paltry wages and under horrible conditions, but their willingness to endure such treatment—or rather their inability to challenge the operators—set the standard for the wages and conditions endured by white miners as well. The observation of one local labor official, that district operators were taking advantage of the fact that "the Negro

Miner usually works a little cheaper than the White Miner" to "keep down the wages [and] to lengthen the hours of labor" for all miners, revealed the centerpiece of the operators' strategy: to deliberately pit blacks against whites, and hope that competition at work, reinforced by the powerful legacy of racial animosity, would frustrate every attempt at union reorganization. Among themselves, operators boasted that their "cheap, docile negro labor" provided them with an important lever for maintaining a low-wage, non-union regime in the Birmingham district. "There is no superior to the negro as a willing, loyal, reasonable and obedient laborer," Sipsey mine boss Milton Fies boasted before a gathering of Alabama operators shortly after the end of World War I. The vulnerability of black labor convinced Fies that black miners were not only "an economic asset" but also "an absolute necessity for the industrial consummation of industrial Alabama."[7]

With the exodus of experienced mine labor out of the district after 1908, Alabama operators were left to choose between two alternatives in trying to meet the industry's insatiable labor demand: they could either import workers in large numbers from outside the district, or they could attempt to discipline and develop the human resources closer at hand. For several years they attempted the former, dispatching labor agents as far away as Ellis Island in an attempt to bring European immigrants to the district. Despite an intensive effort on the part of Birmingham's industrial employers, however, few immigrants voluntarily chose to head South.

The fundamental obstacle to southern immigration during this period was the employers' unwillingness to match the wage scales in the North, but the South's harsh racial order repulsed many as well. Immigrants arriving at Birmingham bearing the hope that they had reached a land of freedom and opportunity were likely to have such illusions dashed very quickly. The editor of the city's Italian newspaper, *L'Avanguardia,* recalled standing "speechless and stupefied, almost incredulous" at his first sight of a chain gang on the city streets. The experience was enough, he thought, to make any visitor "attracted by the reputation of [the district's] wonderful development and modernity" reconsider his decision to call Birmingham home. Immigrant workers' apprehensions about their status in the New South were deepened by white southerners' difficulty in deciding where newcomers figured in the

region's rigid racial hierarchy. In most mining camps, Europeans were segregated from both blacks and native whites, and occasionally their children
were barred from attending white schools.[8]

The contradiction at the heart of southern immigration efforts, in the
view of an unusually candid South Carolina labor commissioner, was the
employers' "cry on the one hand, for only the highest type of immigrant,"
and "on the other, to secure him at the scale of wages paid the Negro."
Editors at the *Labor Advocate* expressed a similar cynicism regarding the district employers' predicament. "What inducement is being offered to bring
the working men to Birmingham?" they asked. "Every pamphlet which is
published by our various boosting clubs holds out to the capitalist the argument that labor can be secured at a lower rate in the Birmingham district
than elsewhere." Unprepared to entice labor southward with material incentives, employers' efforts inevitably developed a coercive edge, borrowing
from the elaborate machinery of control so central to their domination of
black labor. In this sense, as in many others, the racial caste system set the
tone for labor relations generally in the coalfields. A Greek miner brought
south by the Tennessee Coal, Iron, and Railroad Company (TCI) in 1909,
for example, penned a letter within days of his arrival in which he expressed
shock at the abuse being meted out by company officials. "Today during
pay-time the company police beat up a black woman because she complained that they are stealing daily wages from her husband," he wrote;
"then they attacked the workers with revolvers. I did not know that such
atrocities occur here." He complained that "for the next twelve days [the
company] will set us at gun point to work for nine and a half hours a day
instead of eight," and noted that on payday "about five hundred workers"
were "shouting that the company is stealing their salaries."[9]

The failure of their immigration campaign forced area operators back
upon native labor, and in particular upon native black labor. If immigrant
labor could not be cajoled into working at the "Negro's wages" in sufficient
numbers, and if skilled whites would leave the district rather than endure
the conditions imposed after the UMW's defeat, then the operators had
little choice but to employ blacks themselves. Area employers had long employed blacks in unskilled positions, but from 1908 onward, leading com-

panies began a systematic attempt to raise the productivity of native black labor and move blacks into semi-skilled and skilled work.

In its thirty-year history, Birmingham industry had shown itself to be of two minds regarding the large-scale employment of blacks. On the one hand, employers were obviously mindful of the advantages held out to them by the destitution prevalent among black laborers. "Until now," a white UMW member noted in 1917, the operators had "depended on fleecing the negro, getting the negro's labor for a song, and making the negro sing it." Cheap black labor was thus crucial both to maintaining low wages and to warding off the threat of unionization.[10] Before 1908, however, when they embarked on a comprehensive overhaul of labor relations, Alabama operators had frequently expressed their reservations about relying so heavily upon native black labor. Chief among their complaints was the concern that blacks were undependable as a source of steady labor. Unsurprisingly, employers expressed their exasperation with black "shiftlessness" in language loaded with the racial assumptions widely shared by white southern society: blacks were considered peculiarly lazy and undisciplined, woefully deficient in matters of thrift, and singularly prone to restlessness, to "wandering and moving about." "Generally speaking," a reporter for the *Birmingham Age-Herald* fretted, "the colored worker of Alabama is not a success when he is taken from the cotton field and harnessed to the chariot of coal and iron." *Survey* reporter John Fitch, echoing the frustrations of local employers, complained that blacks "appear[ed] to be content to do just that number of days' work each week that will afford them a bare subsistence—and not one day more." Others complained that blacks brought with them into the mines the rhythm of seasonal labor they had known on Black Belt plantations. Few could be induced to work Saturday afternoons, for instance, and many took extended vacations at the years' end to return to the Cotton Belt, where those they had left behind were settling up with planters and celebrating the end of another year's labor.[11]

Although, in the context of a racially divided South, black miners constituted an easy target for operators' complaints about "shiftlessness," some employers admitted that there was no substantial difference between the levels of absenteeism among blacks and those shown by either native whites or European immigrants. One industrial historian notes that the rate of absenteeism among immigrants and native whites was only slightly lower than that for blacks. For mine operatives as a whole, attendance averaged just over eighteen days' work per month in 1913, a figure that reflects both the reluctance of workers of all racial and ethnic backgrounds to "harness" themselves to full-time industrial employment and the inability of employers to guarantee miners steady work. Full-time work was rare throughout the Birmingham district during this period: the operators' unceasing lament over labor's unreliability obscured the fact that what they actually desired was a steady supply of labor that could be put to work whenever the coal market demanded it and laid off just as easily—very often within days of being rehired. Very few black or white Alabamians could count on making a living solely from their mine earnings, therefore, and contemporary newspapers are littered with complaints from miners and their wives about the hardship imposed by the chronic boom-bust character of the coal industry. By necessity, miners kept one foot on the farm or, in the case of many Black Belt refugees, migrated back to the plantation districts during slack times, and this unwillingness of native labor to make itself available on the operators' terms lay behind many of the mine owners' very public complaints about native indolence.[12]

The lack of basic sanitation and medical care in Alabama's mining communities posed another important obstacle to increasing productivity, and no doubt contributed to the high rates of absenteeism. Even official accounts acknowledged that the cause of much absenteeism was "recurring epidemics" resulting from unsanitary conditions and lack of a safe water supply, "which decimated labor forces and threatened to cancel out all the advantages accruing from the ready access to rich mineral deposits." Those few skilled workers who had been relocated to the district were generally "reluctant to bring their families into the area," and after experiencing "the unattractive and unhealthful conditions of surrounding communities," company officials lamented, "men would leave after only a short rest period." Years of employer neglect of the most basic amenities for workers were beginning to take an exacting toll on productivity.[13]

For a number of reasons, TCI would play the leading role in attempting to address the district's long-term labor problem. Most important of these,

Early machine mining, circa 1915. General Collection, Birmingham Public Library Archives.

no doubt, was the company's singular ability to shoulder the financial burden of a comprehensive overhaul. TCI had long dominated the Birmingham district, and company officials had recognized even before the 1908 strike the need for substantial new capital investment. The company's acquisition by U.S. Steel in 1907 brought the technical and financial resources of the world's most powerful industrial corporation to bear on local problems, and even before the strike, officials had embarked on a modest program aimed at raising the productivity of its black and white workers.

A number of chroniclers of TCI's role in the Birmingham district have depicted the company's adoption of welfare capitalism as a story of corporate philanthropy and even racial benevolence. Beyond any humanitarian concern, however, company officials recognized that the successful exploitation of the district's material advantages demanded the establishment of a new order in the area's coal mines. With the only viable threat to their hegemony in the district safely laid to rest, TCI officials led the district's

largest employers in the search for a long-term solution to the chronic problems of labor supply and productivity. Even with the UMW out of the way,
however, coal operators faced a daunting task in devising a solution that
would satisfy their contending labor requirements. On the one hand, their
newly won authority would amount to little if it did not enable them to
hold the line on wages and maintain their competitive position. On the
other hand, by 1910 or 1911, their reluctant realization that significant
gains in productivity would not be forthcoming without substantial long-
term investment in improved industrial technology, remedial training for
native labor, and housing and sanitary facilities added even more pressure to
reduce labor costs.

The urgency of their quest was brought home to TCI officials in 1911,
when state officials denied the company's annual bid for convict labor. Over-
night, company officials were forced to put their sprawling operation on an
exclusively free labor basis, a process they probably would have preferred to
implement gradually over years, possibly decades—if at all. The emergency
situation brought on by its forced abandonment of convict labor, coupled
with the continued exodus of skilled miners out of the district, posed a
serious threat to the company's viability in the district, as well as its long-
term plans to revamp local facilities.

The elusiveness of a quick-fix solution to deficiencies in skill and depend-
ability left the area's major employers with a labor problem "difficult beyond
belief." In a district where, according to one (pro-company) account, "the
original native labor body was indolent, untrained, unreliable, and where
there was no initial desire for regular employment," industrial employers
were left with little choice but to "take what [they] had on hand and work
with that," to adopt a comprehensive approach to developing a sufficiently
skilled, dependable workforce as rapidly as possible. Tight employer control,
low wages, and the development of a skilled, stable body of workers out
of the ragged, illiterate, and disorganized droves of black and white Alabamians fleeing the harsh poverty of rural life—these requirements, rather
than philanthropic considerations, would define the new order that would
take root in the coalfields during the decades ahead.[14]

The defining feature of this new order would be its continuing depen-
dency on black labor—but not, as some of its prominent spokespersons

would later claim, out of a sense of sympathy toward black workers. Stripped of the sugary rhetoric that accompanied their reorientation to native labor, coal operators were interested in pursuing profits. They were astutely aware that the large body of destitute and relatively defenseless blacks at their disposal could serve as a powerful lever with which to contain the grievances of all workers, both white and black. If, as novelist Carl Carmer wrote in *Stars Fell on Alabama,* Birmingham was a "muddle of contradictions," a "new city in an old land," then the most glaring of its many incongruities was the chasm between the rhetoric of industrial progress and the reality of intensive, historically rooted racial and class exploitation. The new order would not discard that legacy, but fasten it more securely. In the process it would graft the most advanced model of labor relations on offer in the industrial world—welfare capitalism—onto a time-honored tradition of racial paternalism rooted in the slave past.[15]

Welfare capitalism was not exclusive to the Birmingham district, of course. Industrial employers elsewhere in the United States and beyond had championed this new, "enlightened" management approach as the best antidote to the bitter antagonism that had marked relations between labor and capital in the decades straddling the turn of the century. For employers who wished to avoid the disruptive effects of labor unrest and develop a workforce that was both productive and loyal, proponents argued, welfare capitalism offered an ounce of prevention where the cure could be very costly indeed. Since it was employee dissatisfaction—and frequently legitimate employee grievances—that opened the door to labor agitators, they perceived, those employers who would demonstrate an interest in the conditions under which their laborers (and their families) worked and lived would reap tangible long-term rewards in terms of greater productivity, lower absenteeism, and immunity from trade unionism.

From the workers' perspective, welfare capitalism proved a double-edged sword. Workers welcomed increased company concern where it delivered real improvements in wages and working conditions, or where it meant that their families lived in better housing, or could attend school or have access to medical care. But to many workers, employer concern felt too much like authoritarian control: what workers gained in material improvements, they sacrificed in personal freedom, since, in return for these benefits, manage-

Alabama mining companies not only rented housing to its employees but also furnished churches (including ministers) and schools. There were wide disparities in the quality of housing in Alabama. Pictured here are quite good white and black housing and churches furnished by the New Castle Coal Company. No date. Photograph courtesy of the Alabama Mining Museum, Dora, Alabama.

ment demanded absolute loyalty. Schoolteachers, social workers, company doctors, even the priests and ministers who conducted services in company-built churches—all were handpicked by company officials, and few employed in positions of authority dared voice dissent, or even independence, from the official pro-company cant. Denied an independent voice, workers were subjected to a near-constant barrage of middle-class morality. With any criticism of the employers or demands for better wages or treatment tabooed, an army of welfare workers preached individual thrift, sobriety,

An armed company guard keeps watch over company housing in Wenonah, circa 1937. Photograph by Arthur Rothstein, courtesy of the Library of Congress.

hard work, and personal responsibility as the solutions to the hardship and alienation faced by many workers.

There was another, more important contradiction at the heart of welfare capitalism. The employers' newfound concern for the health and well-being of their workforce, and their confidence to overcome the exhortations of labor agitators, never completely assured them that their workers would remain loyal. Very often the elaborate apparatus employers constructed to oversee company welfare was matched by an equally formidable structure that oversaw employee surveillance. In the Birmingham district, as elsewhere, the leading proponents of welfare capitalism all maintained extensive internal police systems: TCI, the DeBardeleben empire, and Pratt Consolidated were at least as notorious locally for the elaborate spying systems they maintained as they were for the material improvements they had introduced for their employees. There were few, if any, coal camps in the Birmingham district that did not post company guards to prevent labor agents and union organizers from tampering with their workers. Most operators insisted on the right to regulate visitors to miners' homes, and miners who traveled outside the camps were often required to carry a pass stipulating which roads they were permitted to travel.

Even at its best, then, the potential for company-directed welfare to alleviate the worst conditions suffered by workers was at least qualified by the trade-off it seemed to demand in workers' freedom. The soil into which this new system of labor relations attempted to sink its roots in the Birmingham mineral district—an important element being the region's long history of racial antagonism—proved far more favorable to the cultivation of the seamy, coercive edge of welfare capitalism. Here the traditions associated with the plantation regime were decisive. Harsh methods thought essential to "handling" black labor were imported wholesale into the mines, and the operators' rhetorical commitment to "uplifting" their employees coexisted quite naturally alongside routine brutality and exploitation. Indeed, the truly distinctive feature of company welfare in the Birmingham district was the operators' shrewd appreciation of the racial element in their calculations, evidenced by the deliberation with which they set out to pit black and white miners against one another.

In the context of a growing labor shortage after 1908, black miners found themselves the objects of the operators' much-touted benevolence. TCI again took the lead in bringing black workers into skilled and semi-skilled positions, less out of a commitment to racial fairness than from an appreciation of the necessity of developing a layer of skilled black miners. In a period when black southerners had been completely routed from formal political participation, and where hardening racial lines were frequently enforced with organized racial terror, individual operators put themselves forward as "friends of the Negro," as protectors who would defend black miners against the outrages of local law enforcement officials, low-level managers, and white miners, and who would see to it that black workers were given a "fair show." A number of employers tolerated, and even encouraged, a certain brand of black racial pride and separatism, handpicking acceptable "race leaders" who toured the mining district preaching a conservative message of racial self-help and industrial salvation through loyalty to one's employer. Above all, black miners were subjected to a continual diatribe against having anything to do with the UMW, dubbed the "white man's union" by race leaders tied to the coal companies.

The operators' strategy of racial paternalism formed the centerpiece of what Philip Taft has described as a "deliberate policy of flattering the Negro workers" and "exalting [them] as competitors of the whites." It requires little imagination to understand why such a policy might resonate with black miners in the dreary, sometimes hopeless years of the early-twentieth-century South. Particularly in the absence of an interracial challenge from the UMW after 1908, the racial hostility that permeated every interaction between black and white southerners would have found its way into the coal camps, and it would require but little effort on the part of coal operators to incite racial antipathy. It is not surprising, therefore, that black miners were occasionally willing to hand their allegiance over to a white coal operator. But it would be wrong to equate their acquiescence to the paternalist arrangement with enthusiasm for the operators' designs. What is most remarkable about the history of Alabama miners during this period is that for all the operators' efforts, and despite the tremendous amount of energy poured into solidifying the new regime in the years between 1908 and World War I, black miners deserted their erstwhile benefactors as soon as new conditions provided them with a viable opportunity to do so.

Their desertion of the paternalist arrangement in favor of working-class interracialism can be understood only if one looks beneath the public image crafted by coal operators and their allies in Birmingham's black middle class and examines the reality of life for black miners during the non-union years. Welfare capitalism promised relief from the brutality and poverty of the Black Belt. It offered a haven from racial hostility where black miners would advance in exact accordance with their demonstrated merits. But it delivered neither. The gap between the ACOA's public commitment to "uplifting" the black miner and life in the coal camps is striking. While convict labor had been driven out of the TCI mines in 1911, for example, their competitors at Pratt Consolidated continued employing convicts—the vast majority of whom were black—throughout this period. At the Montevallo mine, one of the few remaining union mines in 1913, new owners prodded by the ACOA and committed to the open shop brought convicts into the mines for the first time in a successful effort to dislodge the UMW.[16]

Miners of both races reported that operators throughout the district employed thugs (commonly known as "shack rousters" or "whipping bosses") whose main job was to drive free black miners daily to work. One Walker County mine veteran recalled that the operators had "fellers, company men that toted guns and [went] to see niggers when they didn't come to work to see what the trouble was, and they'd tell 'em they'd better be there the next day." From the Margaret mine came a protest that the company employed "what is called a company devil here and at all of their mines who rides around and sees that you do not lay off when you are sick." A black miner from Republic complained that "many of the camps" employed a "Shack Rouster" who was "almost inhuman in his treatment of the average Negro man and in many instances he takes unlimited authority with the Negro women." His words echoed those of a black miner in the pages of the *United Mine Workers Journal* who complained that the "shack rouster rides from sunrise until [sunset] with his billy and his revolver hanging to his saddle, and if any negro opens his mouth in protest of his cowardly acts with their women they are either beaten almost to death or shot down like a dog."[17]

The especially harsh treatment accorded black miners was apparently not lost upon all whites in the coal camps. One white miner "of twenty-five years' experience" who had "worked in many mines and with many Negro miners" acknowledged that while "the white miner is treated bad enough" in Alabama mines, "the Negro as a general thing simply catches 'hell' in the big way." The operators "do not send 'Shack Rousters' to any white man's home to drive him out to work, sick or well, but day by day," he feared, "the reins are being drawn tighter and tighter on us and if we continue to hold our peace the day will soon come when we will be catching as much hell as the Negro." The remedy, he concluded, was for white miners to "lay aside prejudice" and reorganize the UMW on an interracial basis.[18]

Miners' inability to mount an effective challenge to the operators during this period was less a manifestation of their satisfaction with the operators' new order than it was a measure of the long-term fallout from the UMW's defeat in 1908. Operators devised a variety of structures, including company unions, which ostensibly offered miners a vehicle for expressing their grievances, but few workers of either race were foolish enough to believe that these had any intention of challenging management prerogatives. "Woe to the man who takes his case to the Mutuality Department," a disgruntled ex-TCI manager complained. "They are always put on a black list in the employment office marked 'NG' ['No Good']."[19]

Absolutely precluded in the paternalist arrangement was any form of independent initiative on the miners' part. Miners and mine management continually battled over implementation of a state law that provided for the election of independent checkweighmen at each mine tipple. Miners routinely complained of shortweighing and won the formal right to elect an independent authority to oversee the weighing of coal. Throughout the district, however, operators attempted to stall the process, either by overseeing the elections themselves or by barring individual candidates. Their resistance seemed less motivated by concern over the weights than by the challenge the arrangement posed to management prerogatives; some even sensed in the campaign for checkweighmen an attempt to revive the union.

While the operators' formidable power and the miners' relative weakness constituted obstacles to a generalized revolt in the mines, such conditions could not completely contain miners' grievances. An incident that occurred at Henry DeBardeleben's Sipsey mine in 1914 reveals both the possibility for local, episodic revolt and the operators' firm hand in dealing with even minor challenges to their authority. Management at Sipsey maintained a policy of "question[ing] all who desire[d] employment . . . very closely, to avoid hiring any men with union sympathies," and when mine boss Milton Fies suspected one of his section foremen of harboring sympathies for trade unionism, he immediately fired the individual and imported ACOA detectives to "make a thorough investigation as to just how much trouble" the man had caused. Some years later, when men in the company's employ at Payne's Bend stopped work to protest a missed payday, company officials instructed supervisors to "find out who is at the bottom of this movement and discharge him." The most striking example of the limits on miners' self-activity occurred in September 1914, however, when a Sipsey night boss brandishing a wagon-wheel spoke beat a black miner to death for failing to show up for shift work. Blacks at Sipsey became "considerably wrought up over the incident," and Fies reported that things "looked squally here for a while" until he imported a deputy from nearby Jasper and discharged "some five or six negroes, who were particularly impertinent and trouble seeking."[20] Under such conditions, racial paternalism could not possibly maintain the long-term allegiance of miners of either race. Little wonder, then, that miners of both races bolted from the paternalist arrangement as soon as new circumstances made it possible.

The resurrection of interracial unionism in the Birmingham district had little to do with events inside Alabama itself. Union stalwarts—both black and white—continued to hold out hope for a revival of the UMW, even in the darkest days of operator control, but the operators kept a close watch over the district and, through the ACOA, maintained a disciplined, sophisticated organization to oversee the fortunes of their open-shop utopia. Cracks began to appear in the non-union monolith, however, from the very outset of World War I. Even before formal U.S. military intervention in the war, increased industrial demand began drawing black and white Alabamians northward. More than any other single factor, their large labor reserve had previously been held in place by a lack of alternatives: work in the district mines was dangerous, unsteady, and underpaid, but even so it seemed to many miners superior to anything else on offer in the immediate vicinity. The new demand for labor in the North presented Alabama blacks and whites, for the first time, with possibilities of paid employment beyond the mines and mills of the Birmingham district. In a trickle at first, and later in a flood, they headed north in search of better wages and relief from the harsh domination of downstate cotton planters.

The effect of this exodus out of the South was dramatic. The resulting labor shortage made it impossible for local operators to hold the line on wages. Wage rates began to rise throughout the district; from an average of 47.5 cents per ton on Pratt Seam coal in 1913, wages climbed steadily, by about 10 cents per year, until district miners were averaging from 80 cents to $1.00 per ton by December 1917. Taking the unprecedented step of attempting to renegotiate prices with long-term clients of the DeBardeleben Coal Company in December 1916, Sipsey mine supervisor Milton Fies complained that with the desertion of their labor force, Birmingham operators confronted "conditions probably without parallel since the Civil War." "It has been necessary for us to offer inducements to our miners to prevent more of them from migrating northward," he explained to a New Orleans buyer, "where manufacturers of war munitions, machinery, [and] automobiles are making very attractive offers to southern labor."[21]

On the whole, however, the material incentives that Birmingham operators were willing to extend fell far short of stemming the exodus. Birmingham wages remained higher than those elsewhere in the South, as they had been for some time before the war, but considerably lower than those on offer in comparable northern cities. As had been their habit, operators substituted coercion where material incentives fell short of success. Especially notable, given the posturing by which they had attempted to prove their benevolence toward the "Negro," were the harsh means employed to prevent black miners from emigrating. The Southern Metal Trades Association issued a bulletin advising employers to "Shut the barn door before the horses all get out!," and a number of operators seem to have applied the journal's directive enthusiastically, as an incident related by the *Labor Advocate* in June 1917 reveals. At a mine located just outside city limits, "many of the colored population had put on their best Sunday clothes and had gathered at the depot intending to come to Birmingham to a big baptizing. Just before the arrival of the train *the superintendent and shack rouster* [emphasis in original] appeared upon the scene and forced all the negroes, without allowing them time to go home and put on their mining clothes, to go into the mines to work." Given such "intolerance," editors reasoned, it was no wonder that "the colored people enter their protests in the way they have."[22]

Under the new conditions brought on by the war, coal operators could not contain the volatile contradictions at the heart of welfare capitalism. While material advances at a few of the more heavily capitalized operations had won the allegiance of some miners to the new system in the years after 1908, events proved that company paternalism could postpone, but not derail, a new challenge to the brutality and deprivation endemic to the operators' new order. Even where it succeeded in alleviating material deprivation, company welfare bred resentment that made unionism an attractive option. Miners' realization that growing industrial demand reinforced their bargaining position injected a new confidence into dealings with their employers, and made many of them eager for a day of reckoning.

With the entry of the United States into the war, the conditions appeared ripe to once again organize Alabama's coalfields. In the spring of 1917, the UMW formally launched a reorganization, and coal miners in every corner of the district responded enthusiastically. Mass meetings of up to 3,000 miners were held at Brookside and elsewhere throughout the Warrior coalfield. Rallies at Jasper, Wylam, Seymour, Maylene, Sumpter, and Blocton drew large turnouts and were everywhere marked by "revival camp enthusiasm." Within just two months, District 20 officials reported having organized 128 new locals, with some 23,000 of 25,000 miners in the district now holding union cards. Over a period of several months, the UMW had managed to achieve what would have been impossible just several years earlier: "almost total organization of the coal mines."[23]

Given the enthusiasm with which district operators had traditionally defended the open shop in the mines, it is not surprising that they resisted the prospect of a UMW revival with every means at their disposal. They enlisted the support of the federal government in labeling the union's demand for higher wages "unpatriotic," and industry spokespeople slandered the UMW as a "pro-German" organization. When, eventually, tensions broke out into a district-wide strike in the fall of 1920, the ACOA succeeded in convincing Alabama governor Thomas Kilby to dispatch state troops to the coalfields to put down the strike forcefully. In some districts the Klan was unleashed on strikers, and miners of both races found themselves the victims of lynch mobs directed by military officials and anti-union operators.

The most conspicuous element in the operators' anti-union arsenal, however, was their flagrant, calculated attempt to split the mine workforce along racial lines. Between 1908 and the outbreak of World War I, leading operators had devoted considerable attention to cultivating a relationship with prominent individuals in Birmingham's black middle class. The ascendancy of Booker T. Washington's accommodationist outlook among city "race leaders" assured astute industrial employers of an important asset in their campaign to inoculate black miners against unionism. With the revival of labor agitation in the district coalfields, prominent employers dispatched an army of black welfare workers throughout the district. Before captive audiences in company-owned halls, speakers like *Birmingham Reporter* editor Oscar Adams railed against the "white man's union," beseeching black miners to spurn the UMW and remain loyal to the mine owners. From his office in the TCI building, a black minister named P. C. Rameau published the *Workmen's Chronicle,* a pro-employer newssheet which operators reportedly bought "by the wagon loads and distributed free of cost to all the colored men in the mines and mills."[24]

This intense propaganda campaign nearly succeeded in its goal of splitting the union along racial lines. U.S. Labor Department agents warned their superiors in Washington of an increasingly perilous descent toward open race war in the district. They attributed the deterioration of race relations to TCI executives, who sensed in the new circumstances brought on by the war an opportunity to "entirely disrupt the union" by "get[ting] the negroes out of the [UMW]," after which "negroes would rapidly and entirely displace white labor in the mines." Observers on all sides increasingly resigned themselves to the likelihood that the tensions arising out of the UMW's effort to reestablish itself would lead to either open race war or "the bitterest and most dangerous kind of conflict between labor and capital."[25] Jefferson County law enforcement officials were banking on a racial conflagration: Sheriff J. C. Hartsfield wired Governor Kilby a request for mounted machine guns, fully expecting that his forces would have to confront "heavily armed negro mobs of six hundred or eight hundred."[26]

That the confrontation, when it finally did erupt in the fall of 1920, took the form of a district-wide, interracial strike and not a murderous showdown between whites and blacks is a testament to the UMW's ability to discipline their ranks against racial provocation and to direct the miners' anger at the operators instead. In the face of a barrage of race-baiting, UMW officials kept their heads, admonishing white miners to stand by the union's commitment to its black membership. Though the union steered clear of endorsing social equality for blacks, it did insist upon full industrial equality for its black members, a stand that flew in the face of southern racial protocol and infuriated the coal operators. A committee of wealthy Birmingham citizens drew up a petition that condemned the "invasion" of the mineral district by "a band of northern negroes and northern whites" who had "for the first time [brought] to the Alabama miners, of whom more than seventy percent are negroes, the news that they were underpaid and ill-treated."[27]

Despite its shortcomings, the union's racial policy contrasted sharply with the steady diet of race-baiting which the operators kept before the public. "These colored men are in the mines because the steel corporations put them there, and they had to go to make a living, the same as you white fellows," UMW organizer Van Bittner told a cheering, mixed assembly of miners early on in the strike. "There is nobody working in these mines for their health. I don't care what a man's color is so long as his industrial relations is all right—so long as he is a good union man. [We cannot] fight this issue on the question of race, and discriminate against the colored man. We are going to get the same wages and the same conditions, industrially, and the same living conditions for these men in these mining camps as we do for the white men." "Certainly," he told a rally of union railway workers several weeks later, "we have taken [the black miners] into the Union, and we are going to keep them in the Union, because we may as well recognize as working men that the wage that the negro worker gets is going to be the wage that the white workmen are forced to take. [There] is only one race question involved and that is the race between the UMW and the ACOA."[28]

The UMW's ability to hold together is also eloquent testimony to the staunch support which black miners showed for their union. Despite their patronizing depiction of black employees as naturally submissive and innately hostile to trade unionism, every experienced operator in the Birmingham district worried that the slightest relaxation of mining camp discipline could prove them wrong. The stereotype around which the mine owners attempted to construct racial paternalism was therefore based more on wishful thinking than on reality. During every previous strike in the Alabama coalfields, black miners had distinguished themselves as loyal union militants, and the events of 1920 and 1921 were no different in this respect. A layer of black union militants, including District 20 vice president Joe Sorsby, kept the interracial tradition alive during the darkest days of the operators' ascendancy, urging black miners to reject the anti-union role that the operators had assigned them in the new order, urging working-class solidarity over the cramped, conservative brand of racial pride peddled by accommodationists, and fighting within the ranks of the UMW to ensure that the union lived up to its formal commitment to equality.

During the strike itself, black and white miners stood shoulder to shoulder for six long months against the combined power of the operators and their allies in Birmingham's business community. In what must rank as one of the most dramatic confrontations between the powerful and the power-less in the post–Civil War South, starving miners, along with their wives and children, endured a vicious race-baiting crusade in the local press and a campaign of terror perpetrated against them by state troops and law en-forcement officials tied to the coal companies. In the end, the union miners of Alabama went down in defeat, unable to prevail against the awesome power ranged against them. But they did not go quietly; and even in their defeat, miners of the Birmingham district left behind a stirring example of the power of interracial solidarity. Many vowed that they would live to fight another day. Angry letters poured in to Governor Thomas Kilby's office in the aftermath of the strike. Wylam miners informed Kilby that they would "not be responsible for any conditions that may arise from this unhappy situation. You have spent thousands of the people's money to protect the coal operators." But the sharpest threat came from a miner's wife at Blocton. "This is our state," she warned Kilby. "We will fight for freedom. There will be a revelution [*sic*] start right in Alabama [and] it won't be weeks about it either."[29]

3

Rising from the Ashes: Alabama Coal Miners, 1921–1941

Peter Alexander

In nineteen hundred an' thirty-two
We wus sometimes sad an' blue,
Travelin' roun' from place to place
Tryin' to find some work to do.
If we's successful to find a job,
De wages wus so small,
We could scarcely live in de summertime—
Almost starved in de fall.[1]

Thus did Uncle George Jones, black miner-cum-minstrel, convey the misery experienced by Alabama coal miners and their families during the worst year of the depression. District 20 had been virtually destroyed by the 1921 defeat, and in 1923, when the top leadership of the United Mine Workers of America fired all the district officers, there were only a few hundred members left in the whole of Alabama.[2] The situation continued to decline, and by 1928 the new district president, George Hargrove, closed the union headquarters.[3] Thereafter, the district became something of a cautionary tale, with the *United Mine Workers Journal* reporting in 1931 that "deplorable conditions [have] developed since the union was driven out . . . miners [are] slowly starving."[4] In 1932, Alabama's coal output was less than half the level recorded ten years before, and the average miner worked half the number of days, only 107.[5] Moreover, the 1921 strike had been followed by broader setbacks for the union—first in West Virginia, then nationally (in 1922, and again in 1927)—and by the end of the decade the UMW was on its knees. Membership was negligible, finances were ruined, and the leadership had been racked by a series of vicious internal disputes. So, it was for good reasons that two astute observers argued in 1931: "It is doubtful if the union will reappear in Alabama within a generation."[6] However, the experts were proved wrong.

To understand the dramatic and successful reestablishment of District 20, it is helpful to begin by considering certain underlying conditions. As well as the depression-related slump in coal output, there was a long-term decline linked to changing energy use. By 1933 only 1.3 percent of electricity in the Alabama area was produced by coal, with 60.5 percent generated by water; by 1934, only 10 percent of ships visiting the major Gulf ports burned coal, compared with 80 percent in 1920; and in the late 1930s there was a sharp move toward purchasing diesel locomotives.[7] Whereas 26,647 Alabama miners produced 21.5 million tons of coal in 1926, in 1939 the respective figures were 22,087 and 12.2 million tons.[8]

The captive mines, most of which were owned by steel and iron companies, were less adversely affected by the decline than the commercial mines, and in 1939 the former were responsible for 56.2 percent of Alabama's coal production, compared with 34.1 percent in 1926.[9] The Tennessee Coal, Iron, and Railroad Company (TCI), a U.S. Steel subsidiary, was the "big boy on the block," and in 1939 it employed nearly 5,000 coal miners, with the three other steel companies employing a total of less than 4,000. The larger commercial operators—those connected to the rail network, as distinct from the truck mines—were organized by the Alabama Mining Institute (previously called the Alabama Coal Operators Association), and in 1939 they were responsible for 38.1 percent of the state's coal output.[10]

Alabama's coal mines were slower to mechanize than was general in the United States, but 71.4 percent of the state's coal was cut by machine and 24.3 percent was mechanically loaded by 1939.[11] The widespread prejudice against employing African Americans in mechanical or supervisory positions had implications for the racial composition of the workforce. Because of mechanization, most black miners engaged in heavy manual work, such as loading, and Earl Brown—who became a coal miner in 1939 and retired in 1997 as secretary-treasurer of District 20—remembered his mine superintendent and foremen collaborating to protect white men's jobs.[12] Census data show the proportion of black miners declining from 53.8 percent of all

Alabama coal miners in 1920, and 53.2 percent in 1930, to 41.7 percent in 1940.[13] Because the overwhelming majority of convict coal miners had been black, the abolition of convict lease in 1928 must also have contributed to this decline.[14] According to the 1920 census, only 4.9 percent of Alabama's "foremen and overseers" were black, and this very low figure slipped to 1.8 percent in 1930 (a mere forty-six employees). In addition to "native whites" and "negroes," the census also recorded "foreign born whites," but by 1930 only 1.5 percent of coal miners were included in this category.[15]

Most Alabama miners lived in company camps (or villages), each with its segregated housing, schools, churches, fraternal orders, and sports teams; its company store (or commissary); and its company-paid doctor and deputy sheriff. Camp life was a mixed experience. Company schools provided better education than county schools (and well-kept UMW minute books attest to literacy and neat handwriting), while churches and fraternal orders assisted people in developing valuable organizational skills, with their buildings offering space for union meetings.[16] The camps were central to a corporate paternalism that aimed at delivering a stable and pliable workforce, and many miners preferred to live elsewhere. Brown, describing his childhood in Booker Heights, an all-black community, said, "I was raised here in freedom," adding: "On the mining camp you was subjected to white supremacy, but in this area we were independent . . . we always thought something of ourselves."[17] A flight to "freedom" was made easier by car ownership (which also made it less troublesome to organize long-distance strike pickets). Although the majority of miners could not afford a car until the 1950s, some obtained one earlier, and during the 1935 Alabama coal strike one dealer complained to the governor that the work stoppage was leading to a large number of car repossessions.[18]

Discussing one of the 1930s strikes, Steven Christian, an African American who first entered the mines in 1933, recalled: "Some of the miners had saved enough to go through the strike; some of them couldn't deal with two or three days."[19] Many miners had a garden plot to sustain them through the strike. Girtley Connell, for example, a white miner who started work in 1926, remembered that his father, also a miner, had about thirty acres "and an ole black man to help him."[20] Corn, peas, beans, greens, okra, and tomatoes were widely grown; cows, hogs, and chickens were often reared; and a

Black miners' housing, circa 1937. Photograph by Arthur Rothstein, courtesy of the Library of Congress.

mule or horse was sometimes kept for plowing.[21] Curtis McAdory, a black miner born in 1907, recalled that "we would raise most of what we eat."[22] Collecting fruit (such as apples, peaches, and berries), fishing, and hunting of rabbits, squirrels, possum, and deer could also make an important contribution to diet (hunting rifles were also useful during strikes).[23] The men plowed, fished, and hunted, gardened, and tended the animals, while women generally gathered fruit, preserved food (by canning in jars), cooked, laundered, and made and repaired clothes and quilts. In addition, some women added to the family income by working as laundresses or housekeepers, and occasionally as teachers or social workers.[24]

Race was an ever-present dynamic in the miners' lives. Alabama's black coal miners were racially segregated yet shared a community of interests with white miners. In the 1930s black miners were effectively disfranchised; according to Steven Christian, "Sheriffs . . . said they would shoot any black man who came to vote."[25] Because of the poll tax and educational quali-

Armed black and white miners protest during the 1933 strike. General Collection, Birmingham Public Library Archives.

fications, only a minority of white miners voted. No more than 28.4 percent of Alabama's white adults voted in the 1932 presidential election (and even this figure assumes that not a single black Alabamian cast a vote).[26] Similarly, as Andrew Ward, a coal miner since 1931, recalled: "All white folks were 'mister,' all of them, don't care how young they was. They'd call you by your name, [but] they didn't put no handle onto your name." At the same time, white as well as black miners were expected to call their bosses "mister," while not, in turn, receiving a "handle" to their own name.[27] In the commissary, blacks and whites would shop at the same counters, but then pay for goods at separate queues, and the black queue would usually be longer; in the larger mines, blacks and whites would share a "mantrip" (a mini-train) to take them to the face, but the blacks would be seated in the front half, where they were more likely to suffer from any accident.[28] At the face, blacks and whites would borrow powder from one another and help

Miners leave the "mantrip" after work, circa 1935. Photograph by Arthur Rothstein, courtesy of the Library of Congress.

each other with pushing cars; they might even share food, but this was not the case everywhere, and there were always limits to cooperation. For instance, Christian, who was sometimes the only black employee at a coal washery, remembered: "We would eat dinner together, [and] specially if it was cold, we'd have a fire together." He added: "[The white workers] decided they'd have . . . a bathhouse, so they built a shed [and] they built one bit for me too. They went in one door and took their bath, and I went in another door and took my bath."[29] The combination of segregation *and* sharing was also present in baseball matches. Blacks never played whites, but a local team, whether black or white, would be enthusiastically supported by all locals, irrespective of race. It was present too in the boyhood stone-throwing "battles" recounted by Aquilla Lowery, whose coal-mining career began in 1934: "Sometimes the whites would come home bloody, sometimes we'd come home bloody, [but] we was looking forward to rock battling on Sunday, [and] we was saving our energy."[30]

From time to time, a white miner might bring a black miner some garden produce, and on other occasions a white man would buy liquor in the black section of a camp, but interracial social relationships were highly restricted.

Indeed, Brown told the author, "There weren't no mixing. Forget about that."[31] However, there were four important aspects of life that underpinned the shared community of interests. First, before unionization, hours were often long, and a fifteen-hour day was common (although not always on a regular basis).[32] Second, although there was some improvement in the safety record of the Alabama mines during the 1920s and 1930s, there was always a danger of death or injury from rockfalls, explosions, and machinery, and between 1921 and 1941–42 there were 1,445 fatalities in Alabama's coal mines.[33] Third, although there was job discrimination, there was equal pay for equal work. Christian recalled a meeting where a naive white miner, having suggested that it was wrong that "the colored can make as much money as the white," was told by a union officer (with the backing of white miners): "If they did that you would be out of a job. They would have all black mans—get the work done real cheap."[34] Moreover, at least until unionization, all pay was appalling; Ward remembered receiving $2.00 per day in 1933, and this was probably typical.[35] Also, some days there was no work, and miners paid by the ton would often have to undertake unpaid labor. The miners' paychecks were also subject to compulsory deductions for such things as explosives, supplies, smithing, rent, schools, the doctor, and the checkweighman.[36] Many miners, unable to survive until the biweekly payday, would have to take an advance in the form of clacker or scrip (which could only be used in the company store).[37] Finally, there were the conditions of life, associated with the camp and the commissary, which were pretty much alike for black and white miners; most lived in similar company housing, and all ate the same kind of food and wore similar clothing.[38]

These hard conditions, made worse by the depression, were experienced by all miners, providing the basis for rapid unionization. Organizing the Alabama coalfields also involved leadership and bravery. As early as August 1930, President John L. Lewis of the UMW International received letters from Alabama urging him to reorganize the state's miners and telling him, for instance, that "the miners are restless and rareing [sic] to go."[39] But Lewis was opposed to a campaign at that stage, and did not intervene in Alabama until 1933. At the beginning of that year, he sent UMW International representative William Dalrymple, the son of an Oklahoma-based Scottish

Bolts replaced timbers in the 1940s to protect against the most common source of injury and deaths, the roof fall. No date. Photograph courtesy of the Alabama Mining Museum, Dora, Alabama.

miner, to Birmingham.[40] Dalrymple's purpose was not to organize miners, but to press legislators to back the Davis-Kelly Coal Bill. The Davis-Kelly bill was one of a number of measures aimed either at stabilizing the coal industry or at broader recovery, all of which were eventually eclipsed by the publication of President Franklin Roosevelt's own National Industrial Recovery Bill. Dalrymple's main concern had been to win resolutions from trade union bodies, and in this he was remarkably successful, with dozens of organizations agreeing to help.[41] One cannot accurately judge the impact of this campaign. It is clear, however, that Lewis was attempting to mobilize labor-movement pressure on President Roosevelt. On May 15, 1933, the final draft of the Recovery Bill was presented to Congress. It contained two elements particularly important for the UMW: Section 7(a), which established the "right of labor to representatives of its own choosing," and a provision for industry-wide codes governing conditions of employment (about which unions and employers would be consulted).

The Recovery Bill was passed by the House on May 27, and Lewis immediately dispersed organizers to rebuild the union. He understood what most union leaders missed, that although the National Industrial Recovery Act (NIRA) would provide greater space for trade unions, organization still had to be built on the ground. His main organizer in Alabama was William Mitch, who became president of District 20, an office he held for more than two decades. Mitch, born in Ohio in 1881, began mining coal at the age of twelve, when his father took him to work at a local mine. The following year the family moved to Indiana, where, while working in different mines around the state, he took various correspondence courses (including accountancy and law) and became a talented cartoonist. Rising through the ranks, he became treasurer of Indiana's District 11 in 1915, holding that post until losing an election in 1931. In 1925 Lewis attempted to become secretary-treasurer of the international union, but in order to retain the support of anthracite miners he backed Thomas Kennedy (who was duly appointed). Although Mitch was a former Socialist, in July 1933 a commissioner of conciliation said of him, and other District 20 leaders, that they were "very conservative in their methods of organization."[42] Mitch's principal lieutenants were Dalrymple and another UMW International representative, William Raney. Dalrymple was removed from the district following complaints that he used profane and aggressive language in meetings with employers.[43] Mitch established his headquarters at the Redmont Hotel, Birmingham, and launched his organizing campaign on June 4, twelve days before the NIRA became law.[44] Within only two months, in line with the UMW's success on other coalfields, Mitch claimed to have signed up 20,000 members, 100 percent of Alabama's miners—adding, however, "our big job now is keeping them in."[45]

The *Birmingham Labor Advocate* reported on large organizing meetings of 4,000 at Dogwood, 2,000 to 3,000 at Turner Town, 1,500 in Jasper, and 1,500 at Boothton, all in early July, and then in late August a total of 10,000 at three meetings in Townley, Cordova, and outside Hull.[46] At first the companies refused the use of premises they owned, forcing miners to meet in the woods or on the highway, or, in the case of the first meeting of Local 6241, under a shade tree in Johns. Steven Christian attended the Johns meeting and recalled that "people that's not working" joined first. Aquilla Lowery remembered that there were more blacks than whites at the meeting: "[The speaker] was telling us . . . we could get our own commit- tee, and if we couldn't work it out with the company, then we'd turn to them and they could work it out. And so we all signed, and finally we got enough signed to get a charter. And after we got a charter, and those whites were seeing we weren't losing our jobs, they begin to sign in too."[47] According to Mitch, an early problem was that some men advocated separate charters for blacks and whites, but he added: "We, of course, overcame this, because the majority of men seem to readily understand."[48]

Popular speakers at the early organizing meetings included Joe Clemo, an Englishman who had been secretary-treasurer of District 20 from 1898 un- til 1923, and Walter Jones, who had been the speaker at the Johns meeting.[49] With the possible exception of Mitch, Jones, an African American, is prob- ably the best-remembered organizer from the 1930s. He was born in 1878 at Montevallo, Alabama, and at sixteen started to work at the local coal mine, where his father also worked. He joined District 20 in 1898, and having held office in his local, was a district organizer between 1917 and 1919. Then in 1920—perhaps to dissuade him from standing for election as a member of the International Executive Board (an election he might well have won)—he was commissioned as an international organizer, a post he held until 1922. Shortly thereafter, he left Alabama and was reassigned by the UMW to Cleveland and Pittsburgh before returning to Birmingham in June 1933.[50] In October of that year, he wrote to Lewis requesting a posi- tion, then wrote again in November, presenting the following argument: "The coal companies and their agents keep it constantly before [the black miners] that the U. M. W. of A. is a white man's organization, and the negro is only used as a tool. We have to fight that propaganda on every side, and it becomes a difficult problem to combat when there is not a single negro that this great host can point to as a legal representative of the U. M. W. of A."[51]

Soon after, Jones was appointed as an organizer. Mitch's son, William, Jr., described Jones as a hard-shell Baptist, "a man of integrity and a very bright fellow." He was clearly a "great orator," and equally important, according to Lowery, "When he git round the company, he didn't chew his words, and eat what he had said to you out there." Brown, for whom Jones acted as something of a "role model," remembered that "it was *Mister* Mitch, but *Walter* Jones."[52] After Jones died, in August 1937, he was given one of the biggest funerals that Birmingham had ever seen, with some twelve hundred people in attendance.[53]

With the passage of the NIRA, negotiations over a bituminous coal code were hastened. These revealed a strong alliance between the UMW and the Illinois and Indiana operators, who retained union contracts and faced stiff competition from non-organized states to the south. To a large extent this alliance was backed by a National Recovery Administration (NRA) that favored increased wages as a means of stimulating the economy to end the Great Depression. The rapid expansion of UMW membership and the first ripples of a potential strike wave in the previously unorganized areas (notably in Pennsylvania) added pressure to reach an agreement.[54] In July 1933 the Alabama Mining Institute delegation was sent to Washington armed with a draft code based on the contention that Alabama should be regarded as a special case (a position which it repeated time and again in the forthcoming years). The institute argued that coal seams in Alabama were relatively thin and dirty, with the result that mining involved more labor per ton than in other coalfields. It added that the main code proposals required Alabama to raise costs far more than in other areas, making it difficult for the state's coal to compete (in particular, with natural gas, hydroelectric power, and oil), and that costs of living were lower in Alabama (a fact acknowledged, it said, by allowances paid by federal relief agencies). It accepted a proposal for an eight-hour workday, but wanted daily wages kept to $2.40 for inside workers and $2.00 for outside labor.[55] The union might have countered that Alabama's labor intensity was a consequence of utilizing cheap labor rather than new machinery, but, understandably, they seem to have concentrated on the justice of equalizing wages. Eventually, the Coal Code—endorsed by Roosevelt on September 18 but not effective in Alabama until October 2, 1933—maintained North/South differentials, while awarding Alabama's miners higher-percentage increases than elsewhere. The state's main minimum rates were to be fixed at $3.40 for inside skilled workers and $2.40 for outside common labor, the former amounting to a 64.3 percent increase, compared with no raise for inside skilled workers in Illinois (who, however, were already paid $5.00 per day).[56]

One might have expected Mitch to have been pleased with the achievement of an eight-hour day and substantial pay increases. He had hoped for higher wage increases, partly because some Alabama operators had refused to sign the code. To make matters worse, the DeBardeleben Coal Company, one of the largest in the state, fired union activists, even though strikes at three of its mines failed to block these victimizations. Informing Lewis about the Alabama code, Mitch reported: "We now have agitation by members of our organization wanting to call a general strike to force action of Coal Companies to put discharged men back to work." But, he added, "I will not sanction any such move as I would fear the results."[57] Then, from October 2, some 1,740 miners, led by men at the Montevallo mine, walked out on strike, complaining about differences over the checkoff and other issues. On October 15, Mitch and a federal representative persuaded the men to return to work, but resentments remained.[58] By the end of the year, the employers had agreed to participate in a local three-man Coal Labor Board—which had Mitch as the employees' representative and Judge James Acuff as the presidential nominee—but there was still widespread dissatisfaction, and Mitch told Lewis: "The operators here are very much concerned throughout the various fields because of the attitude of the men in trying to force full recognition . . . and the check-off. There is a strike program which has been organized under cover and I am opposing the strike program because I feel that they cannot make a successful strike in Alabama. However, I am using the situation as much as possible. . . . I am insisting that the operators should make a contract with us."[59]

Mitch misjudged the situation. The operators would not concede a contract, leading to a rank-and-file rebellion culminating in strike action. Strikes began at two Cahaba mines on February 19, 1933. By February 23, "an armed mob in excess of 1,000 men, white and black, disarmed a force of 15 deputy sheriffs . . . [and] on the following day all roads . . . were guarded by striking miners, and all vehicles were searched for strikebreakers and deputies."[60] Governor Miller rushed a force of National Guards into the strike zone, but this failed to prevent the strike from spreading. On March

5 approximately 1,450 miners in Jefferson and Walker Counties joined the 1,200 men already on strike, and by March 9 more than 10,000 miners had walked out.[61] A. B. Aldridge, one of the state's leading operators, complained to Miller that when he found 250 pickets on his property and informed them that they were breaking the law, they replied that "they did know it, but did not care—that no man was going to work there that day." He also reported "mobs" of 500 at Coal Valley and more than 600 at America, "armed with all kinds of guns" and led by "negroes and white[s]."[62] The miners considered the National Guard a hostile force, and, partly because of the strikers' militancy and resentment, Miller asked General Persons, the force's commanding officer, to mediate a settlement. An agreement was probably made more likely by the provision of some New Deal relief for the strikers, and by the unilateral decision of TCI and two other captive concerns, Republic and Woodward, to introduce a checkoff system. On March 16 operators representing 85 percent of Alabama's commercial production reached an agreement with Mitch, accepting the checkoff and full implementation of the Coal Code (including future amendments). Mitch did not consider the agreement to be ideal, but calculated that "the strike had had the effect of compelling more respect for the miners."[63]

Peace on the coalfield was short-lived. On March 31 the NRA revised the Coal Code, providing a further increase of $1.20 per week in Alabama, thus further reducing the North/South wage differential. The operators responded by closing their mines until they had secured a restraining order in the federal courts, but when they reopened them, on April 4, most miners rejected Mitch's advice and refused to return.[64] The Alabama operators directed their anger at northern owners, with Forney Johnston, their representative at NRA hearings in Washington, D.C., alleging that the amended code was initiated by a triumvirate that included J. D. A. Morrow of the Pittsburgh Coal Company, Charles O'Neill of the Central Pennsylvania Coal Operators, and Lewis. When Johnston went further, and threatened "civil war" if Alabama was forced to implement the revision, Lewis responded by saying that, if this happened, "the United Mine Workers' of America are ready within 15 days to furnish the President with 20 army divisions [to suppress the rebellion]." Nevertheless, on April 17 a gathering of three hundred southern industrialists applauded the statement that "secession may be the ultimate outcome in the fight to preserve Southern industry by the maintenance of a wage differential."[65]

With the closure of the TCI and DeBardeleben Company mines, the Alabama strike included 21,000 men, and it showed definite signs of spreading to other industries.[66] On April 16, Persons informed Miller that at TCI's Docena mine, "75 negroes . . . said they would beat anybody that bothered them," and a group of leading employers told the governor that the general situation was "terrible." One operator argued: "There has never been a time when a Governor of Alabama was faced with a greater crisis."[67] On April 18, despite the presence of National Guardsmen armed with machine guns, a 750-strong picket managed to close down the Porter mine, and the following day the mine's irate vice president informed Miller:

Radical labor agitators and some communists have called the negroes in this district "Mister" and "Brother," and put their arms around them and fraternized with them in public meeting places. . . . As a result the labor situation at the mines in this district has veered entirely away from any question of wage rates and hours of work, and is now a question of whether or not mobs composed of illiterate, ignorant blacks, and some illiterate whites, can continue to ignore and defy all of our laws. . . . [Their attitude] is worse than at any time since reconstruction. . . . If this demoralization is not halted . . . it will undoubtedly spread to the agricultural sections of our state.[68]

The following day, the Red Diamond mine was closed by 1,000 pickets ("mostly negroes") who had arrived in forty-five automobiles and eight trucks.[69] In the end, a compromise was reached providing Alabama miners with a thirty-five-hour week (part of the revised code) and a 40-cent rise, increasing the pay of skilled indoor men to $3.80 per day. By May 2 most miners had returned to work.[70]

Although, once again, there was some disappointment with this outcome, material advances had been won and union organization had been strengthened. However, two of the larger companies refused to sign a contract; these were the DeBardeleben, run by Henry DeBardeleben, and the Alabama Fuel and Iron (AFI), run by his brother, Charlie, which had managed to operate throughout the stoppage. Organizing these two companies was made more difficult, and more bloody, because of the brothers' willingness to make use of machine guns (sometimes placed in "nests"), "organizer traps" charged with dynamite, and copious amounts of tear gas.[71] Nevertheless, Henry DeBardeleben agreed to reinstate the miners he had fired in 1933. In late May 1934 he begrudgingly signed an agreement similar to others in Alabama (permitting, however, some dismissals).[72] By contrast, Charlie DeBardeleben never did sign a contract, but to retain his workforce he was compelled to pay wages equal to those in union mines. In August 1934, after his one mine in Jefferson County, Overton, had been organized by Raney and Jones, he closed it down rather than recognize the union, and this doubtless had an impact on his remaining workers. These were all employed in an isolated part of St. Clair County (where the mines remained non-union until they were closed in 1950).[73] By the end of 1934, only 10 percent of Alabama's coal miners were outside the UMW, and most of these were members of AFI and TCI company unions (disparagingly referred to as "popsicle" unions from the company's habit of providing this icy refreshment at company-dominated union meetings).[74]

At the beginning of May 1934, just as the coal miners' stoppage was ending, the district's 8,000 iron ore miners, members of the Mine, Mill and Smelter Workers Union, went on strike. They demanded equality with coal miners, but despite considerable militancy, they were unsuccessful and returned to work on June 27 with a small wage rise and no union recognition.[75] This failure was probably associated with General Persons's expansion of his National Guard force from the 225 or so deployed in the coal dispute to about 475, thus enabling him to halt effective picketing and prevent the strike from spreading to steel production.[76] Ore mining was regarded as part of the steel industry, and the lack of an industrial code for steel may also have affected the strike's outcome.[77]

The ore stoppage, like the coal strikes, should be seen as part of the broader unrest that marked 1934. Members of the Communist Party helped spread the strike to the TCI coal mines, and then to that company's ore miners.[78] In addition to the impact that Alabama coal miners had on the wider working class through their strikes and rank-and-file contacts, the UMW had influence at an official level. For a short year, Mitch was president of the Alabama State Federation of Labor, leaving that post once the UMW and the other unions of the Congress of Industrial Organization

(CIO) split from the American Federation of Labor (AFL). From June 1936 he was the southern regional director of the CIO's Steel Workers Organizing Committee (SWOC).[79]

For Alabama's coal miners, there was one more major battle before their union was firmly established. The 1934 contract was due to expire at the end of March 1935, and when negotiations failed a strike was called for June 16. However, after the NIRA was invalidated by the U.S. Supreme Court in May 1935, Lewis accepted Roosevelt's request to postpone the stoppage until after the passage of the Guffey-Snyder Bill. By August there was widespread unrest in Alabama, and Mitch complained that he was having "considerable trouble with stampede strikes."[80] From September 21 there was a four-day national strike which lifted the northern skilled rate from $5.00 to $5.50 a day, but the Alabama operators refused to concede any increase, thus forcing District 20 to continue a local stoppage.[81] On October 3 a march by eighteen hundred miners forced the closure of the Red Diamond mine, owned by Charles DeBardeleben, Jr., son of the AFI president. On October 28 a much smaller, peaceful march to AFI's Acmar mine was met with machine gun fire, killing one miner. Charles DeBardeleben, Sr., was among fourteen men held responsible for what the coroner regarded as homicide. When a grand jury refused to charge thirteen of these men, including Charles, Alabama's attorney general concluded that "a small coterie of men are preventing law enforcement in [St. Clair] county."[82]

With the NIRA no longer in force, strike relief was unavailable or meager; by late October, the "morale of the men [was] not good," and a month later some miners were said to be "absolutely starving."[83] The leadership also felt the strain. Former UMW International president Frank Hayes, who had been sent to assist District 20, informed Lewis: "Mitch is quite excitable and 'blows up' at times. . . . The presence of the boys seeking relief seems to get on his nerves." Mitch was also becoming worried that the operators wanted to break the union, as they had done in 1921.[84] However, when the operators threatened to reopen the mines, Governor Bibb Graves, fearing bloodshed, made it clear that he opposed deployment of the National Guard and offered instead to act as a mediator. The ensuing offer provided only a 20-cent increase, to $4.00 a day on the skilled inside rate. The miners, nearing exhaustion, agreed and returned to work on November 17.[85]

The 1935 strike had been a hard one, but the union had survived and demonstrated that it was a force to be reckoned with. Soon after, the truck mine operators reached an agreement with District 20, and on April 1, 1937, Alabama operators agreed to raise the inside skilled rate to $4.50 a day and to introduce an overtime payment (set at time and a half). From 1935, industrial relations in Alabama coal mining became less dramatic (excepting the AFI) because the district was well organized. As Lowery recalled, "When John L. Lewis said 'no contract' you didn't have to put pickets out there—coal miners wouldn't cross a picket line."[86] On April 2, 1939, there was "no contract," and Alabama's miners struck, the only exceptions being the AFI and the truck mines. The latter had pledged to implement changes then being negotiated at the Appalachian Conference, the industry's major contract-making forum, and were exempt. By contrast, Alabama's commercial and captive mines had rejected such a deal, hence the strike. After a two-day Appalachian stoppage in early May, the conference agreed to a union shop, and on May 18 employers representing 90 percent of Alabama's commercial tonnage signed a similar agreement. Mitch smoothed the way to a settlement by conceding a strike penalty clause, and by explaining that all mine workers would now have to be union members, but employers would still be free to select all new employees. TCI, where a significant number of miners were members of the AFL-affiliated Progressive Miners of America, secured a renewal of the old contract. The Republic and Woodward companies had the "captive contract" extended to their mines.[87]

When the 1939 contract came to an end on March 31, 1941, Alabama's commercial and captive operators again refused to accept any settlement emanating from the Appalachian Conference, thereby provoking another strike (with the truck mines once more adopting the opposite stance and avoiding a stoppage).[88] Maintaining that Alabama was part of a national dispute, Mitch refused to appear before a mediation board established by Governor Dixon, thus making it easier for the operators to win local support for their "special case" argument.[89] Back in March, the Appalachian Conference had agreed to a "dollar a day" raise, and after Roosevelt (supported by Dixon) called for new negotiations, Mitch proposed an increase in the basic rate by $1.00, to $5.50, as a "temporary agreement." Commercial operators and then the captive owners accepted the agreement, putting most men back at work by May 14.[90] However, a permanent settlement would depend upon the outcome of a series of complicated maneuvers held at a national level, and these led, on July 5, to the removal of the North/South differential within the Appalachian Agreement, thus boosting the pay of southern Appalachian miners by a further 40 cents.[91] Alabama operators did not participate in the Appalachian Conference, paying lower wages than the southern Appalachian operators, and on August 3, Alabama miners began a new strike, demanding that they too should receive the 40 cents (a modest demand which would not eradicate the substantial differential between Alabama and Appalachian rates). Mitch denounced the action as "an unauthorized, illegal work stoppage," but by September 4 it had spread from its initial base among the captive miners to involve twenty-two thousand men, virtually the whole field. Eventually, with a hearing of the National Defense Mediation Board scheduled for September 10, Mitch was able to order a return to work, paving the way for a 25-cent increase on basic rates.[92]

There was one other issue of importance in 1941, and that concerned the captive mines. On June 30 the National Labor Relations Board conducted a representation ballot at TCI's four coal mines. Out of 5,277 eligible voters, 3,554 voted for the UMW, and only 758 backed the AFL affiliate, now called the Captive Coal Miners Union; as a consequence the UMW became the sole representative of TCI's coal miners.[93] At the national level, the steel companies were still rejecting a union shop for their coal mines. This led to a series of short strikes and, with the war approaching, to a political crisis, which was eventually resolved on November 22 when Roosevelt appointed a three-person arbitration committee that included Lewis and a pro–closed shop federal official.[94] The achievement of a union shop for nearly all the country's miners was a major triumph, but particularly in Alabama where the UMW had long faced great difficulties.

In assessing the reorganization of District 20 during the 1930s, we are faced with a problem: why did the union succeed in this period, when it had failed in 1920–21? One answer, which might be popular with retired miners, would be that this was because of Roosevelt and Lewis.[95] But there are problems with this approach. In particular, it belittles the leadership and courage of rank-and-file miners, whose strikes in 1934, against the wishes of Mitch (and presumably Lewis), were crucial to success. Moreover, Lewis had been the UMW president during the 1920–21 strike, and Roosevelt's administration drew much of its inspiration from that of President Wilson, which stood aside from the earlier conflict, allowing Governor Kilby to destroy District 20. Perhaps we should compare Alabama governors, where Graves, although not Miller, might be regarded as more sympathetic to labor than Kilby. We should acknowledge that Graves's governorship in the New Deal years was very different from his earlier period in office (1927–31), which he began as a member of the Ku Klux Klan. If we focus on Alabama's rank and file, it would be erroneous to believe that a lack of militancy was responsible for the 1921 defeat. The actions of political and labor leaders, and of ordinary miners, certainly played a part in the triumph of the 1930s, but they do not fully explain it.

Anyone who compares newspapers or official archives for the two eras can hardly fail to notice the difference in the political and popular mood. Here, one can acknowledge the contrast, and suggest two specific aspects that seem significant for this history. In 1920 the northern operators did nothing to prevent the defeat of southern miners; perhaps they thought it would help extinguish support for "red" (Communist) politics, then a major concern. In 1933 they were more worried about climbing out of the depression, and doing this in such a way that they did not lose out to southern (especially West Virginia) operators, whose market share had expanded during the intervening dozen years. The split within the ruling class was much deeper in the latter period, providing a crucial opening for southern miners. At the same time, whereas in the earlier years the American labor movement was weakened by a series of bad defeats (associated partly with the onset of a very sharp economic recession), in 1934 workers won a number of impressive victories (in a period when the economy was slowly beginning to recover). These two considerations, important in their own terms, help to explain the very different kinds of pressure felt by political and labor leaders in the early 1920s and in the mid-1930s.

A second important question is this: what impact did the rise of District 20 have on race relations among Alabama coal miners? Union membership and meetings were racially mixed; so was strike activity, and, although it has not been considered here, individual black, as well as individual white, miners could, and did, initiate wildcat stoppages. Earl Brown explained that "the union was the only place where there was equality." In union meetings people would be addressed as "brother."[96] Further, in the organizing campaign black miners were often in the forefront. Also, in meetings and rallies, African Americans usually led the singing and prayers that were a vital part of union culture, and Brenda McCallum has shown how jubilee singers, usually quartets, adapted the gospel tradition to pro-union purposes.[97] Blacks were elected as officers of locals and as members of mine committees, and they sometimes played a more prominent role than their titles suggested. For instance, Lowery recalled that in his local, "the President was a white man but he mostly put [Carlee] Thomas [a black man and vice president] up to speak." Perhaps the following incident, reported to Horace Cayton and George Mitchell during their fieldwork in Alabama (which occurred between March 1934 and March 1935), can be regarded as indicative of the confidence and interracial cooperation that developed among coal miners in this period: "A union man held a gun on a deputy sheriff while a Negro trade unionist was allowed to slap and curse him. The deputy had been 'hard.' The Negro escaped, although the observer thought the man would have been lynched if the white union people in the district had not given him protection."[98]

Although District 20 advanced the cause of racial equality, the walls of union meeting halls were not impervious to southern norms. Cayton and Mitchell provided the following generalized description of union meetings in the Birmingham district: "The chairs or benches for the members are arranged with an aisle between, and as the people drift in they sit on the white side or the colored side, according to race." They added: "On the platform sit the two or three chief officers of the local, usually white, but with a Negro chaplain or another Negro officer sometimes there."[99] Interviews with old miners tend to confirm this picture; the normal practice in UMW meetings being to have union officers—and, hence, virtually always at least one black miner—on the platform. Although blacks represented a majority of Alabama miners, local presidents and a majority of local officers would almost always be white (although Cayton and Mitchell received a report of two black presidents, presumably in locals with virtually no white members). African Americans were elected as vice presidents and/or recording secretaries, and sometimes as financial secretaries. Similarly, whites normally had a two-to-one majority on mine committees and something of the kind on conference delegations.[100] In photographs of the 1935, 1939, and 1940 district conventions, between 31 and 34 percent of the 160 to 226 male faces are black (although it is possible that a few guests and staff, probably predominantly white, may have been included). Another photograph, of the 1941 District 20 scale committee, the union's negotiating body, includes only three black men and fifteen whites, and, although Jones was effectively the district's third most senior leader, he was the only black person out of six officials.[101]

How should we account for this combination of formal equality and black leadership of militancy with white domination of the union? In good measure it was because of the existence, to a greater or lesser degree, of racial prejudice among the whites, but this does not explain why it was tolerated, apparently without complaint, by capable black activists. Partly it was because, as Brown said, "It was the thing that you accepted then, because segregation was just . . . white was white, and white was right." This acceptance of custom is echoed in Lowery's comment that there was "a lot of brain washing an' all going on." Lowery added what was probably crucial: black miners "figured that a white man could get a better deal than a black man could, out of the company." Similarly, Cayton and Mitchell interviewed a white trade unionist who, having just organized a local of sixty-five blacks and fourteen whites, told them that the former had voluntarily elected white officers, arguing that these could "more conveniently bargain with the employers."[102] Thus black miners were making a calculation about what was in their material interest; in their view, for which they doubtless had good evidence, white operators had more respect for white representatives than for black ones. Where black miners were the majority, they held considerable sway through elections and by insisting on committeemen's reporting back to general meetings. Brown noted: "If [a white man] wanted our vote he had to give some overtures. . . . [The black man] had a lot of influence when it came to voting."[103] As with unions in general, there was conflict with societal norms as well as compromise. In the South of the 1930s, District 20 of the UMW was the most successful democratic organization around, and biracial solidarity and unity is the index of that success.

Although one may debate the source and depth of District 20's success with racial solidarity, one must recognize that during the 1930s black and white miners came together to fight for economic justice. By 1941 the Alabama wage differential still existed, mine safety was still appalling, wages and conditions were still poor, and black miners still suffered from discrimination. As a consequence of union pressure between 1933 and 1941, a period of low inflation, the wages of Alabama's coal miners virtually tripled, and in some cases the working day was halved. Indeed, the 1934 strikes deserve to be much better known. Within the United States they were just as significant as the famous industrial battles of that year—Minneapolis teamsters, West Coast longshoremen, and Toledo Autolite workers—all of which occurred after the Alabama conflict started. But the success was not just about measurable economic improvements; it was also about the confidence that miners gained to limit capricious and brutal behavior by employers and foremen. The combination of material advance and increased personal pride, which benefited all Alabama miners, is best conveyed in this verse by Uncle George Jones:

> Now when our union men walks out,
> Got de good clothes on deir backs,
> Crepe de chine and fine silk shirts,
> Bran' new Miller block hats;
> Fine silk socks an' Floriseim shoes,
> De're glitterin' against de sun,
> Got dollars in deir pockets, smokin' good cigars—
> Boys, dis what de union done.[104]

4

Alabama Coal Miners in War and Peace, 1942–1975

Glenn Feldman

Coal miners in Alabama experienced both tragedy and triumph in the first half of the twentieth century, but their prospects looked decidedly brighter after America's entry into World War II. Franklin Roosevelt's New Deal did not solve the riddle of the Great Depression, but for many Americans, including Alabama's coal miners, it improved the quality of life and brightened hopes for the future. Protective New Deal legislation, structural changes in labor law and policy, a friendly and progressive pro-labor governor in Bibb Graves, and assertive federal inquiries of Alabama by Wisconsin senator Bob LaFollette and others combined to make the outlook of work and life much better for Alabama's coal miners and their union, the United Mine Workers of America.[1]

Alabama's miners had always been blessed, of course, with abundant natural resources with which to fuel their livelihoods. If Alabama's governors and politicians had not always been kind to the state's miners, nature, in a more fundamental way, had. During the early 1940s Alabamians mined the same fields that had made their state such an attractive industrial location for more than half a century: the Warrior, Cahaba, and Coosa fields, and the Plateau region comprising the Plateau, Cumberland Mountain, and Lookout Mountain fields stretching from Blount County north to Tennessee and east to Georgia. The Warrior field was by far the largest, comprising some 3,000 square miles of land and supplying 60 percent of the state's coal output. Miners had begun working the 400-square-mile Cahaba field in the 1830s using wagons. The 340-square-mile Coosa field was the smallest, but all three were rich in high-heat-yielding, low-moisture bituminous coal, an ideal resource for industrial use.[2]

During the early 1940s, the state's coal miners faced the prospect of decreased demand for their product because of the decline of the locomotive fuel and domestic fuel markets. But electric power generation more than made up for the loss of the locomotive market, and foreign exports also helped make the 1940s relatively good years for Alabama coal production. Supply was not a problem. Scientists, a notoriously serious breed, are usually not noted for their hyperbole, so the proclamation by one geologist that the Birmingham district was "a geologic Paradise" commands respect. Alabama's reserves were so plentiful in the early 1940s that the Tennessee Coal, Iron, and Railroad Company (TCI) alone ran four coal mines—in Hamilton, Wylam, Docena, and Edgewater—and produced 3 million tons of coal annually.[3]

Although prospects brightened some for Alabama's miners, the nature of their work actually changed very little. Coal mining in the 1940s was still dangerous, dirty, and difficult work. The vast majority of it was done in underground mines where extensive safety regulations were still three decades away. Coal had to be undercut and blasted out with dynamite from the seams before it could be hauled to the surface by electric locomotives traveling vertical shafts. From the surface, coal would be carried to company terminals on the state's rivers for shipping to Mobile and other Gulf ports. Some miners scratched and clawed out livings in tiny seams that ran some three hundred feet away from the main shaft. The prospect of disaster was everywhere, from dynamite going off at the wrong time or in the wrong place, to makeshift roofs caving in, to slower yet equally lethal hazards from years of inhaling coal dust and powder.[4]

Jimmie Crockett, a UMW member who worked mines in Savage Creek, Boothton, and Sayreton, remembered the hazards associated with capping dynamite, tapping holes, and testing the air for content; the carbon dioxide that would cause an explosion or the carbon monoxide that could choke one to death:

You would go in there and put two timbers between every one of them [spaces]. . . . Then you'd have to go and get that old poison powder and cut it half in two,

Each coal miner was assigned a numbered safety tag that was returned at the end of
the shift. Circa 1937. Arthur Rothstein photograph, courtesy of Library of Congress,
Farm Security Administration, Birmingham Public Library Archives.

and you had a drill . . . and you drilled a hole in the timber, every timber
. . . and first put that powder in a hole and then . . . go back and cut a five
foot fuse . . . take it over there and put it in that powder and run the
powder back in there. When you got that done you had to go back over
and tie them [fuses] up close together as you could where you could light
as many as you could get at one time to keep it [the explosion] from
catching you before you could get out. And then you would split the end
of the fuse . . . where three or four of them would light. Then they would
have a man sliding down the conveyor pan with a lamp so if your's went
out he could jump across there and light it . . . and [by] the time I'd . . .
got out of there, buddy . . . why the pieces of timber from them shots,
where it had blowed the timbers in two . . . would whiz by your head.
That's right.[5]

In such an environment, accidents were a matter of course. In 1941 an
explosion at TCI's Docena mine killed five men. Lost fingers and rockfalls
were also common there, remembered union miner Erskine Bonds. W. B.

Turner, a UMW miner at Docena, broke his back in a rockfall in 1941. Six years later a shuttle car crushed and nearly killed a cousin of Charles L. Fuller, later president of District 20 of the UMW. Fuller, who was born in a mine camp in High Level near Parrish, began mining in the 1940s and eventually worked mines in Shortcamp, Corinth, Gorgas, Parrish, and Cordova. He knew five men who were killed in mine accidents and a number of others who had wasted away from the dreaded pneumoconiosis (black lung disease). Fuller's father, Eli, was a black lung victim; he retired in the 1960s after entering the mines in 1906 at age eleven. An uncle died in a mine rockfall in the 1920s. Still, Fuller had no regrets. "I enjoy mining," he said. "Several of us work[ed] together. It was like being a family. You stuck together and helped one another and got real close." William L. "Uncle Bill" Logan, a veteran Pratt City miner, agreed even after witnessing the deaths of several coworkers. Mining "gets in your blood," he explained, "and you keep going back."[6]

But not every Alabama miner was so stoic. "The mines is dangerous," a veteran Jefferson County miner concluded. "I don't care what they [the company] do to it and what they don't do [to try to make it safe]." One of the greatest hazards during the 1940s and 1950s, according to Jimmie Crockett, was mine explosions due to high levels of gas in the underground air. A union fire boss at the Manuel mines, Crockett took pride in knowing more about gas composition and the hazards of explosions than anyone in management, both "for . . . my own safety and the safety of the people that worked around me." He used a glass-topped safety lamp stuffed with two gauzes to evaluate test flames for length and color to determine if an area of the mine was dangerous. "You had to know when you hit gas," he explained, "it caused a little-bitty blue blaze, but you had to tell the difference between [dangerous and safe blazes] you see." At times, even experienced miners misjudged the content of gas in the areas they worked; the results could be lethal. "I seen fire going down the old worked-out place as big as [a] car, just rolling," Crockett recalled, "and they wasn't supposed to have been no [gas] in there."[7]

Health problems after years of service underground brought slower deaths to many miners. One Birmingham district miner who suffered from black lung after retirement recalled the choked atmosphere of work underground: "The way I worked and the coal dust I eat and the poison powder I eat, it might have caused me the trouble I had [later]. . . . [W]hen they would shoot [dynamite], you couldn't see where you was going" because of the smoke and powder. Crockett remembered a retired miner telling him that the sudden death of his seemingly sturdy eighteen-month-old son and the "spasms" of an older boy might very well have been the result of improper nutrition and poor health conditions in Alabama's coal camps.[8]

The constant specter of disaster and the tenuousness of life and health for the coal miner led to community solidarity and, for many, a fatalistic view of the world. "If somebody lost a person in the mines or there was an accident . . . they all understood and they went to each other . . . they were together like one," explained Dr. E. L. McFee, company church pastor in a Walker County village. "But when things were going good," he complained, "the church seemed to mean little."[9]

Coal towns in the 1940s differed little from those in earlier eras. Poverty, poor sanitation, company surveillance, and social control in the guise of company paternalism were common. Miners had to buy their own powder, carbide, and other supplies at overpriced company stores using company money, or "clacker." If they took their scrip to town they could get only eighty cents on the dollar for it. A Pratt City UMW member recalled that "if you didn't trade a whole lot at the store, you didn't get to work." Czech immigrant Annie Sokira, wife and daughter of Brookside coal miners, concurred: "They liked for you to spend all your money with 'em. They didn't like for you to save your money in your [pay] envelope." "They give you the work," Luther Smith recalled, "and they wanted you to trade with them . . . naturally."[10]

The TCI mine at Docena was somewhat of an exception. After it was bought out by U.S. Steel, the company had launched an extensive program of corporate paternalism designed to undercut desires for a union. At Docena the company furnished a physician, hospital, church, baseball teams, bathhouses, and entertainment in addition to the company store. By contrast, the wife of a Brookside miner remembered that the company in her town "never provide[d] anything . . . nothing at all." Reuben Barnes, a miner thrice expelled from the UMW for doing supervisory work, provided perhaps a somewhat sanguine view of life in Docena. TCI "preferred to handle our labor on a 'you like me' basis," he recollected, it "was the only coal company in the state that did anything . . . to help their employees. Just concerned about them. . . . [TCI] was really good to its people." "As odd as you might think," a longtime Docena miner's wife agreed, "TCI made it comfortable for those who worked for the company."[11]

Pressure also existed to use company housing. Elmer Burton remembered that up until the mid-1940s, "everything was bad" at Walker County's Gamble mines. "They could fire a feller whenever they wanted to or . . . cut off [from work] the men that lived outside the mine['s company housing]. They'd let some of 'em work if they'd pay house rent. . . . I've knowed of my daddy to pay four dollars a month house rent, and we lived in our own house. But that [was] the system they had."[12]

Conditions improved the stronger the UMW grew, but Burton recalled having to attend early union meetings in the woods in order to escape company retaliation. "They done just about everything they could . . . to prevent labor from organizing," confirmed Birmingham's Ellis Self. A fifty-year veteran of the mines—he worked as a loader, rock man, roofbolter, shot fireman, and machine operator—Self recalled being threatened with termination by company officials in 1940 for joining the union.[13]

Union organizing and the eradication of company or "popsicle" unions were sometimes turbulent. UMW miners recalled that fistfights and strife accompanied union organizing drives in the early 1940s. Docena miner B. D. Ogletree believed the union served a useful purpose, but resented what he considered the "roughneck" tactics of coercing membership in the early 1940s. "I didn't join them till after I had to. Everybody had to, they made 'em . . . if you didn't you'd get beat up," Ogletree recalled. "'Course I was a Union man and I believed in it, but still I had [to] work and had a family and didn't want to get messed up. So I went the easiest way around."[14]

Other problems confronted Alabama's miners during the 1940s, not the least of which was a political and social environment that catered to the Birmingham district's industrial giants and was hostile to organized labor. The city was home to union-busting attorneys such as Borden Burr and one Burr associate who proudly described himself as "a son-of-a-bitch" who could break any union.[15]

Despite these difficulties, many Alabama miners loved their work and their way of life. "I liked to see the results of my work," UMW leader Charlie Fuller recalled. "It is a challenge to go into the heart of the earth and be able to accomplish something. It's a challenge to produce and to do it correctly." James Lincoln, a veteran union miner from Alabaster, said, "I don't [even] miss the sun. Don't even think about it." Ralph A. "Shorty" Blake, who began mining in 1941 and received thirty-five cents in his first pay envelope, concurred: "I've been below ground so much I don't like to get in the sun."[16]

Yet missing so much daylight presented unique problems for miners and their families. The wife of a Brookside miner explained: "To tell the truth . . . sometimes if it was cloudy [her husband] didn't see the sunshine if it didn't shine on Sunday and actually his kids didn't hardly know him. . . . [T]hey were asleep when he left and they were asleep when he come [back]. . . . [I]t was a hard life." A Docena miner's wife agreed: "It was dark when you went to the mines . . . and it was dark when you came out. The only time you saw the sun was the day they let you off. If something needed to be worked . . . you just stayed on and worked and worked until they got through with you."[17]

American involvement in World War II presented a special kind of problem to miners all over the country: how to maintain their status against operators in the face of overwhelming public pressure not to strike. This was an especially sensitive issue in the patriotic South and a state like Alabama. From 1942 through 1945, though, 7 million American workers participated in 14,000 work stoppages. In 1942 alone there were 3,000 strikes, with the number rising to 3,750 in 1943 and nearly 5,000 in 1944. "The sheer number of strikes," historian Robert Zieger has written, "was impressive testimony to the unwillingness of working people to permit government officials, patriotic slogans, or even their own union leaders to define the terms under which they would toil." In May 1943 the UMW considered a national strike that would have almost surely led to government seizure of the mines. Because of their desire "not to let down the war effort" and their confidence that President Franklin Roosevelt would "give them a square deal," unionists voted two to one in referendum not to strike. But more than 75 percent of them also added that they would walk out of the mines if their leaders called a strike because their loyalty to the union took precedence. The no-strike vote was a reprieve for the Alabama miners, who would surely have encountered fierce public opinion in the hyperpatriotic state. One Walker County miner remembered working double shifts at the Bankhead mines throughout the war years, without time and a half, because "they claimed they needed coal bad" for the war.[18]

Industrial production in Alabama flourished during the war. The Birmingham district was home to 1,230 coke ovens that burned coking coal to produce fuel for the area's iron and steel furnaces. TCI operated 416 ovens; Sloss-Sheffield operated 214, of which 95 were the old beehive type; Woodward Iron had 205; Alabama By-Products, 174; Republic Steel, 161; and DeBardeleben Coal, 60. By the end of the war, Alabama ranked fifth in the United States in coke production, furnishing almost a tenth of the country's supply. Miners also won a midwar boon in 1943 when a U.S. circuit court of appeals ruled that "travel time" spent by underground miners going to and from their work sites had to be considered "work time" under the provisions of the Fair Labor Standards Act.[19]

The war also brought racial tensions on a level unseen since 1919. Union molders and machinists in Mobile resisted having to work alongside blacks, and a serious race riot broke out in the city's shipyards in 1943 over welder promotions. The worst evidence of wartime and postwar racial dissension occurred in the ranks of the Birmingham district's ore miners. By 1950, at the height of McCarthyism, Alabama's white United Steelworkers of America locals had swallowed several black and largely Communist Mine, Mill and Smelter Workers locals. It is unclear whether radicalism or race was a more important factor in the fratricide and annexation, but the national Congress of Industrial Organizations expelled forty-four thousand black Mine, Mill unionists for communism. McCarthyism and the atmosphere of intolerance it bred surely played a role, but so did the heavily black makeup of Mine, Mill. The low point came when joint Klan and steelworker intimidation led to a representation-election victory and an election-eve brawl in which a Birmingham Mine, Mill officer lost an eye.[20]

The UMW, which had a remarkable biracial membership and leadership by the standards of the time period and region, did not experience the racial tensions that roiled within other Alabama unions. Some racial incidents did

The mining industry changed dramatically during the 1970s. By 1976, Alabama began hiring women to work underground, ending a century-long social taboo that blocked their entry. Today close to 10 percent of Alabama's miners are female. Photograph by Dennis K. Hall, courtesy of Jim Walter Resources, Inc.

occur, though, such as the police beating of a black worker in the pay line at Bessemer's TCI plant. But this incident was laid to company complicity, not the union's. The workforce was changing as well. In 1940, for example, only fifty-five women worked in the state's coal mines. By 1950 the number had doubled.[21]

Many Alabama miners recalled significant biracial cooperation. "In the mines, you worked shoulder to shoulder with a man," Walker County's Luther Smith explained. "You go over and help him push his cars up and he'd come over and help you. . . . [W]hen they went into the mines [blacks and whites] was all miners and they held nothing agin nobody. . . . [T]hey went in to . . . make a living and they all helped each other." Docena's B. D. Ogletree remembered that blacks and whites met together in union halls, worked together, and "budd[ied] together," especially when loading coal. W. B. Turner, a white Docena miner, believed that mine work and village life resulted in fewer racial problems "than there are today." Turner also gave

During the 1930s the workforce was almost evenly divided between black and white.
Photograph by Arthur Rothstein, courtesy of the Library of Congress.

credit to black miner militancy—not white—for initially bringing the
UMW to Docena during the early 1940s.[22]

A degree of biracial harmony existed in some company villages as well.
Despite the fact that schools, churches, and living quarters in Docena were
segregated, TCI was "not partial at all," resident Christine Cochran remembered. "They came from out of the state and they were making the money
and they fenced us all in and we all went together then. . . . [M]y house was
always full of [blacks] and all down in there. We just visited and ha-ha'ed."
Her experiences were confirmed by Docena resident Grace Darden, who
recalled that "we got along famously well . . . we didn't keep separately. . . .
We just didn't know what anything to do [racially] against each other was.
Everybody, I would say, almost loved everybody else. . . . [E]verybody
helped you. . . . We worked together and visited each other and, I don't
know, it was just . . . respect for each other."[23]

Because of the strictness and ubiquity of legal segregation, though, some
blacks felt differently about the amount of racial enlightenment present.
While blacks in Docena enjoyed the town's amicable race relations, they
were also acutely aware that their legal status as segregated persons kept

them from being inherently equal in all respects to their white neighbors. "Well, it's always been about the same," Samuel Kelley recalled. "[Whites] would talk and go on with you, but that was just about it."[24]

Soon after the war's end, hard times confronted some in the Alabama mines. Domestic demand for bituminous coal fell dramatically, but supply remained high. Alabama miners produced 18 million tons of coal in 1947 and 19.1 million tons in 1948. As a result, many commercial mines filled orders by operating only three days a week and were able to resist UMW wage demands. Frustration ensued for Alabama's miners, leading to several confrontations in the latter part of the decade. During the summer of 1949, a three-hundred-man mob attacked a small non-union Shelby County mine, assaulted its managers, and destroyed a considerable amount of property with dynamite. In the fall a rifle raid on the Preskitt Brothers non-union mine in Walker County led the Big-Mule editors of the *Alabama Magazine* to brand the violence "among the foulest and most cowardly crimes in modern Alabama history ... two vicious rapes of law and order."[25]

Still, relative to their trying experiences before the war, times were good for Alabama miners. UMW leader Carey Haigler, suitably, served as president of Alabama's state labor council. In May 1949 coal miners averaged $1.95 an hour, the third-highest hourly wage out of 155 American occupations. Historian Wayne Flynt has given credit for the post–World War II prosperity of Alabama coal miners directly to the miners' union. "Thanks to the United Mine Workers of America," Flynt wrote, Alabama "coal miners could no longer be listed among the white poor. . . . [T]hose who lived into the postwar era experienced unprecedented prosperity."[26]

Many others agreed. A host of Alabama miners were convinced that wages, hours, conditions, and safety improved with strong UMW organization. Years later, Iva Goodwin, an Ensley unionist and the daughter of a UMW miner, concurred: "My daddy was a coal miner and we were looked on as poor people [before World War II]. We never had any money, only clacker to buy groceries at the commissary. The union gets blamed for what's happening now, but people forget what the union has done—the union brought them up. We're really . . . middle-class people now."[27]

Federal government activism was another significant factor in improving

The Bensko brothers returning home after work at the Brookside mine in north Jefferson County, circa 1937. Brookside had a large Russian and Greek immigrant community. General Collection, Birmingham Public Library Archives.

the quality of life for Alabama miners and their families. New Deal and postwar spending by the Tennessee Valley Authority in Alabama alone amounted to $448 million, half of which went for coal and coke purchases to provide electric power generation. During the New Deal and World War II, the federal government constantly supervised the bituminous coal industry, and after the war, labor historian Morton Baratz has noted, Washington became "a party, willing or not, to every major dispute in the industry," leading to the revival of the UMW into "the most powerful single labor organization in the United States."[28]

The 1950s began well for Alabama's miners. In 1952 the state legislature, in a rare role as pioneer, passed unprecedented legislation that made black lung disease a compensatory illness. Union leaders reached agreements with Alabama Power Company for safety requirements related to drill operation and the construction of mine roofs. Production during the decade averaged about 12.2 million tons per year, making Alabama the eighth-largest coal producer in the United States.[29]

The most dramatic development, though, revolved around a joint federal government–Alabama Power series of tests at the Gorgas mines. Private and public geologists, engineers, and mine specialists from around the country descended on Alabama during the early and mid-1950s for a series of tests to determine if the underground gasification of coal could be accomplished. If successful, the procedure would have allowed scientists to convert underground coal directly into natural gas without having to extract it. While such a procedure was exciting from a scientific and management point of view, successful implementation would have greatly reduced the need for underground coal miners. Gorgas was selected as the test site because it was considered a model mine. Alabama Power employed five hundred men there who extracted more than a million tons of coal in 1955, making it the second-largest single producing mine in the state. Despite federal funding to the tune of $200,000 per year—and an international conference in Birmingham in 1952 sponsored by Alabama Power, the Southern Research Institute, and the colleges of engineering at the University of Alabama and Auburn University that attracted scientists from England, France, and Belgium—the experiments ultimately failed.[30]

Even though coal miners generally fared better in the postwar period, pockets of poverty remained. Historians have often portrayed the 1950s and early 1960s as a golden age of American prosperity, but for some Alabama miners reality was much more grim. At times during the late 1950s, staunch union miners were simply too poor to pay union dues. Periodic slumps in demand for coal led to uncertain and insecure employment. Coal mining had always been dangerous work, and the hazards continued to be present. But irregularity crept into the lives of Alabama miners at an increasingly alarming rate and the opportunities for work "gyrated wildly between periods of intense labor [and] . . . extended layoffs."[31]

Herbert South, a bivocational coal miner/Methodist preacher from Marion County, made $39.93 a week mining coal in 1958. His weekly wages over the next three years averaged $42.26. To say the least, it was a struggle for South to feed and clothe his wife and eight children. A slumping industry in 1960 led to South's being able to get just two days of work a week. Eventually, he moved his family to Arkansas, where they sharecropped soybeans and cotton. "Brother Carl," South complained to liberal U.S. congressman Carl Elliott before he left, "times was so hard. The coal business was pretty well 'shot,' and . . . good union men, UMW members for years, had to come out of the union in order to get a job and make a living for their families."[32]

Jimmie Crockett was one such miner. Crockett went two years and ten months without a regular mine job and had to drop out of the UMW because he could not afford to pay dues. He worked odd jobs and loaded coal at two north Jefferson County "wagon mines" for a dollar a week. At wagon mines (often called "dogtrots"), miners worked close to the surface where they set blasts and scooped coal out manually. The operations were generally simple, paid little, and were less dangerous than underground mining. The work was still difficult, though. Wagon miners often had to return to the work site after dinner in order to wade in and pump out freezing cold water so that coal could be reached in the morning. Crockett remembered coming home at nine or ten at night, soaking his feet in a tub of hot water, and having only enough time to drink coffee for supper before he returned to the mine and waded up to his chest in ice-cold water, to "try to clear that place up . . . where we could try to get some coal the next day . . . trying to make a living for that woman in there and [that] bunch of kids, and nearly freez[ing] to death."[33]

During his many years as an Alabama miner, Crockett endured a number of layoffs. Years later he recalled them vividly. "I had to go to a housing project, first one place and [then] another, anywhere I could, and try to pick up a dollar here, a dollar there," he said. "Buddy, there ain't . . . a colored man nowhere that has had it any harder than I've had it trying to make a living for my wife and kids. . . . It would get to where it didn't look like there was another meal coming from nowhere and I didn't know which way to turn and what to do." Jobless miners like Crockett wandered down Birmingham's busy Morris Avenue "from one end to the other begging, for work, for anything [they] could get."[34]

Irregularities in the late 1950s led to sporadic mine closings as well. Two mines closed in the Bibb County coal town of Piper. In 1957 miners and

Two men at a mine fall. In all likelihood this was a two- or three-man mining operation, often called a "dogtrot." The primary customers of these small operators were schools and homes. No date. General Collection, Birmingham Public Library Archives.

their families left Bradford in response to a mine shutdown. Some, though, remained behind in the small northeast Jefferson County town. "They just didn't have nowhere else to go," one old-timer explained, "and, too, the company houses are cheap . . . and they're just home to a lot of folks." They were home to Will Allen, a thirty-year veteran of the Bradford mine. Allen stayed behind in 1957 "because [Bradford is] home. . . . I don't want to leave," he explained, "I was raised here and I like to live here." "I just liked to work the mines," another old-timer said. "When I went to work that's about all there was—mining and farming." Through the 1960s a small wagon mine operated in Bradford employing a dozen men. Two others used the Bradford washer to process coal from the surrounding area.[35]

In some ways, mechanization was a bane to Alabama's miners and their union, especially during the 1950s. In 1940 some seventeen thousand miners worked in Alabama. Ten years later the number was virtually the same, but by 1960 only half that number remained.[36] The vast majority of these survivors were white. The number of blacks mining coal in the South fell 50 percent from 1930 to 1950 and another 50 percent in the next ten years, so that by 1960 blacks made up just 6.8 percent of southern coal miners. Some scholars have been critical of the UMW, pointing to mechanization and racism as the prime culprits for this decline, and assigning some responsibility to the racial shortcomings of the UMW. As mechanization increased, prejudiced employers failed to upgrade unskilled black coal cutters or loaders to mechanical cutting and loading jobs. Strip mining only exacerbated this trend. Historian Charles Perry echoed the harsh criticism of Darrold T. Barnum on the issue: "[The UMW,] 'once the most equalitarian of unions,' failed to force equality in upgrading and stood idly by while its Negro members were displaced and not given a fair share of newly opened jobs." Black jobs in the mines were lost, but reminiscences like those of Jimmie Crockett and Herbert South suggest that the late 1950s were hard times for Alabama miners of both colors, and the UMW was not exactly in a position of extraordinary bargaining strength.[37]

There is little question, though, that the world of Alabama's coal operators remained a bastion of white supremacy—even through the civil rights turmoil of the 1950s and 1960s. While UMW biracial cooperation may not have been ideal, it was a far sight more advanced than the racial policies prescribed by Alabama's leading coal operators—even as the controversy over civil rights and massive resistance was reaching a fever pitch. Hugh Morrow, Big-Mule attorney for more than a quarter of a century and vice president of Sloss-Sheffield for another forty years, took a leading role in defending segregation. For his 1958 support of race-baiting gubernatorial candidate John Patterson, Morrow was rewarded with an invitation to speak to the state legislature on the race question. On October 6, 1959, he appeared before a joint session and presented his credentials as a leading member of the Alabama Mining Institute, as well as his degrees from the University of Alabama, where he had played varsity quarterback and allegedly "introduced the curve ball . . . in college baseball in [Alabama]." After a few "nigger" stories, Morrow got down to business by praising Governor Patterson, fellow segregationist Albert Boutwell, demagogue Tom Heflin, and Mississippi senator James O. Eastland, founder of the White Citizens'

Council. Morrow then blamed southern racial woes on northern and federal agitators, the NAACP, a "dastardly" Supreme Court, and "communist
outfits" such as the Southern Conference for Human Welfare that associated
themselves with Franklin Roosevelt, Hugo Black, and Swedish sociologist
Gunnar Myrdal, the "product of one of those South-hating, tax-exempt,
multi-million dollar, leftist, 'intellectual disease carrier' Foundations." After
praising Tuskegee educator Booker T. Washington's "good sense" for defending segregation, Morrow declared: "The South, forever tragic, forever trium-
phant . . . finds herself today, with her back to the wall . . . making a last
stand in defense of her true way of life. If I am any judge, her people will
not surrender to the 'Pinks' and the 'Reds' and the 'Mongrels,' nor to any
foreign conception of sociology flying under the false colors of the law. . . .
Make no mistake about it," Morrow concluded, "if Racial Integration is
forced upon the South . . . there is going to be trouble."[38]

If little in southern society was color-blind during the 1950s and 1960s,
the danger of mining coal was one notable exception. Accidents continued
to take the lives of Alabama miners, leaving families without fathers, hus-
bands, brothers, and sons. In June 1956 an explosion at the Praco mines
killed Clark Hogeland and H. M. Robbins, the latter a sixty-one-year-old
who had been mining since he was thirteen. Hogeland, too, was a veteran
miner who knew well the risks involved in his trade. A sign reading "Jesus
Never Fails" graced his plain front door. The pair daily passed another sign
at the tunnel mouth of the mine that read: "In life, as in baseball, it is the
number of times you reach home safely that counts." At 9:00 on the morning of June 13, an explosion rocked the innards of the Praco mines, but it
was not until 4:00 that afternoon that rescue crews were able to start down-
ward in cable-drawn coal cars. Survivor Amos Reed explained that there was
so much dust, commotion, and debris that it took him a full hour to walk
to the outside after the blast. "I felt a puff of wind," he said, "It hit me on
the back [and] the first thing I knew I was lying on my back." Four years
later, a crew of eight men mining the Alabama By-Product's Maxine mine
set a dynamite blast without knowing that Benjamin Luther Lawson was
working alone in a vein close by. Fortunately, Lawson sustained only a broken leg and injuries to his arm before the crew located him by following his
muffled cries for help. A father of four and a seventeen-year veteran of the

mines, Lawson had previously been injured twice, losing a finger and break-ing his heel, but he planned to return to work as soon as possible.[39]

Safety conditions improved during the 1960s. From 1920 through 1935, Alabama ranked third from the bottom among the Appalachian coal-producing states in terms of safety, with one fatality for every 300,300 tons of coal mined. During the 1960s and most of the 1970s, Alabama rose two places to become the third-safest Appalachian mining state, with only one fatality for every 2.03 million tons of coal produced in the state's under-ground mines. Strip mining, of course, was even safer.[40]

Other improvements marked what was a turbulent decade for the rest of America. Veteran miners such as Walker County's Elmer Burton made $36 a day at the start of the decade. In 1967 the UMW Welfare and Retirement Board in Washington announced a $15 hike in miners' monthly pensions, a gain that translated into an additional $52,500 per month for Alabama's 3,500 retired miners. The following year E. E. Holyfield, president of Dis-trict 20, proudly announced that the UMW had signed a contract with Jasper's Drummond Coal Company to begin surface mining operations in Cullman County. The new strip mine, located in the Black Creek Seam, was slated to produce 20,000 tons of coal per month. Alabama production reached 14.1 million tons in 1966 and topped 15.2 million tons the next year, making 1967 the best year in two decades. By the end of the decade Alabama and the other Appalachian states supplied 70 percent of the coun-try's bituminous coal, and the 1969 national UMW conference was, appro-priately, held in Birmingham. The 1960s had been good years for the union nationally. It began the decade as the wealthiest union in America with $110.3 million in assets, including 40 percent of the National Bank of Washington's capital stock. UMW assets tripled those of the Teamsters and the United Auto Workers, and were five times those of the fourth-wealthiest union, the International Union of Operating Engineers.[41]

Several new mining operations opened during these years. In 1967 Ala-bama Power reopened its No. 7 mine near Gorgas and recalled seventy min-ers. Alabama By-Products opened a new mine at Cheopta, as did U.S. Steel near the confluence of the Big Shoal Creek and the Warrior River. Peabody Coal stepped up operations at its Warrior mine. Shortly thereafter, Alabama Power and Republic Steel announced the opening of a new underground

mine in Fayette County that was slated to tap the North River coal reserves
lying in the Corona Seam of the Pratt field to the tune of 2 million tons
a year. Operators planned to use the mine's output to supply an 850,000-
kilowatt steam electric plant near Wilsonville in Shelby County.[42]

A few moments of turbulence did occur in Alabama's mines during the
1960s, of course, such as the April and May 1966 strike of Alabama Power
Company's Gorgas mine and Southern Company's Shelby County site. The
Birmingham firm of Martin, Balch, Bingham et al. filed suits for $6 million
in damages against UMW District 20 and Local 7813 alleging a host of
labor law violations, including illegal picketing, threats, coercion, violence,
and attempts to keep the firms from purchasing coal from non-union operators.[43] At the conclusion of the strike, Alabama Power Company withdrew
the suit.

Overall, though, coal mining in the 1960s was safer and less turbulent
than it had been in Alabama's stormy past. Lane Horton, a thirty-five-year
veteran at Jim Walter Resources No. 3 in Adger, followed into the mines two
older brothers and a father who had mined for fifty-three years. Jesse Coley,
a third-generation miner at Jim Walter No. 3, dismissed a lot of the hype
associated with the job. "You always read this stuff in the newspapers about
strikes, violence, company repression," he said. "Well, I think that's non-
sense. It's not the way mining is at all. It's like going to any job." "Lotta mining is dead work," Coley continued as he described dusting, maintenance,
shoring up weak areas, and putting up heavy plastic curtains to channel air.
For shuttle car driver Ralph Glenn, a relatively new miner at only four years'
seniority, mining still possessed a certain awe and wonder. "When you cut
into the face you're seeing some place no man's ever seen before," he remarked. "[It] is by far more interesting than anything else I've done."[44]

Increasingly, though, cutting into an underground seam of coal gave way
to the gigantic bulldozers, drills, draglines, front-end loaders, and dump
trucks associated with strip mining. Surface mining became big business in
Alabama by the late 1960s, its success resting on its greater safety and productivity over underground mining and the utility of electric power generation in the light of atomic power's disappointing returns. By 1969 Alabama
strip mines produced three times as much coal per man, per shift, as underground mining. In 1926, when the state produced a record 21.5 million

tons of coal, it took 27,300 men to do it. But in 1970, when Alabamians mined in ninety-five strip mines and only sixteen underground sites, just 5,080 Alabama miners produced 20.6 million tons of coal.[45]

The growth of strip mining weakened the UMW, which had traditionally been strongest in underground bituminous coal mining, where it represented about 90 percent of all miners. But, for a number of reasons, in 1974 only 40 percent of surface miners belonged to the miners' union. Because of strip mining's tremendous productivity, wages and benefits were equal to or better than union wages and benefits underground. Surface mining was inherently safer; thus there was less of a need for union-regulated safety committees. And different skills on the surface led to a loss of membership to rival unions such as the International Union of Operating Engineers.[46]

Strip mining led to other problems as well. Early on, especially, little or no reclamation was done. By the early 1970s, as the environmental controversy over strip mining raged, Alabama operators reclaimed at a much higher rate. State laws in 1969 and 1971 stimulated them, as did public indignation at vast scarred and stripped tracts of land. Reclaiming involved using the overburden to put dirt and topsoil back down, choosing new vegetation to fit in with the environment, and planting trees and shrubs, usually pines.[47]

Despite strip mining's superior productivity, many were unimpressed, and some were outraged. Charles Richardson, a *Birmingham News* staff reporter, wrote in 1971 against "virtually unrestrained strip mining, an industry which in its newfound hunger, is gobbling up mountainsides, blocking rivers, closing streams, and killing off wildlife at a rate undreamed of just a few years ago. . . . Alabama's lasting legacy is a ravished countryside. . . . [The operators] are gutting the earth and leaching life itself from the Alabama soil." Another critic, reporter Waylon Smithey, wrote passionately about strip mining's "million-dollar draglines with 10-story booms that move scoops that hold 15 cubic yards of earth and rock and coal at a time. It is front-end loaders, huge, dusty-yellow mechanical behemoths so massive that each 10-foot tire costs thousands [of dollars]." "It is five-axle trucks each carrying anywhere from 30 to 60 tons of coal and each pounding many hard-surfaced rural roads to dusty oblivion . . . explosives on a massive scale . . . splitting apart great rock strata that have lain undisturbed since the world was very young," Smithey continued. "Faced with this accumulation of might and will power, nature yields. . . . Before even the first ton of coal is reached, the land is laid embarrassingly naked. Then it is carved away, layer by layer . . . pushed into mountains of ragged, dead rubble. . . . [It is the] worst scene on this earth . . . the valley of the shadow of destruction."[48]

Others defended the practice on a variety of grounds. Reynold Q. Shotts, an engineering professor at the University of Alabama, lamented the laxity of reclamation but praised surface mining's productivity and efficiency. Birmingham UMW representative Sam Littlefield criticized attempts by Alabama state attorney general Bill Baxley and state representative Chriss Doss to environmentally regulate the industry as "trying to put strip miners out of business," an action of obvious concern to the state's two thousand union strip miners. William Kelce, executive director of the Alabama Surface Mining Reclamation Council, ironically found himself on the same side as the union on the issue because, he said, "the public is grossly misinformed" about the environmental effects of strip mining. Henry T. Rogers, president of the Alabama Mining Institute, in an apparent fit of amnesia about Tennessee Valley Authority spending and government funding for coal research, declared that "there actually is no reason why the federal government should step into the [coal mining] field at all."[49]

Actually, the federal government had long been involved in the coal mining industry, and continued to be. UMW lobbying led in 1970 to the adoption of stricter federal health and safety regulations concerning poisonous gases and black lung. In truth, without UMW lobbying on the issue, Alabama coal miners would probably still be waiting today for protective black lung legislation and other health and safety regulations. One side effect of the new laws was the closure of a number of Alabama mines that were so small they could not afford to modify their operations to comply. Independent Marion County operators Herschel Springle and C. O. May cut back to half their workforce, while Fred Weeks and Enoc Childers of Warrior closed their mines completely. "I haven't got anything to retire to but Social Security," lamented W. C. Elliott, a fifty-year non-union miner in Marion County. "People who survive are going to do well," the Birmingham district manager of the U.S. Bureau of Mines said. But Springle commented: "It just looks like the end of the road for small operators."[50]

In 1971, though, UMW agitation on the health and safety issue reaped dividends. Only 181 men died in U.S. mines, the lowest figure in the twentieth century, yet coal production was 564 million tons, the third-highest total since 1951. Under the Mine Safety and Health Act the number of mine inspectors leaped from 220 to 1,300, inspections increased 126 percent, and the number of regulations jumped tenfold. New U.S. Bureau of Mines inspectors, such as veteran miner Fay Miller, became federal officials for personal reasons. Miller's father, himself a longtime miner, had died in a 1951 roof fall.[51] Perhaps as important, inspections tended to be less predictable. In earlier eras, a union miner recalled, the "companies . . . they know when the mine inspector was coming and they knew where he was going. . . . [I]t was just kinda like getting ready to go to church . . . you get your best clothes and put them on."[52]

In spite of the stricter provisions, coal mining remained a dangerous occupation. Alabama authorities recorded thirteen mine fatalities in 1970 and 1971. At the U.S. Pipe and Foundry's Bessie mines in 1971 a trolley operator lost control of his car when a wire came loose, leading to a collision with the rear of a vehicle holding four miners who had just repaired a piece of track. Two died and two were seriously injured. In 1972 falling slate killed Alfred Frank Stipes, a forty-nine-year-old loading machine operator at U.S. Steel's Concord mine in west Jefferson County. A company spokesman termed it "just one of those things." That summer a fireball from an explosion rolled through the Concord mine, the state's largest mine and usually a safe site. The fire occurred at 11:22 P.M., just as two hundred men were ending their shift and awaiting transport to the top. The proximity of the miners to portals of escape prevented the underground fire from becoming a terrible tragedy. Still, twenty-seven miners were hospitalized for burns and other injuries, one in critical condition and three in serious condition. A company spokesman termed the explosion "minor" and was quick to take credit for the rapid and efficient evacuation of the mine, although the UMW had traditionally been forced to battle and haggle for increased safety procedures.[53]

The Concord miners remained stoic in the face of what could have been a massive loss of human life. Carlos McCaleb, a thirty-year veteran, described the scene: "I was sitting on a tool box at the foreman's office waiting for the trip car when I felt the earth shake and saw a fireball coming straight at me. It blew my safety glasses off, and I lost my headlight. I crawled 150 yards and found the trip car. We rode on out. I guess I was lucky. . . . I may miss a shift or two." Dennis Stewart, sitting next to McCaleb, caught on fire. Fellow miners ripped off their shirts to put out the flame, but Stewart sustained serious burns. "Talk about pain?" one burned miner said at a Birmingham hospital: "You'd better believe it." "There was just a big jar and a bunch of dust came out of the mine," another said. "It sounded like one heck of a big rock fall," a miner added. LeRoy Oliver, a thirty-year-old Bessemer man, said he never knew what hit him: "I just heard a blast and got knocked down." "There was so much dust, a light wouldn't have been any good any way," pointed out Wayne Sawyer, a Forestdale miner who described how safety glasses, lunch buckets, and headlights flew in all directions. "Nobody said much of anything," crusher operator Jack George recalled, "they just headed for fresh air." Douglas Black, a railcar operator and veteran of the Concord mine for more than a quarter of a century, was knocked off his seat by the blast but kept bringing men out of the darkness and returning below to get thirty or forty more until his supervisor ordered him to go to the hospital. "I figure if that's the way I was meant to go," said the unflappable Black, "then that's the way."[54]

Union politics was rockier in the early 1970s than it had been in some time. The 1972 national UMW election featured W. A. "Tony" Boyle, longtime incumbent president and confidante of John L. Lewis, versus reform candidate Arnold Miller. Miller, an intimate of Boyle's last serious challenger, the slain Joseph A. "Jock" Yablonski, represented, for many, a break from the image of a corruption-ridden union. Yablonski and his wife and daughter had been murdered in their Pennsylvania home shortly after his close defeat by Boyle in the 1969 national UMW election—an election that a federal court had found to be rife with fraud. Rumors persisted that Boyle or his supporters had been involved in the killings.[55]

The federally ordered and federally supervised election, which tore union locals apart all over the country, also bitterly divided Alabama's UMW.

Boyle's supporters dubbed Miller's as "outsiders and left-wing sympathizers" and pointed to their political inexperience: "You can't come up out of the pit and run a million-dollar operation." Miller's people responded by branding Boyle "a dictator" and "a company man" who had compromised mineworker safety and benefits. In October, Miller filed a class-action suit against Boyle on behalf of Alabama's 8,000 UMW miners for the right of District 20 members to elect their own officials instead of the traditional method of having Boyle appoint them. Three Trafford miners filed suit against Boyle in a Jefferson County court, charging that his administration had cheated them and 8,400 other retired Alabama miners out of their pensions. The following month four members of Alabama's "Young Miners for Miller" sent a formal request to President Richard Nixon, Senator James B. Allen, and Labor Secretary James Hodgeson asking for a federal investigation into alleged acts of campaign violence and intimidation in their state.[56]

But Boyle received strong support in Alabama from veteran miners such as Samuel Kelley, a black Docena man who felt Boyle was "a great man" and Miller was the "company man." Olin Lawson of Local 8982 concurred. And Boyle appointee Lloyd Baker, secretary-treasurer of District 20, dismissed the Alabama request for a federal election investigation as a publicity stunt. On December 8, 1972, federal election officials determined that Miller and his reform slate of candidates had defeated Boyle by 150,000 votes nationally. But Alabama remained firmly in the Boyle camp, with the state's miners having given him 78 percent of their vote.[57]

Industrial relations were also turbulent during the early 1970s for Alabama's UMW. A U.S. district court judge imposed a fine of $2,000 on UMW Local 7578 for ignoring an October 1972 back-to-work order issued by Judge H. H. Grooms. The miners had participated in a mid-contract work stoppage at Burgess Mining and Construction's strip mining pits at West Blocton and Boothton in Shelby County. A year later, UMW Local 1164 was fined $1,000 by U.S. district court judge J. Foy Guin, Jr., for ignoring a similar Walker County order. In June 1974, Guin, who was rapidly becoming a judicial thorn in the union's side, issued a temporary restraining order against UMW miners at U.S. Pipe's Bessie mines in Graysville. The miners had begun a three-day wildcat strike after the termination of a union fire boss who had refused to heed an order to work alone in a section of the mine—an order that was in violation of the local's health and safety rules. Guin also imposed a fine of $12,000 on Local 8982 in 1974 for ignoring his back-to-work order for U.S. Steel's Oak Grove mines in Jefferson County. At Oak Grove, union miners had walked out in support of Alabama Gas Company miners who were picketing the importation of South African coal.[58]

As the summer of 1974 wore on, the issue of continued imports of South African and Australian coal by Alabama Power Company and the Southern Company became a major issue for union miners. Cliff Pierson, a father of two, had been laid off in 1967 as an iron-ore miner when Alabama companies began importing ore from Venezuela. After the layoff Pierson turned to coal mining, but, speaking of Alabama Power Company's plans to import 2.5 million tons of coal from South Africa annually, he said: "I've been a victim before. When they shut down the ore mines, I was out in the cold. Now, it could happen again." District 20 staged a series of public rallies and brief shutdowns in response to the imports, and Attorney General Bill Baxley filed suit against the companies under a state law that prohibited imports produced by "slave labor." In late August seventy-five members of the International Longshoremen's Association in Mobile refused to cross the picket line of seven UMW miners to unload a South African freighter. "The union wants that ship stopped," said recently elected national UMW president Arnold Miller. "That coal can be shipped 9,000 miles and still be competitive with Alabama coal [only] because it was produced by slave labor. I don't believe the people of Alabama and the South want to use coal clawed out of the earth by a chain-gang when millions of tons . . . of Alabama coal are readily available." But Judge Guin responded with an injunction to prohibit any continued picketing.[59]

In December 1974, Alabama's union miners took part in a national UMW strike that idled 120,000 miners and won a 64 percent wage hike over a three-year period. During the strike, armed robbers in a Washington, D.C., hotel killed District 20 president Sam Littlefield, who had entered the mines in 1936 at the age of sixteen. UMW membership ratified the contract, and national president Arnold Miller defended it in the court of public opinion. "I don't consider this agreement inflationary," he said. "We had 20 years to catch up." Miller and national UMW secretary-treasurer Harry

Patrick then checked into George Washington University Hospital, suffering from exhaustion. Alabama miners such as Stanley McDale exhibited frustration with public hostility to the strike. "People shouldn't point the finger and blame us for this," McDale reminded the public. "If we had a contract, we'd work. We only become important when we strike." Richard Hedriek, a Sumiton miner, concurred. "Why should we go back without a contract we can live with?" he asked. "Nobody gives a damn about us until we . . . go out, and then . . . it's all our fault. . . . There's no way I want a bad contract. If it takes six months I'm ready to stay out."[60]

Striking miners in the early 1970s found themselves supported by many old-time union miners who had endured conditions much worse than theirs. Black miners such as James Simmons and Samuel Kelley agreed. "As I grow older and I see more and more things," Docena's W. B. Turner remarked, "it makes me a stronger union man. . . . When the union started organizing, I was not a part. I was raised the other way," explained Turner, "but down through the years, it made me stronger and stronger [pro-union] because I see what goes on. . . . I will not cross a picket line. Teach my family that." Turner also took a measure of satisfaction in reporting that his father, who was a mine supervisor for most of his life, spent two years late in life as a mine laborer, joined the UMW, and "reversed his thinking" considerably.[61] Still, union or no union, Turner was not ready to recommend the hard life of an Alabama coal miner. "I don't think so. No," he said, "I would do what my father tried to get me to do, finish school and go to college and get a good education and go into something else. . . . I do everything I can to discourage my grandchildren from going to the coal mines."[62]

But at the midpoint of the 1970s the outlook for those who had decided to enter the Alabama mines was fairly optimistic. Health and safety was better than ever before. Union militancy and solidarity (if not membership), as evidenced by the brief 1974–75 strike, was strong. In 1975 Alabama produced 21 million tons of coal, two-thirds of it from strip mines, making it the eighth-largest coal producer in the country. Firms consumed 16 of the 21 million tons for electric power generation, from which Alabama got 75 percent of its energy. The other 5 million tons were used in coke production, chemical extraction, petroleum-based products, and other forms of industrial power. More than a million tons of Alabama coal left the state via

Mobile, and Alabama's coal reserves were estimated at 18.4 billion tons, the vast majority of it still underground. What is more, national hysteria over the 1973 "oil crisis" had led to a renewed interest in domestic fuels such as coal.[63]

On the whole, the period since World War II had been one of improvement for the state's miners. While the UMW's rank and file shrank because of technological and structural changes, the wages and conditions of those who remained steadily improved. But, as had been the case for miners in Alabama and elsewhere, each step forward was earned, not given—the result of organization, solidarity, and careful attention to changes in politics, society, and the industry.

5

Wildcats, Caravans, and Dynamite: Alabama Miners and the 1977–1978 Coal Strike

Robert H. Woodrum

For almost four months in 1977 and 1978, thousands of union miners struck the country's largest coal producers. The walkout by 160,000 members of the United Mine Workers of America started when their three-year contract expired in early December 1977, and it ended 111 days later in March. Alabama miners, members of UMW District 20, joined fellow union members in twelve states during the strike against the coal companies, organized under the Bituminous Coal Operators Association (BCOA). Rank-and-file miners demonstrated a remarkable militancy in Alabama during the longest national walkout in the UMW's modern history.[1] District 20 miners fanned out across the state in large convoys of cars and trucks in an attempt to shut down the few non-union strip mines that remained open after the walkout. The rank and file were determined that all Alabama coal production would be dug by union miners.

The actions of Alabama miners at the end of the 1970s did not exist in a vacuum. The democratic reform movement that swept the UMW in the late 1960s and early 1970s, though never popular in District 20, inspired a new round of militancy on the part of rank-and-file miners. Alabama miners approached the 1977 contract negotiations with their backs against the wall. They saw the BCOA's demands as a direct assault on the union's health care and retirement system, the "sacred right to strike," and hard-won improvements in mine safety. Alabama miners, like those in much of the rest of the country, perceived the BCOA's demands as a thinly veiled attempt to break their union. "I believe that was the first time the BCOA . . . really had their minds set on breaking the United Mine Workers," miner Gary Pickett remembered when asked about the strike almost two decades later.[2]

The 1977–78 strike ended fifteen years of rank-and-file militancy marked by an extraordinary number of wildcat strikes. In opposition to state and national leadership, the rank and file had long battled for the right to strike. They perceived the contracts negotiated by their national leadership during the 1970s as whittling away that right, substituting it with a flawed grievance and arbitration procedure. The 1970s represented a new era of industrial relations in Alabama coalfields that pitted miners not just against the coal operators but also against their own union leaders.

By the late 1960s the UMW seemed filled with internal political turmoil. Rank-and-file union miners rebelled against autocratic UMW president W. A. "Tony" Boyle in the 1960s and early 1970s. After years of struggle, a reform slate headed by Arnold Miller united under the Miners for Democracy banner to defeat Boyle in 1972. Boyle's removal as union president did not end miner protests, however, as wildcat strikes continued to draw attention to safety and health issues and disciplinary grievances. But wildcats also took overtly political positions, most notably when Alabama miners walked out in 1974 to protest Southern Company's plans to import South African coal for plants at a Florida subsidiary. Alabama's eight thousand union miners walked out in protest of Southern Company's South Africa policy on May 22. Hundreds of miners demonstrated at a company annual meeting in Birmingham that day against the coal imports. The miners connected the imports to the elimination of jobs in District 20 and the use of slave labor in South African coal mines. They further linked concern for their own economic well-being with the low wages and poor working conditions South African miners faced. "We don't want any coal coming in to this country that's got blood on it," said Howard Tedford, a miner from Adger. "The information we got is that the safety conditions in South Africa for the miners is real bad. If it's worked under slave labor, then you know it's as bad as you can get."[3]

District 20 members partially shut down the Alabama State Docks when the first shipment arrived from South Africa in August 1974. A series of legal setbacks, however, forced the miners to remove pickets, and longshoremen eventually unloaded the coal. National UMW officers later failed to convince federal customs officials to block the imports. The union, however, joined with community activists to continue to demonstrate against the South African coal purchase at Southern Company annual meetings through 1976.[4]

Concern about the working conditions black miners faced in South Africa may have united miners in Alabama during the boycott, but race remained a divisive issue in the state's coalfields in the 1970s. After 1930, as companies began to mechanize their mines, the number of black coal miners in the state experienced a steady decline. The most dramatic drop occurred between 1960 and 1970, when the number of black miners plummeted from 3,026, or about 25 percent of the mining workforce, to 806, or about 18 percent. During the 1970s, black miners in District 20 saw their numbers increase to 1,459. This gain failed to keep pace with white miners, however, and the percentage of black miners declined further, to about 17 percent.[5]

Mechanization, the decline in the coal industry between the end of World War II and 1970, and the growth of strip mining accounted for a dramatic drop in overall coal employment. Overall, between 1950 and 1970 white miners saw their numbers decrease from 483,818 to 128,375, a stunning decline of almost 74 percent. During the same time period the overall ranks of black miners dropped by almost 88 percent, from about 30,000 to under 4,000.[6] The introduction of continuous mining technology and the increase of strip mining account for much of the drop among both black and white coal miners. But historians Ronald Lewis and Robert Norrell have both criticized the UMW for its failure to protect the jobs of black coal miners in the face of industry-wide declines and technological change.[7]

Black male coal miners were not the only group in the District 20 coalfields who faced challenges in the 1970s. Affirmative action programs and successful challenges to legal barriers opened the way for female miners to enter Alabama's coal mines in the middle of the decade. In 1975 a group of six women began work at the SEGCO No. 1 mine in Parrish with more than four hundred male miners. Betty Jones, then a thirty-nine-year-old mother of three, found herself fighting a battle on two fronts—harassment from both her fellow miners and, most of all, from company managers.

The most significant change in Alabama mining resulted from improved technology, especially longwall mining introduced in the late 1970s. The new technology tripled to quadrupled production while at the same time reducing the workforce by 40 percent. Pictured above is a continuous mining machine that cuts the pathway for the new longwall technology, circa 1980. Photograph by Dennis K. Hall, courtesy of Jim Walter Resources, Inc.

More than two decades later, Jones recalled that the women received little training and that managers made the women work their first shifts without breaks—a violation of their UMW contract. Union officers, to their credit, eventually forced the company to abide by the contract, Jones said. If UMW officials were supportive, her fellow male workers often were not. "Some of them wouldn't talk to us, then some of them did, and then some of them were real rude and said ugly things, and you just had to ignore it," Jones remembered.[8]

District 20 miners faced other tests in the 1970s. The UMW-BCOA contract signed in 1974 contained a flawed grievance system which allowed companies to delay and draw out the process, and these delays often produced wildcat strikes as miners grew frustrated. When walkouts occurred,

Longwall technology, circa 1980. Photograph by Dennis K. Hall, courtesy of Jim Walter Resources, Inc.

companies took UMW locals to court and obtained federal injunctions to force striking miners back to work. These injunctions often caused strikes to spread, idling thousands of miners. A massive wildcat strike that hit the Alabama coalfields in August 1975 followed this pattern. It began in West Virginia as a dispute over the suspension of a local union president, but spread quickly to coalfields in other states.[9]

Alabama miners joined the 1975 walkout during the last week of August. They interpreted the strike as a show of solidarity for thirty-seven thousand West Virginia miners who were demanding that Miller renegotiate the 1974 grievance procedure.[10] The strike idled UMW members at many of the state's largest operations when roving pickets from West Virginia ar-

rived at mine sites. District 20 president Lloyd Baker, a former Boyle supporter, urged the miners to disregard the out-of-state pickets and return to
the mines, and U.S. Steel obtained a restraining order from a Birmingham
federal court ordering the miners back to work at its Concord mine.[11] The
pleas of union leaders and the court injunction failed to stop the strike,
however, and the miners eventually returned to work on September 3, joining other UMW members throughout the nation.[12]

A year later, Alabama miners idled the coalfields again when roving pickets appeared at large mines in the state. Like the previous walkout, the 1976
strike grew out of a local dispute in West Virginia. From there, the roving
pickets fanned out across the coalfields in several states. At its height, 90,000
miners walked out to protest what they believed was federal judges' unfair
use of court injunctions against the UMW.[13] Alabama miners began walk-
ing out in early August, despite the pleas of District 20 officers to return to
the mines. By August 6, Baker acknowledged that most of the state's 10,500
miners had stopped working.[14] Industry and Alabama UMW officials again
placed most of the blame on out-of-state pickets, but the action had strong
support among the state's rank-and-file miners. At a meeting on August 11
at Birmingham Municipal Auditorium, miners vowed to stay out in a show
of solidarity with miners in West Virginia. "We're not going back to work,"
some shouted. "When West Virginia gets their jobs back we'll go back,"
others cried out.[15] The strike ended in Alabama on August 13 after West
Virginia miners began returning to work.[16]

Miners directed some of their frustration at Miller in the 1977 election. The UMW president won reelection against Boyle loyalist Lee Roy
Patterson and his former Miners for Democracy colleague Harry Patrick,
but only with a plurality of the vote. Miller received 55,275 votes, while
Patterson won 49,042 and Patrick 34,523. In Alabama, Patterson easily won
with 4,395 votes. Miller trailed with 1,070, while Patrick made a surpris-
ingly strong showing of 1,438.[17]

In Alabama, another wave of wildcats began in June 1977. Like many
other unauthorized walkouts, this one—at a Jim Walter Resources mine
near Adger-started as a protest over the firing of a local union officer. By the
end of the week, ten thousand District 20 miners had joined the strike.[18]
Although the company's firing of local union treasurer C. C. Carnes directly

The Lawrence brothers, Bamon, John, and George, all work at the Jim Walter Resources No. 5 mine in Tuscaloosa County. All three work on the same shift, in the same section, and at the same job as continuous mine operators. Photograph by Dennis K. Hall, courtesy of Jim Walter Resources, Inc.

provoked the wildcat, several miners said the strike actually involved the bigger issue of mine safety. During a court hearing on the walkout, a miner testified that the mine had unsafe roofs and high levels of methane gas.[19] Miners began to return to work June 23, after Jim Walter officials agreed to reinstate Carnes.[20]

Strikes idled the Alabama coalfields again two months later, when out-of-state pickets appeared at many operations. Miners in West Virginia and several other states had gone on strike shortly after the 1977 election to protest cutbacks in UMW fund benefits.[21] The departure of the out-of-state pickets failed to end the walkout in District 20, and Baker admitted that Alabama miners made up most of the protesters. The district president attacked the strikers as "a group of people who just don't want to work."[22] The miners began to return to their jobs after ten thousand met at the Walker County Vocational School on Sunday, August 21, following a voice vote.[23]

Baker's poor performance in mediating these wildcat strikes likely hurt his reelection effort that fall. He had become head of District 20 in the fall of 1974, after a hotel robber murdered district president Sam Littlefield during national contract negotiations. Though Baker had won election in 1973 as secretary-treasurer, a position he had held since the 1960s, he faced a tough contest from Charles Fuller in 1977. District 20 miners had often criticized Baker for his lack of experience as a working miner, while Fuller, who had lost a close district president race to Littlefield four years earlier, began work in the Alabama coalfields in the late 1930s and had worked as an organizer and district representative. He defeated Baker by a large margin, 5,099 to 1,932. Miners for Democracy supporter Frank Clements won a close reelection to the union's International Executive Board, garnering 2,855 votes, with his two opponents receiving 2,377 and 1,620 votes.[24] The table was set for the renewal of contract negotiations with the BCOA in the fall of 1977.

Miners braced for the confrontation with the coal operators. Companies saw an opportunity to exert more control over their labor force, and they united behind the desire to eliminate the wildcat strikes. The operators also hoped to dismantle the UMW's health care system for working miners— the jointly administered UMW health and retirement funds—and replace it with company-administered private health insurance plans. They wanted the right to discipline members of union safety committees, and pushed for language in the new contract allowing them to offer incentives designed to boost production.[25] As negotiations dragged on in the fall, neither side seemed willing to give, and thousands of miners across the country walked out when the UMW-BCOA contract expired on December 6.

The strike began quietly enough in District 20, with work reportedly stopped at most facilities. A few strip mines remained open, but officials expected pickets to quickly shut down these operations.[26] Armed with baseball bats and crowbars, union miners fanned out across northern Alabama and closed down several of the mines a week after the strike started. Three to four mines in northeast Alabama, however, remained open.[27]

A caravan of eight hundred miners left Birmingham for northeast Alabama on December 20. The miners drove through Jackson and Dekalb Counties during the early-morning hours, closing down non-union mines. The miners eventually arrived at a Sand Mountain Minerals Company mine in Pisgah, where they burned the operations office and a pair of tractor tires, provoking several fights with mine officials. The miners also went to the Robertson and Associates Fabius mine, where they slashed tires and broke vehicle windshields. State troopers warned non-union miners to stay away from work.[28]

The non-union operators in Alabama, angered by these events, met with Governor George Wallace and state police representatives. Wallace immediately ordered James Fuqua, head of the state highway patrol, to keep the non-union mines open. Fuqua planned to use four elite platoons of fifty state troopers, supplemented by helicopters, to comply with the governor's wishes. He also assigned officers to guard non-union mines.[29]

Wallace's actions marked a change in his relationship with the UMW in Alabama. During major walkouts in 1966 and 1974, the governor had declined to use a heavy state police presence to keep mines open. The 1966 strike provides an interesting point of comparison because of the high level of violence associated with it. The walkout began in April, as then-UMW president Boyle negotiated a national contract with BCOA representatives, and lasted into May. In addition to closing down union mines, District 20 pickets shut down non-union operations and mines where the Southern Labor Union (SLU), an operator-dominated organization, represented the workers.[30]

SLU officials and operators sent a series of appeals to Wallace, urging the governor to intervene in the walkout. "We have been bodily harmed . . . [s]ome hospitalized and kept from our jobs by outside mobs of the United Mine Workers," complained Bobby Peterson in a May 1966 telegram to Wallace. Administration officials claimed they had no authority to arbitrate the dispute. "We regret the relationship between some of the coal companies and the two labor organizations has broken down and will assist in any way possible in cementing the relationship to its former status," labor secretary Arlis Fant coldly replied to one SLU official. Wallace later conferred with a delegation of UMW miners and, according to a Walker County legislator present at the meeting, pledged to seek a peaceful and speedy solution of the dispute. Miners eventually went back to work at the end of May.[31]

Now, in 1977, District 20 officials also likely hoped that their endorsement of Wallace in his 1974 gubernatorial campaign might keep the state police away. By this time, however, Wallace's stance on intervening in strikes clearly had changed. District 20 miners would find the governor much more willing to use the state police to keep non-union mines open. Wallace's meeting with the non-union operators in December was only the beginning.[32]

After meeting with the governor, Fuqua began a surveillance effort of the miners in an attempt to find out when the caravans were moving and where they were headed. The job fell to Billy Wooten, who worked for the state police's intelligence unit. The officer tailed union miners for about three months, attending their meetings and listening in on their conversations in restaurants. Wooten described his not-so-sophisticated method as "going around, sitting in coffee shops with blue jeans and cowboy boots and shirts on, and listening. . . . We were looking for anything where the miners was going to move in a mass movement."[33] Wooten kept state police one step ahead of Alabama's miners during most of the strike.

In January, Wooten attended a meeting at the Walker County Vocational School where leaders briefed about three hundred UMW miners on the progress of the national negotiations. He also listened in on a conversation between several miners at a barbecue restaurant in Jasper. The leaders talked about how the non-union mines were still operating and hurting the contract negotiations by diluting the union's bargaining power. The miners unknowingly tipped Wooten off to a January 9 meeting at the Bessemer Labor Temple. Wooten parked about a block and a half away from the temple and then tailed a caravan of sixty miners to Fayette and Walker Counties, where miners inspected several non-union operations to make sure they were shut down.[34]

District 20 president Charles Fuller wanted the caravans stopped, and he urged local union presidents to rein in their members. Fuller feared the roving pickets could lead to serious violence and confrontations with state police. The local leaders, however, had trouble controlling the rank and file. On January 3, 1978, Fuller met with the governor in Montgomery and explained that he would try to stop the miners from continuing the caravans.[35]

When non-union operators brazenly announced plans to reopen their mines on January 9, the stage was set for a confrontation between state police and UMW miners. Wallace ordered several platoons of the "special operations teams" to Jackson and Dekalb Counties "to preserve law and order." Expected confrontations never occurred because the mines did not reopen on time, but teams of troopers patrolled the area for UMW members.[36]

The troopers waited in northeast Alabama for two weeks. On January 22, state police received information that miners planned to take roving pickets into northern Alabama. At about 11 P.M., Wooten arrived at the Walker County Vocational School, where more than three hundred UMW members had gathered. A miner with a bullhorn addressed the crowd. "And he was telling them they were going up to Mentone," Wooten later claimed. "Whoever was speaking to them over the bullhorn . . . [said] they had non-union mines operating in north Alabama for TVA [Tennessee Valley Authority]. And he said they was going up and close the scabs down, that they [scabs] were hurting their negotiations."[37]

A caravan of automobiles then left Walker County and headed south for Birmingham. More miners joined the procession as it snaked through Jefferson County, then headed north toward Mentone. State police, alerted by Wooten's intelligence report, followed the caravan with a helicopter. As the miners wound their way up Alabama 117 in northeast Alabama, a platoon of heavily armed police met them.

The police ordered the miners to disperse, then descended on them—pulling miners from their vehicles, breaking car antennas, ordering the miners around at gunpoint, and shooting tear gas at them. Troopers arrested between thirty and fifty miners in the incident and confiscated firearms and knives. The aggressive police tactics resulted in the miners' failure to shut down any coal mines in the area.[38] Fuller and other union officials believed that state police used excessive force. "They took and treated them like they were convicts," Fuller remembered.[39] He worried about potential violence if troopers and miners squared off again. In the wake of the incident, worried relatives flooded the District 20 headquarters with anxious telephone calls about miners who had been arrested.[40]

Heavily influenced by the police violence and concerns of family members, and in an effort to avert further violence, Fuller and other District 20 leaders met with Governor Wallace in Montgomery on January 23. They voiced their complaints about police tactics to the governor and other state officials. Fuller accused Wallace of "declaring war" on the UMW in Alabama. Wallace told the miners that he had received information that the non-union operators had placed land mines along roads leading to their operations and stationed snipers in the woods. The state police had the best interests of the miners in mind when they stopped the caravan, the governor said.[41]

The meeting calmed the atmosphere for a few days. But miners and troopers clashed again on February 3 outside a Drummond Coal Company mine in the Winston County community of Natural Bridge. The incident began when miners stopped a convoy of trucks carrying coal for Madison County schools. The miners forced the trucks to dump their coal on the road outside the mine's entrance. Eventually, about two hundred miners gathered at the mine. When a platoon of fifty state troopers arrived, they were met with a barrage of rocks and fire from pellet guns. A few troopers received minor injuries, and miners damaged several patrol cars in the incident.[42]

The largest confrontation occurred during the night and early-morning hours of February 2 and 3 outside the non-union Oakman Mining Company strip mine in Walker County. Miners suspected that company owner Claude Prater planned to resume mining coal. When several union miners approached Prater at the mine, he panicked and fired a rifle at the ground. Prater later claimed that the union miners circled him and made threats before he fired. Alfred Key, who led the group of ten to fifteen miners to the Oakman site, denied threatening Prater. In fact, Key said that he saw several guns pointed at the group of union miners from a building on the mine site. Key said the UMW miners wanted only to convince Prater to join the union.[43]

The union members immediately left Prater's operation and began to congregate a short distance from the mine. When a state trooper arrived, the group of miners demanded that he arrest Prater for shooting at them. The trooper refused. As the afternoon wore on, more miners arrived and gathered in the yard of a nearby house. The strikers used citizens band radios to call for more UMW members. As night fell, the miners lit bonfires along the side of the road. Police estimated that by dark between eight hundred and a thousand miners had gathered at the scene. Prater and his terrified miners took cover in a building near the mine site as state highway patrol helicopters swirled above the area.[44]

State police units rushed to the scene when they received news of the potential confrontation. The troopers, in riot gear, met at Oakman High School. They considered trying to remove the trapped non-union miners by helicopter, but decided against it. Instead, Fuqua and other state police leaders agreed to move the miners back from the road and send a platoon of state police to the mine to bring out the non-union miners.[45] A pitched battle erupted between miners and state police when officers tried to enter the mine site. Police began firing tear gas at the miners. At some point a miner emerged from the house and lobbed two sticks of dynamite at the troopers. The first stick fell before it reached the road, and exploded without causing any injuries. The second stick failed to detonate after it rolled under a state police cruiser.[46]

Fuqua claimed that he ordered his men not to fire on the miners, but a trooper's shotgun blast struck the home.[47] Retired miner Thomas Cook of Empire sat in a car with his son and a friend as the battle raged around them: "They [the troopers] put the gas to us, shot through the windshield of the truck, shot the house," Cook said. "[They] come down here and jerked Gene [Cook's son] out of the car and Jack [the friend] out and several more that was there and kicked them right in the straddle; made them lay down in a mud hole in freezing water."[48]

Despite all of the shooting and dynamite-throwing described by the troopers, no one was injured or arrested in the incident. The troopers eventually moved the miners out of the way, and Prater and his workers were "rescued." The president of the Alabama Mining Institute, an operator association, praised Wallace and the state troopers for their actions and urged the governor to call out the National Guard. Wallace declined the request.[49]

The actions of the state troopers aggravated the situation. Many rank-and-file miners believed that the troopers served the interests of non-union operators like Prater. They regarded the confrontations with state police on the highway near Mentone and in Oakman as a clear pattern: "Every time they tear gas us, every time they beat on us, we learn a lesson. Before long, we'll be smarter than the troopers," a miner told a newspaper the day following the Oakman incident.[50]

Although several smaller incidents followed, the confrontation at Oakman was the last major altercation between state police and union miners during the strike. Troopers broke up a crowd of fifteen to twenty strikers who attempted to prevent two coal trucks from leaving a Jefferson County mine on February 17. Miners eventually allowed the trucks to leave the mine, but state police had to escort the vehicles after strikers attempted to follow them. The miners gathered again at the mine and trapped three workers inside until troopers returned to escort the men out safely.[51] Later that month, troopers dispersed a crowd of seventy-five to one hundred miners who had gathered to prevent a mine in Brookwood from reopening. Though the miners allegedly fired guns and threw rocks, the incident quickly passed without the level of confrontation that characterized the earlier violent outbreaks. The mine never opened.[52]

National events, meanwhile—particularly the UMW-BCOA contract negotiations—began to occupy more of the miners' attention. Disputes over the progress of negotiations quickly drew in District 20's leaders. Most, though not all, joined a movement to oust Miller from his position as the union's lead negotiator. The movement began in earnest after UMW and BCOA negotiators reached a controversial tentative agreement on February 6.

The proposal included a wage increase, but BCOA negotiators refused to back off from their demand for deductibles and co-payments for miners' health insurance plans and from their proposal that companies be allowed to fire and suspend miners who led or engaged in wildcat strikes. The operators also added production incentives to the pact, while union negotiators failed to include safety improvements and pension equity for older retirees. Although the agreement capitulated to the BCOA on crucial issues, Miller submitted the contract to the union's bargaining council with his strong endorsement. The council officially rejected the agreement by a vote of thirty to six on February 12.[53]

Fuller and other District 20 leaders, members of the state executive board, denounced the rejected agreement and issued a resolution calling for

Miller to resign as the union's chief negotiator. "At every turn this contract takes away, in hidden and deceptive forms," the resolution read. "It reduces and removes the union's power to contest unjust firings, to champion safety, to insure that those who work in the mines receive decent retirement benefits, and decent health care. It cannot be tolerated."[54] The group from Alabama sent copies of the resolution to union locals across the country.

As February dragged on, anecdotal evidence emerged that Alabama's miners supported their leaders' opposition to Miller. Most strikers interviewed at the Jim Walter Resources Bessie mine supported the criticism of the UMW president. "We don't want old people or children to have the light and heat cut off on them, but we're human beings too," an unidentified miner said. "We can't spend twenty or thirty years in the mines and then lose our pension and benefits on account of one man. The United Mine Workers is united except for one man, and we're going to get rid of him."[55] The strikers were unified in their determination to remain on strike until their demands were met. The federal government, increasingly alarmed by the length of the strike, was just as determined to maintain the nation's coal supply.

After the bargaining council rejected the agreement, the Carter administration intervened. The administration's initial attempt to broker a truce failed. The union, however, reached a tentative agreement with Pittsburgh and Midway Coal (P&M), a company not affiliated with the BCOA, on February 20. The Carter administration pressured the BCOA and the union's bargaining council to accept the provisions of this agreement. The council voted twenty-five to thirteen to send the "P&M" agreement to the miners for a vote. The coal companies eventually capitulated to administration pressure, and the contract went before the rank-and-file miners.[56]

The "P&M" agreement differed little from the pact rejected a week earlier.[57] Fuller opposed the proposal, although he said he would urge miners to approve it. Nationally, the pact failed by a two-to-one margin. Alabama miners joined fellow UMW members in rejecting the agreement by huge margins, 4,238 to 2,096. The union announced the failure of the "P&M" pact on March 5.[58]

President Carter immediately announced plans to seek a Taft-Hartley injunction to force the miners back to work. Federal district judge Aubrey E.

Robinson of Washington, D.C., granted the president's request on March 9. In part, Judge Robinson based his decision on administration predictions of dire economic consequences if the coal strike continued. Some administration officials believed that a million workers would be unemployed by the end of March and declared that coal stockpiles at many utilities, particularly those in the east-central states, had shrunk to critically low levels.[59]

Later, the administration received harsh criticism for overemphasizing the energy emergency. Electric utilities used western coal and transferred power in from other parts of the country to offset the effects of the walkout. Also, after mid-January, coal production from non-union mines steadily increased. Some utilities developed and imposed voluntary conservation plans, but overall the strike had little effect on power customers. Alabama Power Company and the Tennessee Valley Authority eagerly joined utilities in other parts of the country in sounding warnings about low coal stockpiles. Both companies regularly announced the number of days left in their coal supplies and trumpeted emergency cutback plans.[60]

In one of the more dramatic and bizarre events of the strike, Governor Wallace on March 9 called for the Alabama Public Service Commission to come up with a plan for mandatory blackouts after meeting with Alabama Power officials and consumers. Though Alabama Power vice president Sam Booker stood at Wallace's side during the announcement, the utility quickly sent telegrams to state officials disputing the need for blackouts. Predictably, the commission declined to impose the blackouts. The next day, after the telegrams became public, Wallace backed off his request, saying Alabama Power officials had misled him. "Alabama Power Co. used me as they have used the people of Alabama by charging all these high electric rates," the angered governor said.[61] At an Alabama Public Service Commission meeting on March 10, Booker and other power company officials, including Tennessee Valley Authority representatives, said the rotating blackout plan could be delayed several more days. The state's "energy emergency" seemed to evaporate almost as quickly as it had arisen.[62]

Carter's Taft-Hartley injunction failed to force union members back to the mines, despite harsh penalties for those who actively disobeyed the order. UMW members faced citations for contempt of court, and individuals who tried to keep miners from returning to work faced criminal charges.[63] Picket lines came down, but the union no longer needed them. Union representative Gary Pickett stated, "What I remember, very plainly, is there was one man in District 20 that showed up at one Drummond location, just to see if someone was there, and he drove back home—nobody worked."[64]

Anticipating conflict, Wallace again sent platoons of state troopers into northern Alabama. Strikers fired shots at employees as they worked at the Blackjack Mine No. 1 in Tuscaloosa County, halting work at the mine.[65] State police also began to escort coal trains through northern Alabama after they received reports that miners planned to derail a train as it passed through Winston or Walker County. Vandals struck on March 15 about two miles south of Jasper. Investigators believed that someone had waited for a scout car to pass, then threw the switch to a side track. When the coal train arrived, it was shifted off the main track and onto the spur track. Two of its seven engines struck a string of hopper cars on the spur siding and derailed. "It was definitely sabotage," said state police spokesman Roy Smith.[66]

Meanwhile, union miners continued to ignore Carter's Taft-Hartley injunction. They had been getting by for more than three months, living hand-to-mouth and taking part-time jobs—selling firewood, working retail or construction jobs. "If we have to picket we will," said miner Troy Downs. "They have taken my pension and my hospitalization away from me, so I've got nothing to lose. If Wallace wants to send the cops in, that's alright too. And let 'Peanut Man' [Carter] come after us. I don't care because we've lost everything we have."[67]

The miners received some help from the community. Early in the strike, bankers extended payments and allowed miners to take out installment loans.[68] Many miners also had saved money before the strike, which helped get them through the weeks without paychecks. Walker County's food stamp operations reported that applications had doubled to thirty-two hundred people in mid-January.[69] The long strike took a harsh toll on the miners and their families. Many cut back on health care soon after the walkout started. The Jefferson Health Foundation's clinics reported a 50 percent drop in visits as miners lost their health benefits. "We are definitely suffering a hardship without the insurance," Janice S. Thomas, a coal miner's wife, told a newspaper reporter. "I was hesitant about coming to see the doctor, but my husband convinced me to come, regardless of the strike."[70]

Former local union president John Stewart remembered that many union miners, particularly those who did not have other skills and could not find part-time jobs, went into debt. "There were a lot of people hurt, who were in bad shape that went through it," Stewart said. "We had a couple who had nervous breakdowns, that never was able to return back to work. . . . Some people made it, some people didn't. We had tough times."[71]

While the strikers battled bravely on at the local level—facing the state police, defying Taft-Hartley, and enduring economic turmoil—national leaders continued to disappoint them. UMW leaders negotiated another contract that compromised on many of the key issues that had motivated miners during the strike. Union and company negotiators reached the final agreement in Washington, D.C., on March 14. The BCOA compromised only slightly on its labor stability demands, and companies retained the ability to discipline miners who engaged in wildcat strikes through an Arbitration Review Board ruling attached to the contract. UMW negotiators partially gave up on the health care issue, agreeing to allow working miners to fall under company medical plans but convincing the operators to reduce maximum yearly deductibles. The companies also forced the union to back down on its opposition to production incentives, if local unions approved them. The union's bargaining council, on a close vote, sent the agreement to the rank-and-file miners for their decision.[72]

The agreement, with its compromises, broke the will of Alabama's miners. Exhausted rank-and-file miners and their leaders quickly rallied around the proposal. Although Fuller voted against sending the contract down to the rank and file, he predicted it would pass. At a meeting in Bessemer on March 19, some 250 union officials from dozens of state locals adopted a motion to recommend that miners approve the contract.[73] On March 24, by a vote of 5,183 to 794, District 20 miners overwhelmingly approved the three-year contract. The agreement carried Alabama by its widest margins, 87 percent to 13 percent. Nationally, 58,802, or 57 percent, of the miners voted for the contract, while 44,457, or 43 percent, opposed it.[74] The miners returned to work on Monday, March 27.

Wildcat strikes, the ultimate symbol of rank-and-file militancy, declined by 90 percent after the 111-day strike. Observers attributed this to the new contract language on the wildcat issue, a recession in the coal industry, and simple exhaustion on the part of coal miners.[75] Miners would walk out for seventy-two days in 1981, but the rank-and-file rebellion that swept the UMW in the 1960s and 1970s had ended. The union, however, survived the 1977–78 strike in Alabama, and miners still had an organization that kept them from working at the total mercy of the coal operators. "I'm not totally satisfied with [the contract] because I thought there should have been more in it for the miners—in medical benefits, time off and other areas," Fuller said after the contract passed, "but I am proud of the solidarity of our membership, and the way they stuck together. The coal mine operators were trying to take away a lot of the things we had won in previous bargaining sessions."[76]

The rank-and-file militancy of the 1960s and 1970s that culminated in the 1977–78 strike has left a mixed legacy. Without grassroots leaders or institutions to help sustain it, miners' activism proved vulnerable to economic realities during the 1980s. Union coal production declined in the eastern section of the country, and the operators targeted militants for layoffs. By the middle of the decade the UMW's share of production dwindled to 35 percent of the country's coal supply. Coal companies also began to leave the BCOA, and by the late 1980s the organization had only fourteen members.[77]

Nonetheless, miners realized an important lesson about the value of solidarity and its implications for improving their economic and political power. Alabama miners learned that they could successfully use the wildcat strike to police their contracts, to protest the firing of union officers, to improve poor working conditions, and to increase safety in the mines. The wildcats of the 1970s also demonstrated solidarity with miners in other states and showed that Alabama miners understood the implications of global developments on their jobs. Most importantly, wildcat strikes energized rank-and-file miners and inspired the militancy miners displayed in 1977–78. Rather than being passive victims, Alabama miners in the 1970s took an active role and fought to improve the quality of their working lives and to preserve the union in District 20.

Appendix

Officers of the United Mine Workers
of America District 20, 1898–1998

President

1898–1907	W. R. Fairley
1907–1923	J. R. Kennamer
1924–1929	George Hargrove
1930–1932	Vacant
1933–1962	William Mitch
1963–1966	Thomas Crawford
1967–1970	E. E. Holyfield
1971–1973	C. E. Beane
1974	Sam Littlefield
1975	Lloyd Baker
1976–1981	Charles Fuller
1982–1985	Tom Youngblood
1986–1989	Mike Gossett
1990–1993	Tom Youngblood
1994–1998	John Stewart

Secretary-Treasurer

1907–1923	J. L. Clemo
1924–1962	Vacant
1963–1975	Lloyd Baker
1976–1985	David Richardson
1986–1997	Earl Brown
1998	Wilburn Lollar

Notes

ABBREVIATIONS

ACOA	Alabama Coal Operators Association
ADAH	Alabama Department of Archives and History, Montgomery, Ala.
BPLA	Birmingham Public Library Archives, Birmingham, Ala.
LC	Library of Congress, Manuscripts Division, Washington, D.C.
NA	National Archives, Washington, D.C.
PSULA	Pennsylvania State University Labor Archives, State College, Pa.
SU	Oral History Collection, Samford University Department of Special Collections, Birmingham, Ala.
TCSH	Tutwiler Collection of Southern History, Birmingham Public Library Archives, Birmingham, Ala.
UMW	United Mine Workers of America
WSUAL	Wayne State University Archives of Labor and Urban Affairs, Detroit, Mich.

INTRODUCTION

1. John A. Fitch, "Birmingham District: Labor Conservation," *Survey,* Jan. 6, 1912, p. 1537.

2. John Drain, *The Coal Miner's Son* (Birmingham: Birmingham Printing and Publishing Company, 1985), 15–17.

3. Journal of Thomas Duke Park, Park Papers, BPLA.

4. *Birmingham Labor Advocate,* Apr. 5, 1909, p. 1.

5. Ibid., May 12, 1900, p. 1.

6. Eric Arnesen, *Waterfront Workers of New Orleans: Race, Class, and Politics,*

1863–1923 (Urbana: University of Illinois Press, 1994); Michael Honey, *Southern Labor and Black Civil Rights: Organizing Memphis Workers* (Urbana: University of Illinois Press, 1993); Robin D. G. Kelley, *Hammer and Hoe: Alabama Communists during the Great Depression* (Chapel Hill: University of North Carolina Press, 1990).

7. Philip Taft, *Organizing Dixie: Alabama Workers in the Industrial Era* (Westport, Conn.: Greenwood Press, 1981); Henry M. McKiven, Jr., *Iron and Steel: Class, Race, and Community in Birmingham, Alabama, 1875–1920* (Chapel Hill: University of North Carolina Press, 1995); see also Robert J. Norrell, "Caste in Steel: Jim Crow Careers in Birmingham, Alabama," *Journal of American History* 73 (December 1986): 669–94; Horace Huntley, "Iron Ore Miners and Mine Mill in Alabama, 1932–1952" (Ph.D. diss., University of Pittsburgh, 1976).

8. Robert H. Zieger, ed., *Southern Labor in Transition, 1940–1995* (Knoxville: University of Tennessee Press, 1997); Zieger, ed., *Organized Labor in the Twentieth-Century South* (Knoxville: University of Tennessee Press, 1991); Gary M. Fink and Merl Reed, *Essays in Southern Labor History: Selected Papers* (Westport, Conn.: Greenwood Press, 1977); Fink and Reed, *Race, Class, and Community in Southern Labor History* (Westport, Conn.: Greenwood Press, 1994).

9. Robert David Ward and William Warren Rogers, *Labor Revolt in Alabama: The Great Strike of 1894* (University: University of Alabama Press, 1965).

10. Eric Arnesen, "Up from Exclusion: Black and White Workers, Race, and the State of Labor History," *Reviews in American History* 26 (March 1998): 147.

11. Herbert Hill, "Myth-Making as Labor History: Herbert Gutman and the United Mine Workers of America," *International Journal of Politics, Culture, and Society* 2 (Winter 1988): 132–200. See also Hill, "The Problem of Race in American Labor History," *Reviews in American History* 24 (June 1996): 189–208. For a critique of Hill's position see Stephen Brier, "In Defense of Gutman: The Union's Case," *International Journal of Politics, Culture, and Society* 2 (Spring 1989): 382–95.

12. W. J. Cash, *The Mind of the South* (New York: Knopf, 1941), 249. Oral history interview with retired black miner Moses Hutchins, April 1985, transcript held by Edwin L. Brown, University of Alabama at Birmingham. Hutchins first worked in the mine as a trapper at $1.95 a day. That was in 1922 when he was eleven years old. His father had been "strictly a union man" who reminded his sons that "the union was the best thing."

13. Russell A. Kazal, "Revisiting Assimilation: The Rise, Fall, and Reappraisal of a Concept in American Ethnic Identity," *American Historical Review* 100 (April 1995): 437–71; James R. Barrett, "Americanization from the Bottom Up: Immigration and the Remaking of the Working Class in America, 1880–1930," *Journal of American History* 79 (December 1992): 996–1020; Lizabeth Cohen, *Making a New Deal: Industrial Workers in Chicago, 1919–1939* (Cambridge: Cambridge University

Press, 1990); Gary Gerstle, *Working-Class Americanism: The Politics of Labor in a Textile City, 1914–1960* (New York: Cambridge University Press, 1989); Gerstle, "Liberty, Coercion, and the Making of Americans," *Journal of American History* 84 (September 1997): 524–58. For work on the construction of race see, of course, David Roediger, *The Wages of Whiteness: Race and the Making of the American Working Class* (London: Verso, 1991); and Theodore W. Allen, *The Invention of the White Race,* vol. 1, *Racial Oppression and Social Control* (London: Verso, 1994), 22.

14. *Birmingham Labor Advocate,* May 12, 1900, p. 1.

CHAPTER 1

1. Carl V. Harris, *Political Power in Birmingham, 1871–1921* (Knoxville: University of Tennessee Press, 1977), 12–14; Ethel Armes, *The Story of Coal and Iron in Alabama* (Birmingham, 1910), 11, 48–57, 226–27; John W. DuBose, *Jefferson County and Birmingham, Alabama: Historical and Biographical* (Birmingham: Teeple and Smith, 1887), 123–24.

2. U.S. Bureau of the Census, *Mines and Quarries* (Washington, D.C.: Government Printing Office, 1902), 167; U.S. Bureau of the Census, *Ninth Census of the United States,* vol. 3: *The Statistics of Wealth and Industry in the United States* (Washington, D.C.: Government Printing Office, 1872), 602; U.S. Department of the Interior, *Compendium of the Tenth Census, Pt. 2* (Washington, D.C.: Government Printing Office, 1883), 1140; U.S. Department of the Interior, *Report on the Mining Industries of the United States (Exclusive of Precious Metals), Tenth Census,* vol. 15 (Washington, D.C.: Government Printing Office, 1886), 642; U.S. Treasury Department, *Statistical Abstract of the United States for 1889* (Washington, D.C.: Government Printing Office, 1890), 178; U.S. Department of the Interior, *Report on the Mineral Industries of the United States at the Eleventh Census,* vol. 7 (Washington, D.C.: Government Printing Office, 1892), 347; U.S. Treasury Department, *Statistical Abstract of the United States for 1900* (Washington, D.C.: Government Printing Office, 1901), 349.

3. U.S. Department of the Interior, *Compendium of the Eleventh Census, 1890, vol. 1, pt. 1—Population* (Washington, D.C.: Government Printing Office, 1892), 7; U.S. Census Office, *Abstract of the Twelfth Census of the United States* (Washington, D.C.: Government Printing Office, 1902), 149.

4. In 1880, 42 percent of the 389 miners were black; in 1889, the black presence had climbed to over 46 percent of the nearly 8,000 miners and quarrymen in the state. By the end of the century, African Americans made up 54.4 percent of nearly 18,000 miners, a percentage that would remain approximately the same over the first decade of the twentieth century. U.S. Immigration Commission, *Reports*

of the Immigration Commission (vol. 7): Immigrants in Industries, part 1, Bituminous Coal Mining, vol. 2 (Washington, D.C.: Government Printing Office, 1911), 136, 142.

5. A dearth of hard numbers compels us to reconstruct how race affected the arrangement of labor in Alabama coal mining primarily from the scattered statements of contemporaries. An early-twentieth-century investigation of American labor conditions by the British Board of Trade, for example, yielded this comment on the Alabama coal miners: "Both white and coloured men are employed in the coal mines as pick miners, but practically all the labourers are coloured" (Board of Trade, *Report of an Enquiry by the Board of Trade into Working Class Rents, Housing, and Retail Prices* [London, 1911], 90). See also U.S. Immigration Commission, *Bituminous Coal Mining* (1911), 200.

6. For background on the use of convict labor in the Alabama coalfields, see Alex Lichtenstein, *Twice the Work of Free Labor: The Political Economy of Convict Labor in the New South* (New York: Verso, 1996); and Robert David Ward and William Warren Rogers, *Convicts, Coal, and the Banner Mine Tragedy* (Tuscaloosa: University of Alabama Press, 1987), 26–45.

7. *Chattanooga Republican,* Feb. 18, 1893.

8. These ongoing class tensions are examined in depth in Daniel Letwin, *The Challenge of Interracial Unionism: Alabama Coal Miners, 1878–1921* (Chapel Hill: University of North Carolina Press, 1998), 40–51.

9. *Alabama Sentinel,* May 10, 1890.

10. Letwin, *Challenge of Interracial Unionism,* 51–52. High rates of turnover and absenteeism were a quiet assertion of what Carter Goodrich dubbed the "miner's freedom," a stubborn streak of autonomy deeply embedded in the culture of coal miners (*The Miner's Freedom: A Study of Working Life in a Changing Industry* [Boston: M. Jones, 1925]).

11. Letwin, *Challenge of Interracial Unionism,* 52–54.

12. On the Greenback-Labor Party in the Birmingham district, see Herbert Gutman, "Black Coal Miners and the Greenback Labor Party in Redeemer Alabama, 1878–79: The Letters of Warren D. Kelley, Willis Johnson Thomas, 'Dawson,' and Others," *Labor History* 10 (Summer 1969): 506–35; and Letwin, *Challenge of Interracial Unionism,* 55–67. On Greenbackism in Alabama, see William Warren Rogers, *The One-Gallused Rebellion: Agrarianism in Alabama, 1865–1896* (Baton Rouge: Louisiana State University Press, 1970), 41–55; Allen Johnston Going, *Bourbon Democracy in Alabama, 1874–1890* (University: University of Alabama Press, 1951), 41–60; and Francis Roberts, "William Manning Lowe and the Greenback Party in Alabama," *Alabama Review* 5 (1952): 100–121.

13. On the Knights of Labor in the Alabama coalfields, see John H. Abernathy, Jr., "The Knights of Labor in Alabama" (Master of Science in Commerce thesis,

University of Alabama, 1960); Holman Head, "The Development of the Labor Movement in Alabama Prior to 1900" (Master of Business Administration thesis, University of Alabama, 1955); Jonathan Garlock, *Guide to the Local Assemblies of the Knights of Labor* (Westport, Conn.: Greenwood Press, 1982), 3–9, 588–680; and Letwin, *Challenge of Interracial Unionism,* 67–87. For a general survey of the Knights of Labor in the South, see Melton A. McLaurin, *The Knights of Labor in the South* (Westport, Conn.: Greenwood Press, 1978).

14. May 13, 1882, letter to the *National Labor Tribune* during a strike against the Pratt Coke and Coal Company.

15. Letwin, *Challenge of Interracial Unionism,* 35–40.

16. *Birmingham Age-Herald,* Aug. 15, 1891.

17. See sources cited in notes 11 and 12. Little data survives concerning the precise racial composition of the Greenback-Labor Party, the Knights of Labor, and the UMW in the Birmingham district.

18. Most prominent among these journals were the Greenbackers' *National Labor Tribune,* the Knights' *Alabama Sentinel* and *Journal of United Labor,* and the *Birmingham Labor Advocate* and *United Mine Workers Journal.*

19. *National Labor Tribune,* Aug. 26, 1879; *Birmingham Negro American,* Oct. 9, 1886.

20. On the founding of the UMW, see Chris Evans, *History of the United Mine Workers of America from the Year 1890 to 1900* (Indianapolis: UMW, 1914), 3–29; Andrew Roy, *A History of the Coal Miners of the United States,* 3rd ed. (Columbus, Ohio: J. L. Trauger, 1907), 243–66; Maier B. Fox, *United We Stand: The United Mine Workers of America, 1890–1990* (Washington, D.C.: UMW, 1990), 22–29.

21. *Alabama Sentinel,* Apr. 12, May 3, 10, 17, 24, 1890.

22. Ibid., July 5, 1890; *Birmingham Age-Herald,* July 2, 3, 4, 7, 8, 1890; *Birmingham Daily News,* July 1, 2, 3, 1890.

23. Day-to-day, often conflicting accounts of the strike can be found in the *Birmingham Age-Herald,* the *Birmingham Daily News,* and the *Alabama Sentinel* (which published a daily edition during much of the strike) for the months of December and January. The strike is also described in Ward and Rogers, *Labor Revolt in Alabama,* 32–33; and Letwin, *Challenge of Interracial Unionism,* 91–95.

24. On the post-strike situation at Warrior, see *Alabama Sentinel,* Jan. 31, Feb. 12, 21, 28, Mar. 7, 21, 1891, and *Birmingham Daily News,* Jan. 22, 1891.

25. *Birmingham Daily News,* Jan. 2, 6, 1891. If the *Daily News* can be believed, a bemused DeBardeleben invited the women round the company office, where beer was provided and "everybody drank and felt better than ever"—after which the president reminded his guests that "fun was fun and business was business and they would have to vacate the [company-provided] houses," which was duly done. Perhaps mindful of the implausibility of such good cheer, the article closed with the

caveat that the "story is given as it reached a *News* reporter and for what it is worth" (Jan. 8, 1891).

26. *Alabama Sentinel,* Dec. 6, 13, 19 (Daily Strike Edition), 20, 28 (Daily Strike Edition), 1890, Jan. 10, 1891.

27. Ibid., Dec. 27, 28 (Daily Strike Edition), 1890, Jan. 3, 17, 1891.

28. On the 1891–92 Tennessee coal miners' rebellion, see Karin A. Shapiro, *A New South Rebellion: The Battle against Convict Labor in the Tennessee Coalfields, 1871–1896* (Chapel Hill: University of North Carolina Press, 1998); and Pete Daniel, "The Tennessee Convict War," *Tennessee Historical Quarterly* 34 (Fall 1975): 273–92.

29. *UMW Journal,* Oct. 5, Nov. 16, Dec. 28, 1893; *Birmingham Labor Advocate,* Oct. 21, 28, Nov. 11, 18, 25, Dec. 2, 30, 1893; *National Labor Tribune,* Dec. 7, 1893; *Engineering and Mining Journal,* Feb. 24, 1894.

30. Ward and Rogers, *Labor Revolt in Alabama,* 59–64, 67, 69, 71; *National Labor Tribune,* May 3, 1894. On the 1894 coal strike nationally, see Fox, *United We Stand,* 44–45; and Priscilla Long, *Where the Sun Never Shines: A History of America's Bloody Coal Industry* (New York: Paragon House, 1991), 153–54. The story of the 1894 strike has been told several times, at varying lengths. The most complete account is Ward and Rogers, *Labor Revolt in Alabama.* See also Head, "Development of the Labor Movement in Alabama," 96–105; Richard A. Straw, "'This Is Not a Strike, It Is Only a Revolution': The Birmingham Miners' Struggle for Power, 1894–1908" (Ph.D. diss., University of Missouri, Columbia, 1980), 14–24; Ronald L. Lewis, *Black Coal Miners in America: Race, Class, and Community Conflict, 1780–1980* (Lexington: University of Kentucky Press, 1987), 41–44; Alex Lichtenstein, "Racial Conflict and Racial Solidarity in the Alabama Coal Strike of 1894: New Evidence for the Gutman-Hill Debate," *Labor History* 36 (Winter 1995): 63–76; and Letwin, *Challenge of Interracial Unionism,* 101–11. The general narrative of this strike can be reconstructed from regular coverage in the *Birmingham Age-Herald,* the *Birmingham Daily News,* the *Birmingham Labor Advocate,* and the *United Mine Workers Journal.*

31. DeBardeleben statement in *Birmingham Age-Herald,* Apr. 20, 1894.

32. *National Labor Tribune,* June 21, 1894 (emphasis in original); J. H. F. to Governor Jones, May 27, June 6, 14, 16, 1894, and J. M. P. to Governor Jones, July 22, 1894, in Governor Thomas Jones Papers, "Pinkerton, 1893–94" file, ADAH. On the mingling of black and white strikers in saloons, see also Lichtenstein, "Racial Conflict and Racial Solidarity."

33. T. N. Vallens to Governor Jones, May 21, 1894, in Jones Papers, "Pinkerton, 1893–94" file (300 strikers); Vallens to Governor Jones, June 9, 1894, ibid. ("No blackleg"); *Birmingham Labor Advocate,* Apr. 28, 1894 ("We, the colored").

34. *West End Banner,* May 12, 1894, and Vallens to Governor Jones, Apr. 22, May 8, 1894 (Horse Creek, evictions, rumors), in Jones Papers, "Pinkerton, 1893–94" file.

35. J. M. P. to Governor Jones, Aug. 9, 1894, ibid.

36. *UMW Journal,* Oct. 25, 1894, and *Birmingham Labor Advocate,* Dec. 1, 1894, Feb. 16, 23, Mar. 16, May 4, June 8, 1895 (sporadic employment); *Birmingham Labor Advocate,* Dec. 1, 1894, Feb. 9, Mar. 16, Apr. 27, May 4, July 6, 13, 20, 27, 1895 (excess labor). Average daily earnings around the district hovered between $1.00 and $1.50, but often fell below $1.00 (ibid., Feb. 16, 23, June 29, 1895).

37. *Birmingham Labor Advocate,* Mar. 2, 1895.

38. *Bessemer Journal,* July 22, 1897; *UMW Journal,* July 15, 22, 1897; *Birmingham Labor Advocate,* July 3, 24, 31, 1897; *Bessemer Herald,* July 7, 1897; *Birmingham Age-Herald,* July 3, 4, 14, 21, 1897; Tennessee Coal, Iron, and Railroad Company, *1898 Annual Report,* 3; *Proceedings of the Joint Convention of the Alabama Coal Operators Association and the United Mine Workers of America, 1903, and Arbitration Proceedings* (Birmingham, 1903), 264–66.

39. On the 1897 strike, see Joseph M. Gowaskie, "From Conflict to Cooperation: John Mitchell and Bituminous Coal Operators, 1898–1908," *Historian* 38 (August 1976): 676–77; Philip Taft, *The A.F.L. in the Time of Gompers* (New York: Harper, 1957), 138–40; and Fox, *United We Stand,* 50–52.

40. *Birmingham Labor Advocate,* Sept. 25, Oct. 2, 16, 30, 1897; *Birmingham Age-Herald,* Sept. 25, 1897; *UMW Journal,* Nov. 4, 1897; *Bessemer Journal,* Oct. 28, 1897; UMW, *Minutes of the Ninth Annual Convention, 1898,* p. 26.

41. On rising prosperity in the coal and iron trade and consequent rise of employment at the mines, see *Birmingham Age-Herald,* Aug. 31, Sept. 2, 1897; *Birmingham News,* Jan. 11, 15, 1898; and the regular survey of days worked per week, mine by mine, in the *Birmingham Labor Advocate* for the fall and winter of 1897–98. On organizing drive: *Birmingham Labor Advocate,* May 14, June 11, 18, 1898; *Birmingham Age-Herald,* June 2, 1898; *Birmingham News,* June 10, 20, 21, 1898. On advance: *Birmingham News,* June 29, 1898. On war: *Birmingham News,* Mar. 7, 15, May 7, June 1, 1898; *Birmingham Age-Herald,* Mar. 11, 1898.

42. On the mounting receptiveness among American bituminous coal operators to working with the UMW as a means of stabilizing labor relations, as well as competition among the operators themselves, see Gowaskie, "From Conflict to Competition"; William Graebner, "Great Expectations: The Search for Order in Bituminous Coal, 1890–1917," *Business History Review* 48 (Spring 1974): 53–55. On the trend toward union recognition in American industry generally, see David Brody, *Workers in Industrial America: Essays on the Twentieth-Century Struggle* (New York: Oxford University Press, 1980), 24.

43. On the 1898 organizing drive, see *Birmingham News,* Sept. 2, 1898. For membership figures during 1898–1904, see *UMW Journal,* Sept. 22, Dec. 22, 1898, Dec. 28, 1899, Dec. 18, 1902; *Birmingham Labor Advocate,* May 26, June 23, 1900, Apr. 26, 1902, Dec. 12, 1903, June 14, 1907; UMW, *Minutes of the Tenth Annual Convention, 1899,* p. 27; UMW, *Minutes of the Twelfth Annual Convention, 1901,* p. 61; UMW, *Minutes of the Thirteenth Annual Convention, 1902,* p. 65; UMW, *Minutes of the Fourteenth Annual Convention, 1903,* pp. 62, 448–50; UMW, *Minutes of the Fifteenth Annual Convention, 1904,* pp. 98–99. On Local 664: UMW, *Minutes of the Twelfth Annual Convention, 1901,* p. 20; *Birmingham Labor Advocate,* Mar. 8, 1900, Feb. 3, 1902.

44. On organization throughout the Birmingham trades, see Head, "Development of the Labor Movement in Alabama," 174–80; *Birmingham News,* Mar. 14, 1899; *Birmingham Labor Advocate* generally for 1898–1903; McKiven, *Iron and Steel,* 97–99; Paul B. Worthman, "Black Workers and Labor Unions in Birmingham, Alabama, 1897–1904," *Labor History* 10 (Summer 1969): 383, 395.

45. Between July 1898 and August 1899 the wage for run-of-mine coal rose in a series of 2.5-cent increments from 37.5 cents to 55 cents per ton. From July 1900 through June 1903 the Pratt scale ranged from a minimum of 45 cents to a maximum of 55 cents, depending on the price of pig iron. Shifts of wages paid on the Pratt scale from 1896 to 1908 are provided in UMW, *Proceedings of the Nineteenth Annual Convention, 1908,* pp. 518–19.

46. On weighing of coal: *UMW Journal,* July 18, 1901. On disciplining of miners: *Mineral Belt Gazette,* May 7, 1904; *Proceedings of the Joint Convention,* 249. On company store: *UMW Journal,* Mar. 13, 1902. On three days away rule: *Proceedings of the Joint Convention,* 247–48, 250. On funerals: ibid., 423–24; *Birmingham News,* June 23, 1899. On labor subcontracting: *UMW Journal,* Jan. 2, July 18, 1901; *Proceedings of the Joint Convention,* 257–63, 698, 705–6; *Birmingham Labor Advocate,* Apr. 1, 1899; *Birmingham News,* Mar. 22, 1899.

47. *Birmingham Labor Advocate,* Oct. 28, 1899.

48. Ibid., Sept. 30, 1905.

49. *Birmingham News,* Aug. 17, 22, 1899 (day laborers); ibid., Aug. 19, 1898, *UMW Journal,* Sept. 1, 1898 (subcontracting); *Birmingham News,* July 13, 14, 19, 21, Aug. 30, 1899 (contested firing); ibid., Oct. 19, 20, 1898 (schools and doctors). On TCI strike: *Birmingham Daily Ledger,* Sept. 23, 29–30, Oct. 1–16, 1902; *UMW Journal,* Oct. 16, 1902; *Birmingham Labor Advocate,* Oct. 4, 11, 1902; *Proceedings of the Joint Convention,* 647–48.

50. *Mineral Belt Gazette,* July 2, 1905 (Brookwood); ibid., May 14, 1904 (Republic); *Birmingham News,* Aug. 25, 1898 (Cardiff); ibid., Aug. 12, 1898 (payday); ibid., Aug. 5, 1899, and *Proceedings of the Joint Convention,* 267 (hospital).

51. *UMW Journal,* Feb. 10, 1898. "If I get on a railway train," Davis noted, "I must ride in a separate car, the same on the street car. If I want a drink I must go in to a separate bar, and I can only look at a hotel or restaurant" (ibid., Nov. 25, 1897).

52. At District 20's June 1898 wage scale convention, twenty out of fifty-four delegates were black (*Birmingham News,* June 20, 1898). Between 1900 and 1904, black District 20 delegates to the UMW's national conventions included C. W. Cain and James Swinney (UMW, *Minutes of the Eleventh Annual Convention, 1900,* p. 13, and *Minutes of the Twelfth Annual Convention, 1901,* p. 21); and Benjamin Greer and Silas Brooks (*Minutes of the Thirteenth Annual Convention, 1902,* p. 29, *Minutes of the Fourteenth Annual Convention, 1903,* p. 75, and *Minutes of the Fifteenth Annual Convention, 1904,* p. 18).

53. The district vice presidency, the *Birmingham Labor Advocate* occasionally noted, has been "conceded to the colored membership" (Nov. 2, Dec. 14, 1901, June 7, 1907).

54. *UMW Journal,* May 3, 1900 (West); *Birmingham Age-Herald,* Aug. 15, 1904 (Greer).

55. *UMW Journal,* July 18, 1901.

56. Ibid., July 19, 1900, July 18, 1901; *Birmingham Labor Advocate,* June 30, 1900; *Birmingham News,* June 22, 25, 1900; Worthman, "Black Workers and Labor Unions," 391.

57. On banquets: *Birmingham Labor Advocate,* Dec. 14, 1901, Jan. 4, 1902; *Bessemer Workman,* June 20, 1902. On parks: *Birmingham Labor Advocate,* Sept. 12, 1903. On convention delegations: *Birmingham Age-Herald,* June 11, 1904.

58. This cautious, often carefully calibrated expression of labor interracialism in the UMW emerged at the national level. On the UMW's racial record nationally, see Herbert Gutman, "The Negro and the United Mine Workers," in *Work, Culture, and Society in Industrialized America* (New York: Vintage, 1976), 121–208; Hill, "Myth-Making as Labor History"; R. Lewis, *Black Coal Miners in America;* and Sterling D. Spero and Abram L. Harris, *The Black Worker: The Negro and the Labor Movement,* 3rd ed. (New York: Atheneum, 1968), 352–82.

59. Chaired by Delaware federal judge George B. Gray, who had conducted the landmark anthracite arbitration of the previous year, the board delivered a mixed judgment. It granted the miners a 2.5-cent increase and twice-monthly paydays, while granting the operators stricter penalties for absenteeism (*Proceedings of the Joint Convention*).

60. On Walker County: *Birmingham Labor Advocate,* Sept. 12, Oct. 17, 1903; *UMW Journal,* Oct. 17, 1903. On Blue Creek: ibid., Sept. 3, Dec. 31, 1903; *Birmingham Labor Advocate,* Sept. 26, Oct. 31, Nov. 21, 1903, Feb. 6, 13, Mar. 5, 1904.

61. On the Pratt company conflict: *Birmingham News,* May 20, 24, June 3, 10, 13, 1904; *Birmingham Labor Advocate,* June 11, 1904; *Mineral Belt Gazette,* June 18, 1904. On the Little Warrior strike: *Birmingham Labor Advocate,* May 14, 28, 1904; *Birmingham News,* May 20, 24, 28, June 13, 1904; *Mineral Belt Gazette,* June 18, 1904. On the Blocton strike: ibid., May 7, 14, 21, 1904; *Birmingham Labor Advocate,* May 21, 28, June 4, 1904; *Birmingham Age-Herald,* May 14, 18, 20, 1904; *Birmingham News,* May 17, 23, 24, 26, 27, June 18, 1904; *Bessemer Workman,* May 20, 1904; *Mineral Belt Gazette,* May 14, 1904.

62. On economic downturn: W. David Lewis, *Sloss Furnaces and the Rise of the Birmingham District: An Industrial Epic* (Tuscaloosa: University of Alabama Press, 1994), 286; Geoffrey H. Moore, "Business Cycles, Panics, and Depressions," in *Encyclopedia of American History,* vol. 1, ed. Glenn Porter (New York: Scribner, 1980), 152. On open-shop drive: David Montgomery, *The Fall of the House of Labor: The Workplace, the State, and American Labor Activism, 1865–1925* (New York: Cambridge University Press, 1987), 269–75. On Alabama anti-boycott legislation: *Birmingham Labor Advocate,* Oct. 3, Nov. 7, 21, Dec. 5, 1903, Feb. 13, 1904; McKiven, *Iron and Steel,* 97–104.

63. *Birmingham News,* June 13, 20, 25, July 1, 2, 25, Aug. 17, 1904; *Birmingham Age-Herald,* June 29, July 2, 1904; *Birmingham Labor Advocate,* July 2, 1904; Tennessee Coal, Iron, and Railroad Company, *1905 Annual Report,* 7–10; W. A. Davis to Charles H. Marshall, July 29, 1904, in Alabama Mineral Land Company Collection, Letter Book, 1903–4, BPLA. The story is drawn primarily from regular coverage in the *Birmingham News, Birmingham Age-Herald, Birmingham Labor Advocate, Mineral Belt Gazette,* and *United Mine Works Journal.* See also Letwin, *Challenge of Interracial Unionism,* 141–45.

64. On Blocton barbecue: *Birmingham Labor Advocate,* July 22, 1905; *Mineral Belt Gazette,* July 22, 1905.

65. *Birmingham Labor Advocate,* Aug. 25, 1906; UMW, *Proceedings of the Eighteenth Annual Convention, 1907,* pp. 52, 322.

66. On blacklisting: *Birmingham Labor Advocate,* June 14, 1907. On newcomers: *Bessemer Weekly,* July 22, 1905. On panic: David Brody, *Steelworkers in America: The Nonunion Era* (New York: Harper Torchbooks, 1969), 151; G. H. Moore, "Business Cycles," 153; *Birmingham Labor Advocate,* Nov. 29, 1907. On U.S. Steel: Brody, *Steelworkers in America.* For membership figures: *Birmingham Labor Advocate,* June 14, 1907; UMW, *Proceedings of the Eighteenth Annual Convention, 1907,* pp. 31–32, 103–4; UMW, *Proceedings of the Nineteenth Annual Convention, 1908,* p. 402. On union contracts: *UMW Journal,* June 22, 1905, June 28, Aug. 2, 1906, June 20, 1907.

67. *Birmingham Labor Advocate,* Jan. 10, 24, 1908; *Birmingham News,* Jan. 17, June 13, 1908.

68. On launching of district-wide strike: *UMW Journal,* July 16, 23, 1908; *Birmingham News,* June 26, July 2, 6, 1908. The story of the 1908 coal strike has been told by a number of historians, most extensively in Straw, "This Is Not a Strike," and Richard A. Straw, "The Collapse of Biracial Unionism: The Alabama Coal Strike of 1908," *Alabama Historical Quarterly* 37 (Summer 1975): 92–114; Richard A. Straw, "Soldiers and Miners in a Strike Zone: Birmingham, 1908," *Alabama Review* 38 (October 1985): 289–308; and Nancy Ruth Elmore, "The Birmingham Coal Strike of 1908" (Master's thesis, University of Alabama, 1966); Letwin, *Challenge of Interracial Unionism,* 145–56. The narrative can be reconstructed chiefly from the newspapers and periodicals listed in note 62.

69. On governor's proclamation: *UMW Journal,* Aug. 20, 1908.

70. *Birmingham News,* July 25 ("most unusual"), 27 ("haven't any governor"), 1908; *UMW Journal,* Aug. 6 ("tramp of the soldiers"), 20 ("just as bad"), 1908; *Birmingham News,* July 27, 1908.

71. *Birmingham Age-Herald,* Aug. 24, 1908 ("Social Equality Horror"); *Birmingham News,* Aug. 31, 1908 (tent colonies); *Birmingham Age-Herald,* Aug. 8, 25, 1908 (Evans; see also Aug. 22, 26); Alabama Coal Operators Association Minute Book, number 1, Sept. 24, 1908, entry 25, ACOA Papers, BPLA.

72. *Birmingham Age-Herald,* Aug. 7, 1908 (Evans); *Birmingham News,* Aug. 25, Aug. 31, 1908 (Comer).

73. *Birmingham Age-Herald,* Aug. 22 (Evans), Aug. 30 (Dalrymple), 1908.

74. Birmingham *Labor Advocate,* Sept. 4 (McDonald), 25 (White), Aug. 28 (editorial), 1908.

75. On the active role of women in major coal strikes around the United States during the late nineteenth and early twentieth centuries, see Long, *Where the Sun Never Shines,* 140–65, 217–304, passim; and Montgomery, *The Fall of the House of Labor,* 338.

76. UMW, *Proceedings of the Twentieth Annual Convention, 1909,* p. 873 ("racial problem"); Gilson Gardner, "Charged Governor Whipped Miners—Destroyed Homes" (typescript), in Edward A. Wieck Collection, box 1, folder L-32 to L-33, WSUAL (Republic); *Birmingham News,* Aug. 28, 1908, *Birmingham Labor Advocate,* Aug. 28, 1908 (hygiene); UMW, *Proceedings of the Twentieth Annual Convention, 1909,* p. 865 ("niggers idle").

77. *UMW Journal,* Sept. 10, 1908 ("it is hard"); UMW, *Proceedings of the Twentieth Annual Convention, 1909,* pp. 865 (ultimatum), 870 (warning).

78. *Birmingham Labor Advocate,* Sept. 4, 1908 ("serfs"); *UMW Journal,* Mar. 11, 1909 ("goodbye").

79. For membership figures: UMW, *Proceedings of the Twentieth Annual Convention, 1909,* p. 70; *UMW Journal,* Jan. 21, 1909.

80. *UMW Journal,* Feb. 4, 1909. Beyond conveying the poignant aftermath of

the 1908 defeat, Leach's letter substantially revises our knowledge of the origins of the civil rights anthem "We Shall Overcome." Historians and folk singers have long traced the evolution of the old southern spiritual "I Will Overcome" into a song of collective protest (first "We Will Overcome," then "We Shall Overcome") to 1940s labor struggles among textile workers of Piedmont Carolina and black tobacco workers of Charleston, South Carolina. Leach's letter, however, indicates that "I Will Overcome" had been transformed into a movement standard (with the significant shift in pronoun from "I" to "We"), at least in the Birmingham coalfields, as far back as the early twentieth century. His passing reference to "that good old song," though remarkable, is also tantalizing. While he hints that the singing of the song at union gatherings was customary, this study has uncovered no other mention of it.

CHAPTER 2

1. Fitch, "Birmingham District," 1527; ACOA Executive Board Minutes, Sept. 24, 1908, Feb. 11, June 3, 1909, ACOA Papers, BPLA.

2. *Birmingham Labor Advocate,* July 22, 1910; Fitch, "Birmingham District," 1538; U.S. Senate, *Report of the Federal Commission on Immigrants in Industries: The Bituminous Coal Mining Industry in the South,* 61st Cong., 2nd sess., 1910, S. Doc. 633, 363; Moran et al., "Report of the Committee on Conditions in the Alabama Coal Mines," 1913, cited in Taft, *Organizing Dixie,* 46.

3. ACOA Executive Board Minutes, June 3, 1909, ACOA Papers, BPLA.

4. Rupert B. Vance, *Human Geography of the South* (Chapel Hill: University of North Carolina Press, 1932), 279.

5. *Birmingham Labor Advocate,* Oct. 30, Sept. 4, 1908.

6. Armes, *Coal and Iron in Alabama,* 467; *Birmingham Age-Herald,* Jan. 28, 1907; C. Vann Woodward, *Origins of the New South* (Baton Rouge: Louisiana State University Press, 1951), 307.

7. *Birmingham Labor Advocate,* June 3, 1916; Milton Fies, "Industrial Alabama and the Negro," in *Proceedings of the Institute Meeting of the Executive and Operating Officials of the Members of the Alabama Mining Institute,* Birmingham, Oct. 31, 1922, 44, ACOA Papers.

8. *Birmingham Age-Herald,* Aug. 18, 1907; on immigrants and segregated schools, see James C. Cobb, *The Most Southern Place on Earth: The Mississippi Delta and the Roots of Regional Identity* (New York: Oxford University Press, 1992), 110.

9. Roland T. Berthoff, "Southern Attitudes toward Immigration, 1865–1914," *Journal of Southern History* 17 (1951): 357; *Birmingham Labor Advocate,* Nov. 12, 1909; Xaridimos to Stefane, June 12, 1909, "Peonage Files," RG 60, Records of the Department of Justice, NA.

10. *Birmingham Labor Advocate,* June 21, 1917.

11. *Birmingham Age-Herald,* Aug. 16, 1903, cited in Harris, *Political Power in Birmingham,* 103; Fitch, "Birmingham District," 1527.

12. W. D. Lewis, *Sloss Furnaces and the Birmingham District,* 316, reports that "immigrants [at TCI] reported for work about twenty days per month, blacks not quite seventeen. For operatives as a whole, the average was just over eighteen, indicating the TCI's native whites were not well disciplined either." See also *Birmingham Age-Herald,* Jan. 28, 1920. Fitch explained the high rates of absenteeism by noting that "industry is young in all the South" and "there has not been time for the development of a body of skilled labor in Alabama." It was "also true," he wrote, "that the Southern whites who come to work in the mines and the mills are generally of the poorer sort" ("Birmingham District," 1528).

13. Quote from Arthur W. Wiebel, *Biography of a Business* (Birmingham: Tennessee Coal, Iron, and Railroad Co., 1960), 44–45.

14. Ida M. Tarbell, *The Life of Elbert H. Gary: The Story of Steel* (New York: Appleton and Company, 1925), 310–11.

15. Carl Carmer, *Stars Fell on Alabama* (New York: Hill and Wang, 1934), 80, 81.

16. See "The Coal Miners' Union during the War and Post-War," 4, in Philip Taft Research Notes (hereafter Taft Papers), BPLA, for an account of the Montevallo strike.

17. Elmer Burton, interview by Sybil Burton, Walker County, Alabama, Nov. 27, 1974, p. 12, SU; *Birmingham Labor Advocate,* Aug. 19, July 1, 1916; *UMW Journal,* June 1, 1916.

18. *Birmingham Labor Advocate,* Aug. 5, 1916.

19. J. L. Westwood to Governor Kilby, Mar. 9, 1921, Governor Thomas Kilby Administrative Files (hereafter Kilby Files), ADAH. The ACOA adopted similar procedures for entertaining workers' grievances. See 1914 President's Annual Report, 188, in ACOA Papers.

20. UMW officials quoted in Taft, "Coal Miners' Union during the War," 3, 2, Taft Papers; *Birmingham Labor Advocate,* July 11, 1913 (see official UMW notice of same in this issue); Fies to DeBardeleben, ca. 1920, Feb. 23, 1914, DeBardeleben to Fies, Feb. 25, 1914, and Fies to R. H. Franklin, June 13, 1920, all in "Fies File," DeBardeleben Coal Company Records (hereafter DeBardeleben Records), BPLA.

21. "Migration Study—Birmingham Summary," 9, Papers of the Urban League, LC; Fies to F. L. Davidson, Dec. 21, 1916, DeBardeleben Records.

22. Robert J. Norrell, ed., *James Bowron: The Autobiography of a New South Industrialist* (Chapel Hill: University of North Carolina Press, 1991), 244; *Birmingham Labor Advocate,* June 21, 1917, Oct. 7, 1916.

23. Taft, "Coal Miners' Union during the War," 4, Taft Papers; *Birmingham Labor Advocate,* June 9, 1917; Joseph Anthony McCartin, "Labor's 'Great War': American Workers, Unions, and the State, 1916–1920" (Ph.D. diss., State University of New York, Binghamton, 1990), 149–50.

24. H. P. Vaughn to George Haynes, "Memorandum for Mr. Haines [*sic*] on the Birmingham Race Situation," Mar. 5, 1919, in Chief Clerk's files, "Special Problems—Birmingham," RG 174: Records of the Department of Labor, 1907–1942, NA.

25. Statement of Field Agent E. Newdick, "Bitter and Dangerous Alignment—Employers Foster Race Prejudice," Feb. 24, 1919, ibid.

26. Hartsfield to Kilby, Sept. 13, 1919, Kilby Files.

27. "Statement of Facts Concerning the Alabama Coal Strike," ca. December 1920, ibid.

28. "Bittner Speech," ca. October 1920, and "Speech of Van A. Bittner," Nov. 7, 1920, ACOA Papers.

29. *Birmingham News,* Apr. 20, 1921; Mrs. Nona Bates to Kilby, Apr. 1, 1921, Kilby Files.

CHAPTER 3

1. Recorded by George Korson, Trafford, Alabama, Mar. 19, 1940. Jones, born in 1872, was a coal miner from 1891 until 1914, when he went blind; during the 1930s his minstrelsy was supported by the union. George Korson, *Coal Dust on the Fiddle: Songs and Stories of the Bituminous Industry,* 2nd ed. (Hatboro, Pa.: Folklore Associates, 1965), 26–27, 301–2, 445.

2. John L. Lewis to John Kennamer, Oct. 26, 1923, President/District 20 Correspondence, UMW Papers, PSULA; UMW, *Proceedings of the 1924 Convention,* vol. 1, UMW Headquarters, Washington, D.C.

3. George Hargrove to Thomas Kennedy, Oct. 1, 1928, Secretary-Treasurer Files, UMW Papers. Hargrove died in office in 1930, and was not replaced.

4. *UMW Journal,* June 1, 1931.

5. U.S. Bureau of Mines, cited in Walter N. Polakov, "Notes on Mechanization, Rates and Employment in Alabama (District 20)," District 20 Papers, UMW District 20 Headquarters, Birmingham, Ala.

6. Spero and Harris, *The Black Worker,* 362.

7. "District 20 Annual Convention (1935)," 14, Secretary-Treasurer Files, UMW Papers; Bureau of the Census, cited in "Alabama's Coal Mining Industry: Report of the Board of Mediation," May 19, 1941, Governor Frank Dixon Papers, ADAH.

8. Alabama Department of Industrial Relations, *Annual Report to the Governor, 1939* (Birmingham: Department of Industrial Relations), 101, 157.

9. Ibid, 101; *UMW Journal,* July 1, 1934. The captive mines were located in Jefferson County, close to the iron and steel industry, and in 1939 this one county contributed 58.8 percent of Alabama's coal output, compared with 47.5 percent in 1921. See also State of Alabama, *Annual Report of Coal Mines, 1921,* p. 40.

10. State of Alabama, *Annual Report of Coal Mines, 1921,* pp. 101, 137–38. The truck mines contributed 5.7 percent of production in 1939. See also Judith Stein, "Southern Workers in National Unions: Birmingham Steelworkers, 1936–1951," in Zieger, *Organized Labor,* 185.

11. H. H. Chapman et al., *The Iron and Steel Industry of the South* (University: University of Alabama Press, 1953), 178. These figures compared with respective national figures of 88.2 percent and 31.0 percent. In 1913 only 23 percent of the state's coal had been mechanically cut, and in 1929 only 0.5 percent had been machine-loaded.

12. Earl Brown, interview by Peter Alexander, tape recording, Booker Heights, Alabama, Sept. 4, 1997. See also *Southern Worker,* March 1934; Steven Christian, interview by Peter Alexander, tape recording, Belle Sumpter, Alabama, Aug. 29, 1997; Cleatus Burns, interview by Cliff Kuhn, Jasper, Alabama, Dec. 6, 1984, "Working Lives Project," University of Alabama, Tuscaloosa; Stein, "Southern Workers," 185; Joe W. Trotter, Jr., "Class and Racial Inequality: The Southern West Virginia Black Coal Miners' Response," in Zieger, *Organized Labor,* 61–63.

13. U.S. Bureau of the Census, *Fourteenth Census: Occupations,* (Washington, D.C.: Government Printing Office, 1920), Table 1; *Fifteenth Census: Occupations by States* (Washington, D.C.: Government Printing Office, 1930), Table 11; *Sixteenth Census: The Labor Force* (Washington, D.C.: Government Printing Office, 1940), Table 18. A wide range of anecdotal evidence suggests a higher proportion of African Americans, perhaps two-thirds of Alabama coal miners, in the early 1930s. The most likely explanation for this discrepancy is that the higher figures were based on observations in Jefferson County, where, according to the census, 63.3 percent of coal miners were African Americans in 1930. See Peter Alexander, "Interracial Unionism and Bifurcated State Power: Alabama Miners 1917–37" (Conference on Labour and Difference, Paper No. 31, St. Antony's College, Oxford, 1997), 16 n. 22; Works Progress Administration, *Gainful Workers, by Occupational Groups, and by Race, in Southeast, 1930* (Birmingham: Works Progress Administration, 1938); reports of fatal accidents, giving "race" of victim, in Alabama's annual reports on coal mines (see notes 9 and 10 above).

14. One reason for the higher proportion of blacks in Jefferson County mines is that convict miners had been concentrated in the TCI and Sloss mines. However, by

1913 only about 5 percent of Alabama's miners were convicts. See also Lichtenstein, *Twice the Work of Free Labor,* 85.

15. U.S. Bureau of the Census, *Fourteenth Census: Occupations,* Table 1; *Fifteenth Census: Occupations by States,* Table 11. In the 1920s, Italians were probably the largest overseas contingent in Alabama's coal mines, and according to Aquilla Lowery, "At Adger we had about six white people and two Italian[s], the rest was black" (interview by Peter Alexander, Belle Sumpter, Alabama, Sept. 3, 1997).

16. Evelyn Howard, interview by Peggy Hamrick, ca. 1984, "Working Lives Project"; Samuel Kelley, interview by Belinda Mardis, Mar. 13, 1979, SU; Brown, interview; Lowery, interview; Curtis McAdory, interview by Peggy Hamrick, Aug. 23, 1984, "Working Lives Project."

17. Brown, interview. Probably more white miners than black miners lived away from the camps.

18. Don Drennen to Governor Graves, Nov. 12, 1935, Governor Bibb Graves Papers, ADAH. See also, Sheriff of St. Clair County to Governor Miller, Apr. 20, 1934, Governor Benjamin Miller Papers, ADAH; Burton, interview; Brown, interview; Andrew Ward, interview by Peter Alexander, tape recording, Mulga, Alabama, Sept. 9, 1997; Lowery, interview; Christian, interview.

19. Christian, interview. See also Lowery, interview; Ward, interview.

20. Girtley Connell, interview by Peter Alexander, tape recording, Black Lung Project, Birmingham, Alabama, Sept. 9, 1997.

21. Gardening was encouraged by the operators, who provided advice and sometimes loaned a company mule. Annual Report of Jas. L. Davidson, Secretary-Treasurer, Alabama Coal Operators Association, June 4, 1918, ACOA Papers; Marie Butler, *"And Now There's Gold": A Brief History of a Unique Community* (Birmingham: n.p., 1989), 10–12; Lowery, interview; Kelley, interview.

22. McAdory, interview.

23. Brown, interview; Ila Hendrix, interview by Ben Hendrix, May 1, 1976, SU; Louise Burns, interview by Cliff Kuhn, June 12, 1984, "Working Lives Project."

24. Particularly, Louise Burns, interview; "Working Lives," No. 11, radio program produced by Brenda McCallum, University of Alabama, Tuscaloosa.

25. Christian, interview. See also Ward; interview; Brown, interview.

26. Based on 1930 census data. See document dated Dec. 29, 1939, District 20 Papers.

27. Ward, interview; Brown, interview.

28. Ward, interview; Brown, interview; State of Alabama, *Annual Report of Coal Mines, 1935,* p. 72 (photograph).

29. Christian, interview. Also, Luther V. Smith, interview by Benny Hendrix,

Quinton, Alabama, Nov. 27, 1974, SU; Lowery, interview; Connell, interview; Brown, interview.

30. Lowery, interview. Also, Louise Burns, interview; Marlene Hunt Rikard, "An Experiment in Welfare Capitalism: the Health care Services of the Tennessee Coal, Iron and Railroad Company" (Ph.D. diss., University of Alabama, 1983), 322.

31. He added: "Only time that black and white were together was when they worked in the mine." Brown, interview. Also, Lowery, interview; Ward, interview.

32. *Birmingham Labor Advocate,* July 8, 1933; Pollard Jones, interview, Sept. 3, 1983, "Working Lives Project"; Clarence Darden, interview by Steve McCallum, May 24, 1983, ibid.

33. Alabama Department of Industrial Relations, *Annual Statistical Report, 1942–43* (Montgomery: Department of Industrial Relations), 59. See also Brown, interview.

34. Christian, interview.

35. Ward, interview. Also, "Wage Scale, January 1, 1933," District 20 Papers; Lowery, interview.

36. Fred Jones, interview by Cliff Kuhn, June 16, 1984, "Working Lives Project"; "Meeting of Mine Agreement Committee, July 25, 26 and 28, 1934," District 20 Papers.

37. Clarence Darden, interview; Christian, interview.

38. Brown, interview. See also Earl Brown, interview by Cliff Kuhn, June 29, 1984, "Working Lives Project."

39. President/District 20 Correspondence, particularly John Lillich, Carbon Hill, to Lewis, Aug. 6, 1930. In July 1932 there was a strike at Sayreton that ended in partial victory, and this was followed by a successful stoppage at Bankhead. See Taft, *Organizing Dixie,* 83.

40. *UMW Journal,* Oct. 15, 1934.

41. President/District 20 Correspondence, particularly Lewis to Dalrymple, July 8, 1933, and Ike Robinton to Lewis, July 8, 1933.

42. *Terre Haute Post,* Jan. 15, 1931; Lewis to William Mitch, telegram, Jan. 5, 1925, and two unidentified press cuttings, District 20 Papers; *UMW Journal,* Dec. 1, 1933; biographical sketch, William Mitch Papers, PSULA; Taft, *Organizing Dixie,* 86.

43. Mitch to Lewis, Oct. 23, 1933, President/District 20 Correspondence. See also C. L. Richardson, Commissioner of Conciliation, to H. L. Kerwin, Director of Conciliation, July 19, 1933, Case Files 170-9178, Federal Mediation and Conciliation Service (RG 280), National Archives 2, Silver Spring, Maryland; Sheriff Barrentine to Lewis, Oct. 28, 1933, President/District 20 Correspondence.

Dalrymple seems to have been popular among the miners because the President/District 20 files contain a number of letters in his support. Raney died in office in 1937 and was replaced by James Terry, a former president of Mitch's old district, Indiana. See "Report of William Mitch, President, District 20, January 29, 1937," in box 1, folder 24, Taft Papers.

44. Press cuttings, and Lewis to Mitch, June 10, 1933, President/District 20 Correspondence.

45. Mitch to Lewis, Aug. 2, 1933, ibid.

46. *Birmingham Labor Advocate,* July 8, Aug. 26, 1933.

47. Christian added that the union dues (or "tax") were set at $1.00 per month. Lowery, interview; Christian, interview. See also Burton, interview; Cleatus Burns, interview.

48. Mitch to Lewis, June 16, 1933, President/District 20 Correspondence. I am grateful to Judith Stein for reminding me of this document.

49. For a short obituary on Clemo see a press cutting (probably *UMW Journal,* ca. Mar. 1, 1941), District 20 Papers.

50. Unidentified press cutting, District 20 Papers; *UMW Journal,* ca. June 1, 1934; Walter Jones to Lewis, Oct. 5, 1933, President/District 20 Correspondence; Fred Jones (brother of Walter), interview. See also Kennamer to Lewis, Nov. 11, 1920, President/District 20 Correspondence; Constance Price (daughter of Walter Jones), interview by Cliff Kuhn, July 18, 1984, "Working Lives Project."

51. Jones to Lewis, Nov. 15, 1933, President/District 20 Correspondence. Joe Sorsby, the former District 20 vice president, also applied to Lewis for a position, but was unsuccessful.

52. William Mitch, Jr., interview by Cliff Kuhn, June 22, 1984, "Working Lives Project"; Kelley, interview; Lowery, interview; Brown, interview by Alexander.

53. Unidentified press cutting, District 20 Papers. Jones's fellow district representatives were J. W. Heathcock, W. H. Huey, and J. O. Parsons. After Jones died, Hartford Knight, an African American from Dolomite, Alabama, was appointed as his successor. Circular to District 20 locals, Aug. 7, 1935, President/District 20 Correspondence; *UMW Journal,* Aug. 15, 1940.

54. My analysis here is drawn largely from James P. Johnson, *The Politics of Soft Coal: The Bituminous Industry from World War I through the New Deal* (Urbana: University of Illinois Press, 1979), 150–64.

55. Taft, *Organizing Dixie,* 83–84; "Extracts from the Alabama Commercial Coal Industry Code of Fair Competition, July 24, 1933," President/District 20 Correspondence.

56. *UMW Journal,* Oct. 1, 1933; "Bituminous Coal Code Information for Local Unions, Birmingham, October 24, 1933," District 20 Papers; Johnson, *Politics of Soft Coal,* 161, 183.

57. Mitch to Lewis, Sept. 30, 1933, President/District 20 Correspondence. Also, *Birmingham Labor Advocate,* Aug. 26, Sept. 30, 1933.

58. Eugene Dunnigan to Kerwin, telegram, Oct. 15, 1933, Taft Papers. See also unidentified press cutting, UMW Papers; Taft, *Organizing Dixie,* 87–88.

59. Mitch to Lewis, Dec. 30, 1933, President/District 20 Correspondence; James Acuff to Mitch, Dec. 25, 1933, District 20 Papers.

60. Taft, *Organizing Dixie,* 88, citing, in particular, a report in the General Persons Papers, ADAH.

61. *Birmingham News,* Mar. 3, 1934; Ralph Howell, Local 5795, to General Hugh Johnson, NRA, telegram, Mar. 9, 1934, President/District 20 Correspondence.

62. A. B. Aldridge to Miller, Mar. 15, 1934, Miller Papers.

63. Mitch to Lewis, Mar. 15, 1934, President/District 20 Correspondence. Also, Carter Quinn to Miller, telegram, Mar. 12, 1933, and folder 21, containing nearly seven hundred names calling for withdrawal of the troops from Walker County, Miller Papers; Wayne Flynt, *Poor but Proud: Alabama's Poor Whites* (Tuscaloosa: University of Alabama Press, 1989), 323; *Birmingham News,* Mar. 12, 19, and Apr. 4, 1933. The fourth captive concern, Sloss, also accepted the March 16 agreement. One outcome of the settlement was the abolition of subcontracting. See "Interpretation, Mine Agreement, March 23, 1934," Alabama By-Products Papers, BPLA. During the strike, black middle-class leaders, including Oscar Adams, grand chancellor of the Knights of Pythias, and Charles McPherson, secretary of the NAACP, held the annual conference of the Alabama Federation of Colored Civic Leagues, at which Robert Gregg, president of TCI, and Charles DeBardeleben, but not Mitch, or even Jones, were "outstanding persons on the program." *Birmingham News,* Mar. 14, 1933.

64. Taft, *Organizing Dixie,* 89; Kelley, *Hammer and Hoe,* 64. The shutdown also affected other areas. See *Birmingham News,* Apr. 4, 10, 13, 1934.

65. *Birmingham News,* Apr. 12, 18, 1934. The operators' assessment of events was substantially endorsed by the Communist Party. See "Miners. Fight to Win!," CPUSA leaflet, ca. Apr. 20, 1934, Mitch Papers. There were, however, southern liberals who favored increased pay. See *Birmingham News,* Apr. 18, 1934.

66. *Birmingham News,* Apr. 16, 17, 18, 1934; Darius Thomas et al. to Miller, telegram, Apr. 16, 1934, Miller Papers.

67. "Phone Conversation with Governor Miller," Apr. 16, 1934, Thomas et al. to Miller, telegram, Apr. 16, 1934, and David Roberts, Jr., to Miller, Apr. 17, 1934, all in Miller Papers.

68. W. Carson Adams to Miller, Apr. 19, 1934, ibid. See also James Hawkins, Sheriff of Jefferson County, to Miller, Apr. 20, 1934, ibid.; *UMW Journal,* May 15, 1934.

69. Sheriff of St. Clair County to Miller, Apr. 20, 1934, and Hawkins to Miller, Apr. 20, 1934, Miller Papers. Altogether there were three fatalities during the stoppage, and one of them was a miner shot after this picket. See ibid.; *Birmingham News,* May 14, 1934.

70. *Birmingham News,* Apr. 23, May 2, 1934; "Alabama Commercial Mines Agreement," Apr. 24, 1934, President/District 20 Correspondence.

71. For example, *Birmingham News,* Apr. 13, 22, May 12, 1934; Taft, *Organizing Dixie,* 91–92; findings of LaFollette Committee, unidentified press cutting, District 20 Papers. TCI and Republic also had huge arsenals. See also *Southern Worker,* July and September 1934.

72. *Birmingham News,* Apr. 4, May 23, 1934; note in Taft Papers, citing Acuff to N. W. Roberts, NRA, May 24, 1934; *Southern Worker,* November 1934.

73. Butler, *"And Now There's Gold,"* 16, 18; *Birmingham News,* Aug. 25, Sept. 8, 1934. *UMW Journal,* press cutting, ca. Dec. 1, 1939; *Gadsden Tribune,* Aug. 26, 1941 (reporting Charlie's death).

74. Polakov, "Notes on Mechanization," 4. The AFI "popsicles," and possibly those at TCI, had separate associations for black and white workers. Presidents, White Welfare Society and Black Welfare Society, AFI, to Brotherhood of Captive Mine Workers, Jan. 25, 1936, TCSH.

75. "Working Lives," No. 4; Kelley, *Hammer and Hoe,* 67.

76. Numerous reports by Persons in Miller Papers.

77. Moreover, Mine, Mill was not a powerful national union like the UMW. The author is grateful to Judith Stein for discussion on these points.

78. Kelley, *Hammer and Hoe,* 65–67. See also Alexander, "Interracial Unionism," 10–11. Indeed, Mitch seems to have coupled the party with the ore stoppage, informing Lewis: "Communism is creeping in down here. The ore miners are on strike." Mitch to Lewis, May 8, 1934, President/District 20 Papers. See also Persons to Miller, Apr. 27, 1934, and report by Persons, Apr. 28, 1934, Miller Papers. Mitch himself was an anti-Communist, and in 1935 he branded the party as "labor's greatest enemy," so it is ironic that in 1941 Congressman Martin Dies, chairman of the House Un-American Affairs Committee, named him as either a member or fellow-traveler of the party. See *Birmingham Labor Advocate,* Apr. 20, 1935.

79. In March 1937, following a signal victory by workers at General Motors, in which Lewis had played a leading part, U.S. Steel signed an agreement with SWOC, and insisted that TCI do the same. However, unlike unionization in Alabama's coal mines, local recognition had not been won by the members themselves, and it was not until a successful strike in 1941 that SWOC became well organized in Birmingham. "Report of William Mitch"; *Birmingham News,* Apr. 1, 1937; Stein, "Southern Workers," 188–89, 191; Alan J. Singer, "'Something of a Man': John L. Lewis, the

UMWA, and the CIO, 1919–1943," in *The United Mine Workers of America: A Model of Industrial Solidarity?* ed. John H. M. Laslett (University Park: Pennsylvania State University Press, 1996), 127.

80. Mitch to Lewis, Aug. 7, 1938, President/District 20 Correspondence. Also Fox, *United We Stand,* 322.

81. Negotiating Committee, Alabama Coal Operators, to Mitch, Oct. 2, 1935, and Local 5827 to Lewis, Nov. 13, 1935, President/District 20 Correspondence.

82. A. A. Carmichael to Governor Graves, Nov. 7, 1935, Graves Papers. Also *Birmingham Post,* Oct. 30, 1935; Taft, *Organizing Dixie,* 93.

83. Mitch to A.D. Lewis, Oct. 21, 1935, and Presidents of TCI Locals to John L. Lewis, telegram, Nov. 1, 1935, President/District 20 Correspondence. Lowery and another black miner, Burns, recalled collecting food in the countryside, probably during this dispute (with the latter adding that a lot of the people they collected from belonged to the union). See Lowery, interview; Cleatus Burns, interview.

84. Hayes to John L. Lewis, Oct. 23, 1935, and Mitch to John L. Lewis, Nov. 11, 1935, President/District 20 Correspondence.

85. *Birmingham Post,* Nov. 15, 1935; "Report of William Mitch."

86. Lowery, interview. Also "Report of William Mitch"; Polakov, "Notes on Mechanization"; Taft, *Organizing Dixie,* 93.

87. *Birmingham Age-Herald,* Apr. 5, 1939; unidentified cutting, April 1939, District 20 Papers; *Birmingham News,* May 12, 14, 18, 20, 1939; *Birmingham Post,* June 20, 1939.

88. *Birmingham Post,* Apr. 4, 1941; Alabama Department of Industrial Relations, "Official Report of Proceedings before the Board of Mediation," Apr. 15, 1941, p. 79, Dixon Papers.

89. Unidentified press cutting, District 20 Papers; "Release," Apr. 29, 1941, Dixon Papers.

90. *Birmingham News,* May 11, 1941; *Birmingham Post,* May 12, 13, 1941.

91. Melvyn Dubofsky and Warren Van Tine, *John L. Lewis: A Biography,* abridged ed. (Urbana: University of Illinois Press, 1986), 282–85.

92. *Birmingham Post,* Aug. 3, Sept. 4, 1941; unidentified press cutting, and data on wage scales, District 20 Papers.

93. National Labor Relations Board, "Certification of Representatives," and "TCI Agreement," Oct. 31, 1941, District 20 Papers.

94. Dubofsky and Van Tine, *John L. Lewis,* 287–94.

95. For instance, Mitch, Jr., observed that Lewis was "revered—legendary to local old coal miners," and for Uncle George Jones, improvements begin with: "When de President and John L. Lewis had signed deir decree, . . . " Mitch, Jr., interview; Korson, *Coal Dust on the Fiddle,* 302. See also "Working Lives," No. 7.

96. He added: "[That's] while we were in the union hall, but outside they was 'mister.'" Brown, interview by Alexander. Also, Ward, interview.

97. Brenda McCallum, "Songs of Work and Songs of Worship: Sanctifying Black Unionism in the Southern City of Steel," *New York Folklore* 14, nos. 1–2 (1988): 9.

98. Horace R. Cayton and George S. Mitchell, *Black Workers and the New Unions* (Chapel Hill: University of North Carolina Press, 1939), 347. Also, Lowery, interview.

99. Cayton and Mitchell, *Black Workers,* 344.

100. Brown, interview by Alexander; Lowery, interview; Christian, interview; Cayton and Mitchell, *Black Workers,* 349.

101. Photograph of 1935 delegates in Mulga UMW Local meeting hall, District 20, UMW; *UMW Journal,* Feb. 1, 1939; *Union News,* Oct. 10, 1940; *Birmingham News,* May 11, 1941; Mitch to John L. Lewis, July 19, 1935, and Circular to District 20 locals, President/District 20 Correspondence.

102. Brown, interview by Alexander; Lowery, interview; Cayton and Mitchell, *Black Workers,* 350.

103. Brown, interview by Alexander.

104. Korson, *Coal Dust on the Fiddle,* 303.

CHAPTER 4

1. William Warren Rogers, Robert David Ward, Leah Rawls Atkins, and Wayne Flynt, *Alabama: The History of a Deep South State* (Tuscaloosa: University of Alabama Press, 1994), 500.

2. Reynold Q. Shotts, "Some Significant Recent Changes in the Pattern of Coal Production and Markets in Alabama," *Journal of the Alabama Academy of Science* 33 (April 1962): 62–82; "Let's Put America Back in the Black," film by the Alabama Coal Association (ACA), 1982, University of Alabama at Birmingham Archives (hereafter cited as ACA Film). Miners found coal in the three seams: the Pratt Group closest to the surface, the Mary Lee Group about 500 feet below, and the Black Creek Group another 300 feet below that.

3. "Is Another Man's Hell," 51, in box 2, folder 20, Erskine Ramsay Papers, BPLA; *Birmingham News,* Dec. 19, 1971, clipping in "Coal Industry and Trade—Alabama" file, clipping files, TCSH.

4. "Is Another Man's Hell," 51, Ramsay Papers.

5. Jimmie Crockett [pseud.], interview by D. G. M., Jan. 28, 1980, pp. 43–45.

6. Erskine Bonds, interview by Bob Baggett, Docena, Alabama, May 22,

1979, p. 3, and W. B. Turner, interview by Don Sullivan, Docena, Alabama, Mar. 2, 1979, p. 4, both at SU; "UMW—Alabama" file, clipping files, TCSH; *Birmingham News,* May 19, 1980, clipping in "Coal Industry and Trade—Coke—Birmingham" file, clipping files, TCSH.

7. Crockett, interview, pp. 47, 50–51.

8. Ibid., 41–43.

9. Dr. E. L. McFee, interview by Jim Nogalski at Birmingham, Alabama, Apr. 1, 1979, pp. 5–7, SU.

10. Burton, interview, p. 5; Mrs. John (Annie) Sokira, interview by Sybil Burton, Brookside, Alabama, Nov. 27, 1974, p. 3, SU; Smith, interview, p. 9; *Birmingham News,* May 19, 1980, clipping in "Coal Industry and Trade—Coke—Birmingham" file, clipping files, TCSH. Italian immigrant John Gioeillo, a TCI miner for thirty-nine years, expressed a positive, distinctly minority, opinion of the company store and its prices. John Gioeillo, interview by Selena Cason, Aug. 7, 1975, at Republic, Alabama, p. 10, SU.

11. Mr. and Mrs. Reuben Barnes, interview by Randy Barnes at Docena, Alabama, Mar. 14, 1979, pp. 15, 19–20, SU; Annie Sokira, interview, p. 4; Christine Cochran, interview by Jerry Tapley at Docena, Alabama, May 24, 1979, p. 2, SU.

12. Burton, interview, pp. 4, 12–13.

13. Ibid., p. 11; Ellis Self, interview by Selena Cason, Birmingham, Alabama, July 20, 1975, pp. 2, 7–8, SU.

14. Self, interview, p. 10; B. D. Ogletree, interview by Ronnie Boulware, Docena, Alabama, Feb. 28, 1979, pp. 9–10, SU; Turner, interview, p. 1, 7–8. Turner felt that TCI eventually appreciated union organization as a way to reduce confusion and chaos in industrial relations.

15. Mike P. Angelo [pseud.], interview by T. T. C., Birmingham, Alabama, Jan. 27, 1977, pp. 27, 31, 33, SU. See also Alan Draper, "The New Southern Labor History Revisited: The Success of the Mine Mill and Smelter Workers Union in Birmingham, 1934–1938," *Journal of Southern History* 62 (February 1996): 97–99.

16. "UMW—Alabama" file and "Coal Industry and Trade—Coke—Birmingham" file, both in the clipping files, TCSH.

17. Annie Sokira, interview, pp. 9–10, 13; Cochran, interview, p. 7.

18. Robert H. Zieger, *The CIO, 1935–1955* (Chapel Hill: University of North Carolina Press, 1995), 150; Morton S. Baratz, *The Union and the Coal Industry* (Port Washington, N.Y.: Kennikat Press, 1973), 79; Burton, interview, pp. 15–16; *Alabama Federationist* 2, no. 5 (January 1943), and 4, no. 10 (May 1944), at the Alabama headquarters of the AFL-CIO, Birmingham, Alabama.

19. *University of Alabama Business News* 17 (May 1947) clipping, and *Birmingham Post,* July 15, 1943, clipping, both in "Coal Industry and Trade—Coke—Ala-

bama" file, clipping files, TCSH; Harris to Murray, March 23, 1943, in box 1, folder 18, Taft Papers.

20. Angelo, interview, pp. 16, 23–24; Sally Furse, "History of the International Union of Mine, Mill and Smelter Workers in the Jefferson County, Alabama, Area" (Unpublished seminar paper, Samford University, Nov. 26, 1974), 20–21, in possession of Glenn Feldman; Finch to Colvin, July 31, 1942, Stevenson to Green, Aug. 6, 1942, and Haas to Griger, June 2, 1943, in box 1, folder 18, Haigler to Brophy, Mar. 9, May 4, 1948, in box 1, folder 19, and Beddow to Murray, Jan. 3, 1950, and Farr to Murray, May 19, 1950, both in box 1, folder 20, Taft Papers; Zieger, *The CIO*, 281–82, 375; Huntley, "Iron Ore Miners and Mine Mill," 109–10.

21. Beddow to Kelley, Nov. 13, 1941, box 1, folder 18, Taft Papers; Flynt, *Poor but Proud*, 339.

22. Smith, interview, p. 2; Cochran, interview, p. 7; Ogletree, interview, p. 12; Turner, interview, pp. 7, 11.

23. Cochran, interview, p. 6; Grace Darden, interview by Scott Gloor at Docena, Alabama, Mar. 15, 1979, pp. 3–4, SU.

24. James Simmons and Samuel Kelley, interview by Belinda Mardis, Birmingham, Alabama, Mar. 13, 1979, p. 2, SU.

25. Baratz, *The Union and the Coal Industry*, 82; *Alabama Magazine,* Oct. 7, 1949, in "UMW—Alabama" file, and *Annual Statistical Reports* (Division of Safety and Inspection, Department of Industrial Relations, State of Alabama), clipping in "Coal Industry and Trade—Alabama" file, both in clipping files, TCSH.

26. Proceedings of the Tenth Constitutional Convention of the Alabama State Industrial Union Council–CIO, Pickwick Club, Birmingham, Ala., Apr. 11–13, 1949, vol. 1949–50, p. 142, AFL-CIO headquarters; Goodwin quoted in Flynt, *Poor but Proud*, 338.

27. John Sokira, interview by Selena Cason, July 24, 1975, Brookside, Alabama, p. 16, SU; Bonds, interview, p. 10; Self interview, p. 8; Cochran, interview, p. 7; Flynt, *Poor but Proud*, 348.

28. Self, interview, p. 10; *Birmingham News,* Oct. 10, 1971, clipping in "Coal Industry and Trade—Alabama" file, clipping files, TCSH; Baratz, *The Union and the Coal Industry*, 48.

29. "Joint Statement of the Alabama Power Company and the UMW," Apr. 20, 1960, Alabama By-Products Corp. File on the UMW, box 1, folder 2, BPLA; *Annual Statistical Reports* in "Coal Industry and Trade—Alabama" file, and *Birmingham Post-Herald,* Dec. 11, 1950, clipping, "Accidents" file, both in clipping files, TCSH; Joseph E. Finley, *The Corrupt Kingdom: The Rise and Fall of the United Mine Workers* (New York: Simon and Schuster, 1972), 224; Fox, *United We Stand,* 463.

30. Program of the First International Conference on the Underground Gasi-

fication of Coal at Birmingham and Gorgas, Alabama, Feb. 12–14, 1952; October 1955 clipping; Program of the 24th Annual Joint Solid Fuels Conference, Oct. 5–7, 1961, Birmingham, Alabama; George F. Bator, "Underground Gasification of Coal" (Report published by the Alabama State Mine Experiment Station, University of Alabama, January 1950); Milton H. Fies et al., "An Experiment in the Underground Gasification of Coal at Gorgas," and "The Second Underground Gasification Experiment at Gorgas, Alabama"; Bureau of Mines, Dept. of the Interior Memo, Nov. 26, 1957; *Birmingham News,* Feb. 12, 17, 1952, June 12, 1955, Nov. 20, 1971; *Birmingham Post-Herald,* Nov. 12, 1952; *Gadsden Times,* Mar. 9, 1957; all materials in the "Coal Industry and Trade—Alabama" file, clipping files, TCSH. One forty-nine-year veteran of the mines who worked at the Gamble, Praco, Calumet, Nauvoo, and Bankhead mines recalled that Gorgas was "one of the best places that I ever worked . . . conditions was good"; Burton, interview, pp. 18–19.

31. Flynt, *Poor but Proud,* 339.

32. Ibid., 339, 348.

33. Crockett, interview, pp. 55–56; Annie Sokira, interview, p. 11.

34. Crockett, interview, pp. 57–58.

35. *Birmingham News,* July 6, 1969, clipping in "Coal Mines and Mining—Alabama" file, clipping files, TCSH; Marie Samsal Fancher, interview, October 1990, in James H. Walker, *The Struggle and the Joy: An American Coal Town, Piper, Alabama* (Birmingham: Birmingham Public Library Press, 1993), 139–41, 158. See also Clarence G. Studdard, "History of Moss & McCormack Coal Mines and Their Employees at the Howard Mines" (Birmingham, ca. 1990), 18 (found in the Special Collections Department at Samford University).

36. Flynt, *Poor but Proud,* 338.

37. Charles R. Perry, *Collective Bargaining and the Decline of the United Mine Workers* (Philadelphia: University of Pennsylvania Press, 1984), 54.

38. Address of the Hon. Hugh Morrow, Oct. 6, 1959, box 3, folder 46, ACOA Papers.

39. *Birmingham News,* June 14, 1956, and *Birmingham Post-Herald,* Mar. 27, 1960, in "Accident" file, clipping files, TCSH.

40. Flynt, *Poor but Proud,* 338–39.

41. Burton, interview, p. 19; *Birmingham News,* Apr. 19, 1960, May 11, 1967, Sept. 28, 1969, clippings in "UMW—Alabama" file, and *Birmingham News,* Jan. 7, 1968, in "Coal Industry and Trade—Coke—Birmingham" file, both in clipping files, TCSH; Perry, *Collective Bargaining,* 18.

42. In 1972 Southern Company did close its No. 2 mine at Maylene in Shelby County. See *Birmingham News,* Apr. 23, 1967, Dec. 29, 1971, and clipping, n.d., in "Coal Industry and Trade—Alabama" file, clipping files, TCSH.

43. *Birmingham Post-Herald,* May 10, 1966, in "UMW—Alabama" file, clipping files, TCSH.

44. *Birmingham News,* Sept. 14, 1979, in "Coal Industry and Trade-Coke-Birmingham" file, clipping files, TCSH. Earlier in the decade, "a poor relationship between labor and management" had led to the burning of forty-two houses and the black and white schools in the Bibb County coal towns of Piper and Coleanor. See Walker, *The Struggle and the Joy,* 159.

45. ACA Film; Mineral Resources Institute–State Mine Experiment Station, "Orientation Session on Surface Mining for the State Legislature" (University of Alabama, May 5, 1975), TCSH; *Birmingham News,* Dec. 1, 1971; miscellaneous clippings in "Coal Industry and Trade—Alabama" file, clipping files, TCSH.

46. Perry, *Collective Bargaining,* 18.

47. ACA Film.

48. *Birmingham News,* Nov. 7, 1971, July 30, 1972, in "Coal Mining and Mines—Strip" file, clipping files, TCSH.

49. *Birmingham Post-Herald,* Aug. 11, 1971, and *Birmingham News,* Nov. 26, 1971, July 30, Sept. 23, Oct. 7, 1972, all in "Coal Mining and Mines—Strip" file, clipping files, TCSH.

50. *Birmingham News,* Mar. 29, 1970, in "Accidents" file, clipping files, TCSH.

51. *Birmingham Post-Herald,* Feb. 14, 1972, in "Accidents" file, clipping files, TCSH.

52. Smith, interview, p. 5.

53. Ibid.; *Birmingham News,* Nov. 19–20, 1971, Mar. 23, June 15, 1972, Apr. 12, 1973, in "Accidents" file, clipping files, TCSH.

54. *Birmingham News,* June 14, 1972, in "Accidents" file, clipping files, TCSH.

55. A Pennsylvania court indicted Boyle and his associates for murder, and a federal court also found Boyle guilty of making illegal political contributions totaling $49,500. See *Birmingham News,* Nov. 26, 1972, and other clipping dated Dec. 23, 1972, in "UMW—The Miners' Fight for Democracy Alabama" file, clipping files, TCSH; Paul F. Clark, *The Miners' Fight for Democracy: Arnold Miller and the Reform of the United Mine Workers* (Ithaca: Cornell University Press, 1981), 35–37. In 1968 Boyle and Yablonski had attended a District 20 rally in Alabama together; see Fox, *United We Stand,* 482.

56. *Birmingham Post-Herald,* Oct. 21, Nov. 20, 25, 1972, *Birmingham News,* Nov. 26, 1972, and other clippings dated Oct. 21 and 24, 1972, all in "UMW—Alabama" file, clipping files, TCSH.

57. Despite his poor showing in Alabama, Miller responded to a March 1973 delegation from the state by visiting District 20 personally in July 1973. See

Simmons and Kelley, interview, p. 16; *Birmingham Post-Herald,* Dec. 1, 15, 1972, *Birmingham News,* Dec. 22, 1972, and other clippings dated Nov. 25, Dec. 23, 1972, Mar. 5, 8, July 28, 1973, and Oct. 10, 1974, all in "UMW—Alabama" file, clipping files, TCSH.

58. *Birmingham News,* Sept. 1, 1973, and clippings dated Oct. 20, 1972, and June 20, Sept. 13, 1974, in "UMW—Alabama" file, clipping files, TCSH.

59. *Birmingham News,* Aug. 11, 1974, and clippings dated Aug. 20, 26, 29, 1974, in "UMW—Alabama" file, clipping files, TCSH.

60. *Birmingham Post-Herald,* Nov. 14, 1974, and clippings dated Nov. 19, Dec. 6, 17–18, 1974, in "UMW—Alabama" file, clipping files, TCSH.

61. Turner interview, pp. 3, 6, 11; Simmons and Kelley, interview, pp. 5–16.

62. Turner, interview, p. 18.

63. ACA Film; James S. Browning, "Recovering Fine-Size Coal from Alabama Surface Mine Washer Wastes Using the Humphrey's Spiral" (University of Alabama Mining Resources Institute, 1977), 1; Frank P. Scruggs, "Coal in Alabama" (Montgomery: Alabama Energy Management Board, September 1974); both reports in the clippings files, TCSH.

CHAPTER 5

1. Fox, *United We Stand,* 498.

2. Gary Pickett, interview by Robert Woodrum, tape recording, Birmingham, Alabama, Jan. 23, 1997. For accounts of this period in the UMW's history, see Curtis Seltzer, *Fire in the Hole: Miners and Managers in the American Coal Industry* (Lexington: University of Kentucky Press, 1985); Clark, *The Miners' Fight;* Perry, *Collective Bargaining;* George William Hopkins, "The Miners for Democracy: Insurgency in the United Mine Workers of America, 1970–1972" (Ph.D. diss., University of North Carolina at Chapel Hill, 1976); Paul Nyden, "Miners for Democracy: Struggle in the Coal Fields" (Ph.D. diss., Columbia University, 1974); Daniel Marschall, "The Miners and the UMW: Crisis in the Reform Process," *Socialist Review* 8 (July–October 1978): 65–115; and Jim Green, "Holding the Line: Miners' Militancy and the Strike of 1978," *Radical America* 12 (May–June 1978): 2–27.

3. "The Rank and File Speaks: South African Coal Imports," and Don Stillman, "UMWA Launches Campaign to Stop South African Coal imports," *UMW Journal,* June 1–15, 1974.

4. For coverage of the UMW's actions at the Alabama State Docks, see Bill Sellers, "South African Coal Arrives, UMW Sets up Picket Lines," Aug. 26; Sellers, "UMW Removes Docks Pickets," Aug. 27; Sellers, "Unloading of Coal Continues:

Longshoremen Return to Jobs at State Docks," Aug. 28; and Sellers, "UMW With-draws Pickets at Docks," Aug. 29, 1974, all in *Mobile Register.* For a description of national union efforts to stop the coal imports, see Don Stillman, "Customs Refuses Bar on South African Coal," *UMW Journal,* Feb. 16–28, 1975. An in-depth examination of the protests against Southern Company can be found in Robert H. Woodrum, "Reforming Dixie: Alabama Coal Miners and Rank-and-File Rebellion in the United Mine Workers of America, 1963 to 1978" (Master's thesis, Georgia State University, 1997).

5. R. Lewis, *Black Coal Miners in America,* 192–93. For statistics on Jefferson County, see Norrell, "Caste in Steel," 676; and Nyden, "Miners for Democracy," 779. All of these sources offer different numbers based on different sources and perspectives. I have followed Lewis here because he takes a statewide perspective and bases his figures on federal statistics.

6. R. Lewis, *Black Coal Miners in America,* 180.

7. Ibid., 171; Norrell, "Caste in Steel," 686.

8. Betty Jones, interview by Robert Woodrum, tape recording, Jasper, Alabama, Feb. 6, 1997; "New Miners," *UMW Journal,* Mar. 1–15, 1975; Marat Moore, "Women Go Underground," in Laslett, *United Mine Workers of America,* 484, 494, 495. For in-depth accounts of the conditions women faced in mines in Alabama and elsewhere, see Marat Moore, *Women in the Mines: Stories of Life and Work* (New York: Twayne Publishers, 1996).

9. Clark, *The Miners' Fight,* 69–72.

10. Peggy Roberson, "Coal Miners Stay Off Jobs in Alabama," *Birmingham News,* Aug. 26, 1975.

11. Chris Conway, "State Miners Ordered to End Strike," *Birmingham Post-Herald,* Aug. 27, 1975.

12. Peggy Roberson, "6,000 Coal Miners in Area Join Wildcat Strike," *Birmingham News,* Aug. 27, 1975; Chris Conway, "Alabama Coal Miners Back on Job," *Birmingham Post-Herald,* Sept. 3, 1975.

13. Clark, *The Miners' Fight,* 71, 72.

14. Phil H. Shook, "Wildcat Mine Strike Hits Alabama Hard; Thousands Idled," *Birmingham News,* Aug. 5, 1976.

15. Phil H. Shook, "End of State Mine Strike May Be Near," ibid., Aug. 12, 1976.

16. Clark, *The Miners' Fight,* 73.

17. Ibid., 109, 110.

18. "Coal Mine Health, Pension Cuts May Hurt Try to End State Strike," *Birmingham Post-Herald,* June 21, 1977.

19. Frank Morring, Jr., "Miners Tell Court Reasons for Strike," ibid., June 22, 1977.

20. "State Coal Strikers Begin Return as Miner Reinstated," ibid., June 24, 1977.

21. "3,000 Birmingham Area Coal Miners Stay Off Job," ibid., Aug. 19, 1977.

22. "Baker Says Pickets Will Be Asked 'Why?'" *Birmingham News,* Aug. 20, 1977.

23. Bruce Patterson, "Miners Vote to End Strike," *Birmingham Post-Herald,* Aug. 22, 1977.

24. For election results see *UMW Journal,* October 1977. Also, Charles Fuller, interview by Robert Woodrum, tape recording, Jasper, Alabama, Jan. 24, 1997. For an account of the issues in 1973 District 20 election, see *Alabama UMWA Miner,* Sept. 15, 1973, folder 100-10, box 100, Miners for Democracy Collection, WSUAL. For an example of early criticism of Baker, see T. M. Ray to John Owens, Feb. 22, 1963, District 20 folder, District 1 to District 31 Series, UMW Papers, PSULA.

25. For discussions of the issues in the 1977–78 negotiations, see Seltzer, *Fire in the Hole,* 148–51; Clark, *The Miners' Fight,* 67–69; and Perry, *Collective Bargaining,* 127–33, 215–29.

26. "14,000 Alabama Miners Leave Jobs," Dec. 6, 1977; Chris Conway, "Coal Pickets Still in Short Supply at Most City Mines," Dec. 8; Chris Conway, "Most State Mines Idled by Strike," Dec. 8, 1977, all in *Birmingham Post-Herald.*

27. "Pickets Armed with Bats and Crowbars Close Mines," ibid., Dec. 14, 1977.

28. Chris Conway, "Strikers Close Mines in State, Start Fire, Threaten Officials," ibid., Dec. 21, 1977.

29. Testimony of James L. Fuqua, Oct. 3, 1984, *Oakman Mining Company and Prater Equipment Company v. United Mine Workers of America, Districts 20 and 23,* U.S. District Court, Birmingham, Alabama (hereafter cited as *Oakman Mining v. UMW*). These records are housed at the National Archives and Records Administration in East Point, Georgia.

30. "UMWA Drives SLU out of Alabama," *UMW Journal,* May 16–31, 1976. The SLU remains a sketchy organization, but former UMW International Executive Board member Joseph A. "Jock" Yablonski had identified its presence at small mines in Alabama as early as 1963. Union officials had vowed to wage a vigorous campaign to oust the SLU from the state, but it was not until 1976 that they could proclaim victory in that effort. For information on the SLU, see John Gaventa, *Power and Powerlessness: Quiescence and Rebellion in an Appalachian Valley* (Urbana: University

of Illinois Press, 1980), 172. For Yablonski's observations, see UMW, Minutes of International Executive Board meeting, June 12–14, 1963, folder 70-5, box 70, Miners for Democracy Collection.

31. Telegram, Bobby Peterson to George Wallace, May 5, 1966, Labor Department, Oct. 1, 1964–May 9, 1966, folder, and Arlis Fant to Donald Peters, May 10, 1966, and newspaper clipping, "Delegation Calls: Governor Vows Aid in Strike," *Jasper (Ala.) Daily Mountain Eagle,* May 13, 1966, Labor Department, May 10, 1966–Sept. 30, 1966, folder, box SG 22408, George Wallace Papers, ADAH. Also "UMW Said Ready to Sign Pact," *Birmingham News,* May 12, 1966; and UMW, Minutes of International Executive Board meeting, June 6–8, 1966, folder 72-25, box 72, Miners for Democracy Collection.

32. Memo, Sam Littlefield, district president, and Lloyd Baker, secretary-treasurer, to All Local Unions, District 20 UMW, Apr. 10, 1974–May 1974 Press Releases folder, box SG 22491, Wallace Papers. For analysis of Wallace's relations with organized labor in Alabama, see Taft, *Organizing Dixie;* Alan Draper, *Conflict of Interests: Organized Labor and the Civil Rights Movement in the South, 1954–1968* (Ithaca: ILR Press, 1994); and Robert J. Norell, "Labor Trouble: George Wallace and Union Politics in Alabama," in Zieger, *Organized Labor,* 250–72.

33. Testimony of Billy R. Wooten, Oct. 9, 1984, *Oakman Mining v. UMW.*

34. Ibid.

35. Testimony of Charles L. Fuller, Oct. 3, 1984, ibid.

36. John Northrop, "State Troopers Mass to Prevent Strikers from Closing Mines," Jan. 9, and Northrop, "Troopers Prepare for Confrontations in Coal Mine Strike," Jan. 10, 1978, both in *Birmingham Post-Herald.*

37. Wooten testimony.

38. Chris Conway and Frank Bruer, "Wallace and UMW to Seek Strike Halt," *Birmingham Post-Herald,* Jan. 24, 1978.

39. Chris Conway, "Union Chief Fears Trooper Clashes," *Birmingham Post-Herald,* Jan. 25, 1978; Fuller, interview.

40. Fuller, interview; Fuller testimony.

41. "Miners Force Coal Dumping, Imperil Schools in Madison," Feb. 1, and Chris Conway, "Troopers Hurt Guarding Mine," Feb. 2, 1978, both in *Birmingham Post-Herald.*

42. Testimony of Alfred Key, Oct. 1, 1984, and Deposition of Claude Prater, Aug. 5, 1984, *Oakman Mining v. UMW.* Also Bruce Parsons, "Riot-Ready Troopers Face Angry Miners in Walker County," Feb. 3, and Bill Cornwell and Bruce Patterson, "Wallace to Keep Troopers at Mines, Won't Use Guard," Feb. 4, 1978, both in *Birmingham Post-Herald;* Frank Truchon, "Events Leading to Battle: 'Came to Do

Some Head-Knocking,'" Feb. 4, and Tom Scarritt, "Somber Union Miners Recall Violence; Vow No 'Scab' Coal," Feb. 4, 1978, both in *Birmingham News.*

43. Key testimony; Prater deposition; testimony of James L. Fowler, Oct. 3, 1984, *Oakman Mining v. UMW;* Truchon, "Events Leading to Battle"; Cornwell and Patterson, "Wallace to Keep Troopers at Mines."

44. Fuqua testimony.

45. Ibid.

46. Scarritt, "Somber Union Miners Recall Violence."

47. Testimony of Thomas I. Cook, Oct. 2, 1984, *Oakman Mining v. UMW.*

48. Cornwell and Patterson, "Wallace to Keep Troopers at Mines"; Truchon, "Events Leading to Battle."

49. Scarritt, "Somber Union Miners Recall Violence."

50. "Troopers Rescue Truck Drivers," *Birmingham News,* Feb. 19, 1978; "Would Prefer Seizure, Local UMW Says," *Birmingham Post-Herald,* Feb. 20, 1978.

51. Chris Conway, "Local Coal Strike Violence Erupts," *Birmingham Post-Herald,* Feb. 28, 1978.

52. Clark, *The Miners' Fight,* 126; Seltzer, *Fire in the Hole,* 155, 156; Perry, *Collective Bargaining,* 221.

53. "Miller Is Urged to Resign," *Birmingham Post-Herald,* Feb. 15, 1978; Larry Corcoran, "State Miners Also after Miller's Head," *Birmingham News,* Feb. 14, 1978.

54. Frank Morring and Chris Conway, "What It's All About: Local Miners Fear Loss of 'Everything We Fought For,'" *Birmingham Post-Herald,* Feb. 17, 1978.

55. Corcoran, "State Miners Also after Miller's Head."

56. Seltzer, *Fire in the Hole,* 156, 157; Clark, *The Miners' Fight,* 127, 128; Perry, *Collective Bargaining,* 225, 226.

57. Clark, *The Miners' Fight,* 128.

58. Chris Conway, "Local UMW Officials Uncertain over Pact," *Birmingham Post-Herald,* Mar. 1, 1978; Byron Davis, "Alabama UMW Will Study Carter Action and 'Abide by Law,'" *Birmingham News,* Mar. 6, 1978; Seltzer, *Fire in the Hole,* 157.

59. Robert H. Woodrum, "Confronting Coal: The Carter Administration and the 1977–1978 Strike," paper presented to "The Carter Presidency: Policy Choices in the Post–New Deal Era," Jimmy Carter Library and Presidential Center, Atlanta, Georgia, Feb. 20–22, 1997, 28. For an overall look at Carter's administration, see Burton I. Kaufman, *The Presidency of James Earl Carter, Jr.* (Lawrence: University Press of Kansas, 1993). For an overview of the administration's relationship with labor, see Taylor Dark, "Organized Labor and the Carter Administration: The Origins of Conflict," and Gary M. Fink, "Fragile Alliance: Jimmy Carter and the

American Labor Movement," both in *The Presidency and Domestic Policies of Jimmy Carter,* ed. Herbert D. Rosenbaum and Alexj Ugrinsky (Westport, Conn.: Greenwood Press, 1994).

60. Seltzer, *Fire in the Hole,* 161; Perry, *Collective Bargaining,* 156–58.

61. Stan Bailey, "Wallace Rescinds Blackouts Call," *Birmingham News,* Mar. 11, 1978; Frank Bruer and Chris Conway, "APC Used Him, Wallace Says," *Birmingham Post-Herald,* Mar. 11, 1978.

62. Bruer and Conway, "APC Used Him, Wallace Says."

63. Peggy Riley, "UMW Won't Say If Miners Will Return," *Birmingham Post-Herald,* Mar. 13, 1978.

64. Pickett, interview.

65. Chris Conway, "Guns Fired at State Mine," *Birmingham Post-Herald,* Mar. 15, 1978.

66. Testimony of Ben Gamel, Oct. 4, 1984, *Oakman Mining v. UMW;* Frank Morring, Jr,. and Chris Conway, "Derailed Jasper Coal Train Was Sabotaged," *Birmingham Post-Herald,* Mar. 16, 1978.

67. Frank Morring, Jr., and Peggy Riley, "State Picketing Ends, but Most Mines Idle," *Birmingham Post-Herald,* Mar. 14, 1978.

68. Byron Davis, "Merchants in Walker Going All-out to Aid UMW Miners Hurting for Cash," *Birmingham News,* Feb. 13, 1978.

69. Chris Conway, "Despite Coal Strike, Economy of Area Seems Healthy So Far," *Birmingham Post-Herald,* Jan. 10, 1978.

70. Bonnie Davis, "Strike Places Coal Miners in Medical Care Bind," ibid., Jan. 10, 1978.

71. John Stewart, interview by Robert Woodrum, tape recording, Birmingham, Alabama, Jan. 23, 1997.

72. Seltzer, *Fire in the Hole,* 163, 164; Clark, *The Miners' Fight,* 129, 130; Marschall, "Miners and the UMW," 72, 73.

73. Larry Corcoran, "Fuller Predicts Pact OK, Early Return to Work," *Birmingham News,* Mar. 20, 1978; Peggy Riley, "District UMW Backs Pact," *Birmingham Post-Herald,* Mar. 20, 1978.

74. *UMW Journal,* March 1978.

75. Clark, *The Miners' Fight,* 158; Seltzer, *Fire in the Hole,* 167.

76. Byron Davis, "State Coal Miners Say They Can Live with New Contract," *Birmingham News,* Mar. 25, 1978.

77. This discussion draws heavily on Seltzer, *Fire in the Hole,* 138–40; and Paul F. Clark, "Legacy of Democratic Reform: The Trumka Administration and the Challenge of the 1980s," in Laslett, *United Mine Workers of America,* 467, 468, 475, 476.

Bibliography

PRIMARY SOURCES

MANUSCRIPT COLLECTIONS

Alabama Department of Archives and History, Montgomery, Ala.
    Dixon, Governor Frank. Papers.
    Graves, Governor Bibb. Papers.
    Jones, Governor Thomas. Papers.
    Kilby, Governor Thomas. Papers.
    Miller, Governor Benjamin. Papers.
    Persons, General. Papers.
    Wallace, Governor George. Papers
Birmingham Public Library Archives, Birmingham, Ala.
    Alabama By-Products Papers.
    Alabama Coal Operators Association Papers
    Alabama Mineral Land Company Collection. Letter Book, 1903–4.
    DeBardeleben Coal Company Records.
    Park, Thomas Duke. Papers.
    Ramsay, Erskine. Papers
    Taft, Philip. Papers.
    Tutwiler Collection of Southern History.
Library of Congress, Manuscripts Division, Washington, D.C.
    Papers of the Urban League.
National Archives, Washington, D.C.
    Federal Mediation and Conciliation Service. Case Files 170-9178.

RG 60: Records of the Department of Justice
RG 174: Records of the Department of Labor, 1907–1942.
Pennsylvania State University Labor Archives, University Park, Pa.
    Mitch, William. Papers.
    United Mine Workers of America Papers.
United Mine Workers District 20 Headquarters, Birmingham, Ala.
    District 20 Papers.
Wayne State University Archives of Labor and Urban Affairs, Detroit, Mich.
    Miners for Democracy Collection
    Weick, Edward A. Collection.

U.S. Government Documents

U.S. Bureau of the Census. *Mines and Quarries.* Washington, D.C.: Government
    Printing Office, 1902.
———. *Ninth Census of the United States,* vol. 3, *The Statistics of Wealth and Industry
    in the United States.* Washington, D.C.: Government Printing Office, 1872.
———. *Abstract of the Twelfth Census of the United States.* Washington, D.C.: Gov-
    ernment Printing Office, 1902.
———. *Fourteenth Census: Occupations.* Washington, D.C.: Government Printing
    Office, 1920.
———. *Fifteenth Census: Occupations.* Washington, D.C.: Government Printing
    Office, 1930.
———. *Sixteenth Census: Occupations.* Washington, D.C.: Government Printing
    Office, 1940.
U.S. Department of the Interior. *Compendium of the Tenth Census, Pt. 2.* Wash-
    ington, D.C.: Government Printing Office, 1883.
———. *Compendium of the Eleventh Census, 1890, Vol. 1, Pt. 1—Population.* Wash-
    ington, D.C.: Government Printing Office, 1892.
———. *Report on the Mining Industries of the United States (Exclusive of Precious Met-
    als), Tenth Census,* vol. 15. Washington, D.C.: Government Printing Office,
    1886.
———. *Report on the Mineral Industries of United States at the Eleventh Census.* Vol.
    7. Washington, D.C.: Government Printing Office, 1892.
U.S. Department of Justice. *Records R 60 "Peonage Files."* National Archives,
    Washington, D.C.
U.S. Department of Labor. *RG 174: "Special Problems—Birmingham", 1907–
    1942.* National Archives, Washington, D.C.

U.S. Immigration Commission. *Reports of the Immigration Commission: Immigrants in Industry, pt. 1, Bituminous Coal Mining, vol. 2.* Washington, D.C.: Government Printing Office, 1911.

U.S. Senate. *Report of the Federal Commission on Immigrants in Industries: The Bituinous Coal Mining Industry in the South,* 61st Cong., 2nd sess., 1910. S. Doc. 633.

U.S. Treasury Department. *Statistical Abstract of the United States for 1889.* Washington, D.C.: Government Printing Office, 1890.

———. *Statistical Abstract of the United States for 1900.* Washington, D.C.: Government Printing Office, 1901.

Works Progress Administration. *Gainful Workers, by Occupational Groups, and by Race, in Southeast, 1930.* Birmingham: Works Progress Administration, 1938.

State Documents

Alabama Department of Industrial Relations. *Annual Report to the Governor, 1939.* Birmingham: Department of Industrial Relations.

———. *Annual Statistical Report, 1942–1943* Montgomery: Department of Industrial Relations.

———. "Official Report of Proceedings before the Board of Mediation." Apr. 15, 1941.

State of Alabama. *Annual Report of Coal Mines, 1921.*

———. *Annual Report of Coal Mines, 1935.*

Minutes, Annual Reports, and Proceedings

Alabama State Industrial Union Council—CIO. *Proceedings of the Tenth Constitutional Convention.* Apr. 11–13, 1949.

Oakman Mining Company and Prater Equipment Company v. United Mine Workers of America Districts 20 and 23. U.S. District Court.

Proceedings of the Joint Convention of the Alabama Coal Operators Association and the United Mine Workers of America, 1903, and Arbitration Proceedings (Birmingham, 1903).

Tennessee Coal, Iron, and Railroad Company. *1898 Annual Report.*

———. *1905 Annual Report.*

United Mine Workers of America. *Minutes of the Ninth Annual Convention, 1898.*

———. *Minutes of the Tenth Annual Convention, 1899.*

———. *Minutes of the Eleventh Annual Convention, 1900.*

————. *Minutes of the Twelfth Annual Convention, 1901.*
————. *Minutes of the Thirteenth Annual Convention, 1902.*
————. *Minutes of the Fourteenth Annual Convention, 1903.*
————. *Minutes of the Fifteenth Annual Convention, 1904.*
————. *Proceedings of the 1924 Convention.*
————. *Proceedings of the Eighteenth Annual Convention, 1907.*
————. *Proceedings of the Nineteenth Annual Convention, 1908.*
————. *Proceedings of the Twentieth Annual Convention, 1909.*

NEWSPAPERS AND PERIODICALS

Alabama Federationist
Alabama Magazine
Alabama Sentinel
Bessemer Herald
Bessemer Journal
Bessemer Workman
Birmingham Age-Herald
Birmingham Daily Ledger
Birmingham Daily News
Birmingham Labor Advocate
Birmingham Negro American
Birmingham News
Birmingham Post
Birmingham Post-Herald
Birmingham State Herald
Chattanooga Republican
Engineering and Mining Journal
Gadsden Times
Gadsden Tribune
Journal of United Labor
Mineral Belt Gazette
National Labor Tribune
Southern Worker
Terre Haute Post
Union News
United Mine Workers Journal
University of Alabama Business News
West End Banner

Interviews

Brown, Earl. Interview by Peter Alexander. Tape recording. Booker Heights, Alabama, Sept. 4, 1997.

Christian, Steven. Interview by Peter Alexander. Tape recording. Belle Sumpter, Alabama, Aug. 29, 1997.

Connell, Girtley. Interview by Peter Alexander. Tape recording. Sept. 9, 1997.

Crockett, Jimmie. Interview by D. G. M. Jan. 28, 1980. In possession of Glenn Feldman.

Fuller, Charles. Interview by Robert Woodrum. Tape recording. Jasper, Alabama, Jan. 24, 1997.

Hutchins, Moses. Interview by Edwin L. Brown. Transcript. Apr. 1985.

Jones, Betty. Interview by Robert Woodrum. Tape recording. Jasper, Alabama, Feb. 6, 1997.

Lowery, Aquilla. Interview by Peter Alexander. Belle Sumpter, Alabama, Sept. 3, 1997.

Pickett, Gary. Interview by Robert Woodrum. Tape recording. Birmingham, Alabama, Jan. 23, 1997.

Stewart, John. Interview by Robert Woodrum. Tape recording. Birmingham, Alabama, Jan. 23, 1997.

Ward, Andrew. Interview by Peter Alexander. Tape recording. Mulga, Alabama, Sept. 9, 1997.

Working Lives Project, University of Alabama, 1983–84

Brown, Earl. Interview by Cliff Kuhn. June 29, 1984.

Burns, Cleatus. Interview by Cliff Kuhn. Jasper, Alabama, Dec. 6, 1984.

Burns, Louise. Interview by Cliff Kuhn. June 12, 1984.

Darden, Clarence. Interview by Steve McCallum. May 24, 1983.

Howard, Evelyn. Interview by Peggy Hamrick. Ca. 1984.

Jones, Fred. Interview by Cliff Kuhn. June 16, 1984.

Jones, Pollard. Interview. Sept. 3, 1983.

McAdory, Curtis. Interview by Peggy Hamrick. Aug. 23, 1984.

Mitch, William, Jr. Interview by Cliff Kuhn. June 22, 1984.

Price, Constance. Interview by Cliff Kuhn. July 18, 1984.

Oral History Collection at Samford University

Angelo, Mike P. Interview by T. T. C. Birmingham, Alabama, Jan. 27, 1977.

Barnes, Mr. and Mrs. Reuben. Interview by Randy Barnes. Docena, Alabama, Mar. 14, 1979.

Bonds, Erskine. Interview by Bob Baggett. Docena, Alabama, May 22, 1979.

Burton, Elmer. Interview by Sybil Burton. Walker County, Alabama, Nov. 27, 1974.

Cochran, Christine. Interview by Jerry Tapley. Docena, Alabama, May 24, 1970.

Darden, Grace. Interview by Scott Gloor. Docena, Alabama, Mar. 15, 1979.

Gioeillo, John. Interview by Selena Cason. Republic, Alabama, Aug. 7, 1975.

Hendrix, Ila. Interview by Ben Hendrix. May 1, 1976.

Kelley Samuel. Interview by Belinda Mardis. Birmingham, Alabama, Mar. 13, 1979.

McFee, Dr. E. L. Interview by Jim Nogalski. Birmingham, Alabama, Apr. 1, 1979.

Ogletree, B. D. Interview by Ronnie Boulware. Docena, Alabama, Feb. 28, 1979.

Self, Ellis. Interview by Selena Cason. Birmingham, Alabama, July 20, 1979.

Simmons, James. Interview by Belinda Mardis. Birmingham, Alabama, Mar. 13, 1979.

Smith, Luther V. Interview by Benny Hendrix. Quinton, Alabama, Nov. 27, 1974.

Sokira, Annie. Interview by Sybil Burton. Nov. 27, 1974.

Sokira, John. Interview by Selena Cason. July 24, 1975.

Turner, W. B. Interview by Don Sullivan. Mar. 2, 1979.

SECONDARY SOURCES

Abernathy, John H., Jr. "The Knights of Labor in Alabama." Master of Science in Commerce thesis, University of Alabama, 1960.

Alexander, Peter. "Interracial Unionism and Bifurcated State Power: Alabama Miners, 1917–37." Conference on Labour and Difference, Paper No. 31, St. Antony's College, Oxford, 1997.

Allen, Theodore W. *The Invention of the White Race.* Vol. 1, *Racial Oppression and Social Control.* London: Verso, 1994.

Armes, Ethel. *The Story of Coal and Iron in Alabama.* Birmingham, 1910.

Arnesen, Eric. "Up from Exclusion: Black and White Workers, Race, and the State of Labor History." *Reviews in American History* 26 (March 1998): 146–174.

———. *Waterfront Workers of New Orleans: Race, Class, and Politics, 1863–1923.* Urbana: University of Illinois Press, 1994.

Baratz, Morton S. *The Union and the Coal Industry.* Port Washington, N.Y.: Kennikat Press, 1973.

Barrett, James R. "Americanization from the Bottom Up: Immigration and the Remaking of the Working Class in America, 1880–1930." *Journal of American History* 79 (December 1992): 996–1020.

Berthoff, Roland T. "Southern Attitudes toward Immigration." *Journal of Southern History* 17 (1951): 328–60.

Bethea, Jack. *The Deep Seam.* New York: Houghton Mifflin, 1926.

Brier, Stephen. "In Defense of Gutman: The Union's Case." *International Journal of Politics, Culture, and Society* 2 (Spring 1989): 382–95.

Brody, David. *Steelworkers in America: The Non-union Era.* New York: Harper Torchbooks, 1969.

———. *Workers in Industrial America: Essays on the Twentieth-Century Struggle.* New York: Oxford University Press, 1980.

Browning, James. "Recovering Fine Size Coal from Alabama Surface Mine Washer Wastes Using the Humphrey's Spiral." Tuscaloosa: University of Alabama Mining Resources Institute, 1977.

Butler, Marie. *"And Now There's Gold": A Brief History of a Unique Community.* Birmingham: n.p., 1989.

Carmer, Carl. *Stars Fell on Alabama.* New York: Hill and Wang, 1934.

Cash, W. J. *The Mind of the South.* New York: Knopf, 1941.

Cayton, Horace R., and George S. Mitchell. *Black Workers and the New Unions.* Chapel Hill: University of North Carolina Press, 1939.

Chapman, H. H., et al. *The Iron and Steel Industry of the South.* University: University of Alabama Press, 1953.

Clark, Paul F. "Legacy of Democratic Reform: The Trumka Administration and the Challenge of the 1980s." In *The United Mine Workers of America: A Model of Industrial Solidarity?* ed. John H. M. Laslett. University Park: Pennsylvania State University Press, 1996.

———. *The Miners' Fight for Democracy: Arnold Miller and the Reform of the United Mine Workers.* Ithaca: Cornell University Press, 1981.

Cobb, James C. *The Most Southern Place on Earth: The Mississippi Delta and the Roots of Regional Identity.* New York: Oxford University Press, 1992.

Cohen, Lizabeth. *Making a New Deal: Industrial Workers in Chicago, 1919–1939.* Cambridge: Cambridge University Press, 1990.

Daniel, Pete. "The Tennessee Convict War." *Tennessee Historical Quarterly* 34 (Fall 1975): 273–92.

Dark, Taylor. "Organized Labor and the Carter Administration: The Origins of Conflict." In *The Presidency and Domestic Policies of Jimmy Carter,* ed. Herbert D. Rosenbaum and Alexj Ugrinsky (Westport, Conn.: Greenwood Press, 1994.

Drain, John. *The Coal Miner's Son.* Birmingham: Birmingham Printing and Publishing Company, 1985.

Draper, Alan. *Conflict of Interests: Organized Labor and the Civil Rights Movement in the South, 1954–1968.* Ithaca: ILR Press, 1994.

———. "The New Southern Labor History Revisited: The Success of the Mine Mill and Smelter Workers Union in Birmingham, 1934–1938." *Journal of Southern History* 62 (February 1996): 97–99.

Dubofsky, Melvyn, and Warren Van Tine. *John L. Lewis: A Biography.* Abridged ed. Urbana: University of Illinois Press, 1986.

DuBose, John W. *Jefferson County and Birmingham, Alabama: Historical and Biographical.* Birmingham: Teeple and Smith, 1887.

Elmore, Nancy Ruth. "The Birmingham Coal Strike of 1908." Master's thesis, University of Alabama, 1966.

Evans, Chris. *History of the United Mine Workers of America from the Year 1890 to 1900.* Indianapolis: United Mine Workers of America, 1914.

Feldman, Glenn. "Labor Repression in the American South: Corporations, State, and Race in Alabama's Coal Fields, 1917–1921." *Historical Journal* 37, no. 2 (1994): 343–64.

Fink, Gary M. "Fragile Alliance: Jimmy Carter and the American Labor Movement." In *The Presidency and Domestic Policies of Jimmy Carter,* ed. Herbert D. Rosenbaum and Alexj Ugrinsky. Westport, Conn.: Greenwood Press, 1994.

Fink, Gary M., and Merl Reed. *Race, Class, and Community in Southern Labor History.* West Port: Greenwood Press, 1994.

———. *Essays in Southern Labor History: Selected Papers.* Westport: Greenwood Press, 1977.

Finley, Joseph E. *The Corrupt Kingdom: The Rise and Fall of the United Mine Workers.* New York: Simon and Schuster, 1972.

Fitch, John A. "Birmingham District: Labor Conservation." *Survey,* Jan. 6, 1912, pp. 1527–40.

Flynt, Wayne. *Poor but Proud: Alabama's Poor Whites.* Tuscaloosa: University of Alabama Press, 1989.

Fox, Maier B. *United We Stand: The United Mine Workers of America, 1890–1990.* Washington, D.C.: United Mine Workers of America, 1990.

Furse, Sally. "History of the International Union of Mine, Mill and Smelter Workers in the Jefferson County, Alabama, Area." Unpublished seminar paper, Samford University, Nov. 26, 1974.

Garlock, Jonathan. *Guide to the Local Assemblies of the Knights of Labor.* Westport: Greenwood Press, 1982.

Gaventa, John. *Power and Powerlessness: Quiescence and Rebellion in an Appalachian Valley.* Urbana: University of Illinois Press, 1980.

Gerstle, Gary. "Liberty, Coercion, and the Making of Americans." *Journal of American History* 84 (September 1997): 524–58.

——. *Working-Class Americanism: The Politics of Labor in a Textile City, 1914–1960.* New York: Cambridge University Press, 1989.

Going, Allen Johnston. *Bourbon Democracy in Alabama, 1865–96.* University: University of Alabama Press, 1951.

Goodrich, Carter. *The Miner's Freedom: A Study of Working Life in a Changing Industry.* Boston: M. Jones, 1925.

Gowaskie, Joseph M. "From Conflict to Cooperation: John Mitchell and Bituminous Coal Operators, 1898–1908." *Historian* 38 (August 1976): 676–77.

Graebner, William. "Great Expectations: The Search for Order in Bituminous Coal, 1890–1917." *Business History Review* 48 (Spring 1974): 53–55.

Green, Jim. "Holding the Line: Miners' Militancy and the Strike of 1978." *Radical America* 12 (May–June 1978): 2–27.

Gutman, Herbert. "Black Coal Miners and the Greenback Labor Party in Redeemer Alabama, 1878–79: The Letters of Warren D. Kelley, Willis Johnson Thomas, 'Dawson,' and others." *Labor History* 10 (Summer 1969): 506–35.

——. "The Negro and the United Mine Workers." In *Work, Culture, and Society in Industrialized America,* 121–208. New York: Vintage, 1976.

Harris, Carl V. *Political Power in Birmingham, 1871–1921.* Knoxville: University of Tennessee Press, 1977.

Head, Holman. "The Development of the Labor Movement in Alabama Prior to 1900." Master of Business Administration thesis, University of Alabama, 1955.

Hill, Herbert. "Myth-Making as Labor History: Herbert Gutman and the United Mine Workers of America." *International Journal of Politics, Culture, and Society* 2 (Winter 1988): 132–200.

——. "The Problem of Race in American Labor History." *Reviews in American History* 24 (June 1996): 189–208.

Honey, Michael. *Southern Labor and Black Civil Rights: Organizing Memphis Workers.* Urbana: University of Illinois Press, 1993.

Hopkins, George William. "The Miners for Democracy: Insurgency in the United Mine Workers of America, 1970–1972." Ph.D. diss., University of North Carolina at Chapel Hill, 1976.

Huntley, Horace. "Iron Ore Miners and Mine Mill in Alabama, 1932–52." Ph.D. diss., University of Pittsburgh, 1976.

Johnson, James P. *The Politics of Soft Coal: The Bituminous Industry from World War I through the New Deal.* Urbana: University of Illinois Press, 1979.

Kaufman, Burton I. *The Presidency of James Earl Carter, Jr.* Lawrence: University Press of Kansas, 1993.

Kazal, Russell A. "Revisiting Assimilation: The Rise, Fall, and Reappraisal of a Concept in American Ethnic Identity." *American Historical Review* 100 (April 1995): 437–71.

Kelley, Robin D. G. *Hammer and Hoe: Alabama Communists during the Great Depression.* Chapel Hill: University of North Carolina Press, 1990.

Korson, George. *Coal Dust on the Fiddle: Songs and Stories of the Bituminous Industry.* 2nd ed. Hatboro, Pa.: Folklore Associates, 1965.

Laslett, John H. M., ed. *The United Mine Workers of America: A Model of Industrial Solidarity?* University Park: Pennsylvania State University Press, 1996.

Letwin, Daniel. *The Challenge of Interracial Unionism: Alabama Coal Miners, 1878–1921.* Chapel Hill: University of North Carolina Press, 1998.

Lewis, Ronald L. *Black Coal Miners in America: Race, Class, and Community Conflict, 1780–1980.* Lexington: University of Kentucky Press, 1987.

Lewis, W. David. *Sloss Furnaces and the Rise of the Birmingham District: An Industrial Epic.* Tuscaloosa: University of Alabama Press, 1994.

Lichtenstein, Alex. "Racial Conflict and Racial Solidarity in the Alabama Coal Strike of 1894: New Evidence for the Gutman-Hill Debate." *Labor History* 36 (Winter 1995): 63–76.

———. *Twice the Work of Free Labor: The Political Economy of Convict Labor in the New South.* New York: Verso, 1996.

Long, Priscilla. *Where the Sun Never Shines: A History of America's Bloody Coal Industry.* New York: Paragon House, 1991.

Marschall, Daniel. "The Miners and the UMW: Crisis in the Reform Process." *Socialist Review* 8 (July–October 1978): 65–115.

McCallum, Brenda. "Songs of Work and Songs of Worship: Sanctifying Black Unionism in the Southern City of Steel." *New York Folklore* 14, nos. 1–2 (1988): 9–33.

McCartin, Joseph Anthony. "Labor's 'Great War': American Workers, Unions, and the State, 1916–1920." Ph.D. diss., State University of New York, Binghamton, 1990.

McKiven, Henry M., Jr. *Iron and Steel: Class, Race, and Community in Birmingham, Alabama, 1875–1920.* Chapel Hill: University of North Carolina Press, 1995.

McLaurin, Melton A. *The Knights of Labor in the South.* Westport, Conn.: Greenwood Press, 1978.

Montgomery, David. *The Fall of the House of Labor: The Workplace, the State, and American Labor Activism, 1865–1925.* New York: Cambridge University Press, 1987.

Moore, Geoffrey H. "Business Cycles, Panics, and Depression." In *Encyclopedia of American Economic History,* ed. Glen Porter. New York: Scribner, 1980.

Moore, Marat. "Women Go Underground." In *The United Mine Workers of America: A Model of Industrial Solidarity?* ed. John H. M. Laslett. University Park: Pennsylvania State University Press, 1996.

———. *Women in the Mines: Stories of Life and Work.* New York: Twayne Publishers, 1996.

Norrell, Robert J. "Caste in Steel: Jim Crow Careers in Birmingham, Alabama." *Journal of American History* 73 (December 1986): 669–94.

———, ed. *James Bowron: The Autobiography of a New South Industrialist.* Chapel Hill: University of North Carolina Press, 1991.

Nyden, Paul. "Miners for Democracy: Struggle in the Coal Fields." Ph.D. diss., Columbia University, 1974.

Perry, Charles R. *Collective Bargaining and the Decline of the United Mine Workers.* Philadelphia: University of Pennsylvania Press, 1984.

Rikard, Marlene Hunt. "An Experiment in Welfare Capitalism: The Health Care Services of the Tennessee Coal, Iron and Railroad Company." Ph.D. diss., University of Alabama, 1983.

Roberts, Francis. "William Manning Lowe and the Greenback Party in Alabama." *Alabama Review* 5 (1952): 100–121.

Roediger, David. *The Wages of Whiteness: Race and the Making of the American Working Class.* London: Verso, 1991.

Rogers, William Warren. *The One-Gallused Rebellion: Agrarianism in Alabama, 1865–1896.* Baton Rouge: Louisiana State University Press, 1970.

Rogers, William Warren, Robert David Ward, Leah Rawls Atkins, and Wayne Flynt. *Alabama: The History of a Deep South State.* Tuscaloosa: University of Alabama Press, 1994.

Roy, Andrew. *A History of the Coal Miners of the United States.* 3rd ed. Columbus, Ohio: J. L. Trauger, 1907.

Scruggs, Frank P. "Coal in Alabama." Montgomery: Alabama Energy Management Board, 1974.

Seltzer, Curtis. *Fire in the Hole: Miners and Managers in the American Coal Industry.* Lexington: University of Kentucky Press, 1985.

Shapiro, Karen A. *A New South Rebellion: The Battle against Convict Labor in the*

Tennessee Coalfields, 1871–1896. Chapel Hill: University of North Carolina Press, 1998.

Shotts, Reynold Q. "Some Significant Recent Changes in the Pattern of Coal Production and Markets in Alabama." *Journal of the Alabama Academy of Science* 33 (April 1962): 62–82.

Singer, Alan J. "'Something of a Man': John L. Lewis, the UMWA, and the CIO, 1919–1943." In *The United Mine Workers of America: A Model of Industrial Solidarity?* ed. John H. M. Laslett. University Park: Pennsylvania State University, 1996.

Spero, Sterling D., and Abram L. Harris. *The Black Worker: The Negro and the Labor Movement.* 3rd ed. New York: Atheneum, 1968.

Stein, Judith. "Southern Workers in National Unions: Birmingham Steelworkers, 1936–1951." In *Organized Labor in the Twentieth Century South,* ed. Robert Zieger. Knoxville: University of Tennessee Press, 1991.

Straw, Richard A. "The Collapse of Biracial Unionism: The Alabama Coal Strike of 1908." *Alabama Historical Quarterly* 37 (Summer 1975): 92–114.

———. "Soldiers and Miners in a Strike Zone: Birmingham, 1908." *Alabama Review* 38 (October 1985): 289–308.

———. "'This Is Not a Strike, It Is Only a Revolution': The Birmingham Miners' Struggle for Power, 1894–1908." Ph.D. diss., University of Missouri, Columbia, 1980.

Studdard, Clarence G. "History of Moss and McCormack Coal Mines and Their Employees at the Howard Mines." Birmingham, ca. 1990.

Taft, Philip. *The A.F.L. in the Time of Gompers.* New York: Harper, 1957.

———. *Organizing Dixie: Alabama Workers in the Industrial Era.* Westport, Conn.: Greenwood Press, 1981.

Tarbell, Ida M. *The Life of Elbert H. Gray: The Story of Steel.* New York: Appleton and Company, 1925.

Trotter, Joe W., Jr. "Class and Racial Inequality: The Southern West Virginia Black Coal Miners' Response." In *Organized Labor in the Twentieth-Century South,* ed. Robert Zieger. Knoxville: University of Tennessee Press, 1991.

Vance, Rupert B. *Human Geography of the South.* Chapel Hill: University of North Carolina Press, 1932.

Walker, James H. *The Struggle and the Joy: An American Coal Town, Piper, Alabama.* Birmingham: Birmingham Public Library Press, 1993.

Ward, Robert David, and William Warren Rogers. *Convicts, Coal, and the Banner Mine Tragedy.* Tuscaloosa: University of Alabama Press, 1987.

———. *Labor Revolt in Alabama: The Great Strike of 1894.* University: University of Alabama Press, 1965.

Wiebel, Arthur W. *Biography of a Business.* Birmingham: Tennessee Coal, Iron, and Railroad Co., 1960.

Woodrum, Robert H. "Confronting Coal: The Carter Administration and the 1977–78 Strike." Paper presented to "The Carter Presidency: Policy Choices in the Post–New Deal Era," Jimmy Carter Library and Presidential Center, Atlanta, Feb. 20, 1997.

———. "Reforming Dixie: Alabama Coal Miners and Rank-and-File Rebellion in The United Workers of America, 1963–1978." Master's thesis, Georgia State University, 1997.

Woodward, C. Vann. *Origins of the New South.* Baton Rouge: Louisiana State University Press, 1951.

Worthman, Paul B. "Black Workers and Labor Unions in Birmingham, Alabama, 1897–1904." *Labor History* 10 (Summer 1969): 383–95.

Zieger, Robert H.. *The CIO, 1935–1955.* Chapel Hill: University of North Carolina Press, 1955.

———, ed. *Organized Labor in the Twentieth-Century South.* Knoxville: University of Tennessee Press, 1991.

———. *Southern Labor in Transition, 1940–1995.* Knoxville: University of Tennessee Press, 1997.

Contributors

Peter Alexander is senior lecturer in sociology and industrial sociology at Rand Afrikaans University in South Africa. He has a Ph.D. from London University, and until recently he was a research fellow at Oxford University, where he was working on the comparative history of mine workers in Alabama and the Transvaal. He is the author of *Racism, Resistance, and Revolution* (1987), and a new book, *Workers, War, and the Origins of Apartheid*, is forthcoming.

Edwin L. Brown is associate professor of labor studies at the University of Alabama at Birmingham. He is the author of two books, *The Painting Craftsman* (1983) and *The Brotherhood of Carpenters in Alabama* (1987). His current research topics include analysis of multinational labor relations and collective bargaining outcomes in the United States.

Colin J. Davis is associate professor of history at the University of Alabama at Birmingham. He is author of *Power at Odds: The 1922 National Railroad Shopmens Strike* (1997). He is currently working on a comparative study of New York City and London dockworkers entitled *Revolt on the Waterfront*.

Glenn Feldman is assistant professor at the Center for Labor Education and Research at the University of Alabama at Birmingham. He received his Ph.D. in history from Auburn University in 1996. Feldman is the author of *Politics, Society, and the Klan in Alabama, 1915–1949*, forthcoming from the University of Alabama Press. He is also the author of *From Demagogue to*

Dixiecrat: Horace Wilkinson and the Politics of Race (1995), and the editor of *Whistlin' Dixie: Essays on the South's Most Notable Historians* (forthcoming).

Brian Kelly is a lecturer in American history at the Queens University of Belfast, Northern Ireland. He received his doctoral degree from Brandeis University in 1997 and is the author of a forthcoming book in the University of Illinois Press series on The Working Class in American History, entitled *Up Against It: Race, Class, and Power in the Alabama Coalfields, 1908–1921.*

Daniel Letwin is associate professor of history at Pennsylvania State University. He is the author of *The Challenge of Interracial Unionism: Alabama Coal Miners, 1878–1921* (1998). He is currently working on a book entitled *The Specter of Social Equality: The Politics of Race in the Jim Crow Era.*

Robert H. Woodrum is pursuing a doctorate in history at Georgia State University in Atlanta. He received a master's degree from Georgia State in 1997.

Index

Adamsville, Ala., 31
Alabama Coal Operators Association (ACOA), 34, 38, 39, 53, 55–56, 58, 60
Alabama Fuel and Iron Company (AFI), 75, 78
Alabama Magazine, 94
Alabama Mining Institute, 63, 72, 104
Alabama Public Service Commission, 126
Alabama Sentinel, 18
Alabama State Docks, 112
Alabama State Federation of Labor, 25, 76
Alabama Surface Reclamation Council, 104
Alexander, Peter, 7
American Federation of Labor, 25, 77
Appalachian Agreement, 79
Appalachian Conference, 78
Arcadia, Ala., 30
Arnesen, Eric, 5
Avenguardia, L', 43

Baker, Lloyd (President District 20), 116–18
Baratz, Morton, 95
Baxley, Attorney General Bill, 108
Birmingham Age-Herald, 16, 20, 34, 45
Birmingham Labor Advocate, 23, 36, 38, 40, 44, 57, 70

Birmingham Negro American, 16
Birmingham News, 33–34, 103
Birmingham Reporter, 58
Birmingham Trades Council, 28
Bittner, Van, 60
Bituminous Coal Operators Association (BCOA), 9, 111, 114, 118–19, 124–25, 128–29
Black miners, 21, 42, 45–46; decline in numbers, 63–64, 82, 89, 99, 113; welfare capitalism, 52–53
Blocton, Ala., 17, 26, 30–32, 58, 61
Blossburg, Ala., 20–21, 31
Blue Creek, Ala., 17, 21, 30–31
Booker Heights, Ala., 63
Boothton, Ala., 85
Boyle, W. A. "Tony" (President of United Mine Workers Union), 106–7, 112
Brookside, Ala., 17, 21, 31
Brookwood, Ala., 17
Brown, Earl, 63–64, 68, 80, 82
Brown v. Board of Education, 8

Carbon Hill, Ala., 17
Cardiff, Ala., 17
Carmer, Carl, 49
Carter, Jimmy, 125–27
Cash, W. J., 6
Cayton, Horace, 81–82

Coalburg, Ala., 17, 21, 31
Coalfields, 11, 63, 84–85
Comer, Governor Braxton Bragg, 34–37
Commissary ("pluck me's"), 2, 25; segre-
    gated, 66, 88
Communist Party, 76, 80
Company guards, 33, 35. See also Evic-
    tions
Company spies, 51. See also Wooten,
    Billy
Company union ("popsicle"), 89
Congress of Industrial Organization
    (CIO), 76, 91
Convicts, 22
Cordova, Ala., 17, 30, 70, 87
Corinth, Ala., 87
Corona, Ala., 17
Cotton Belt, 42

Davis-Kelly Coal Bill, 69
DeBardeleben, Charles, 76–77
DeBardeleben, Charles, Jr., 77
DeBardeleben, Henry F., 18–20, 75–76
DeBardeleben Coal and Iron Company,
    18, 51, 56, 73
District 20, 1, 7, 17, 19, 23–25, 27–29,
    32, 38, 58, 62–63, 78, 82, 111–12,
    114, 118–20, 129
Dixon, Governor Frank M., 78
Docena, Ala., 86–88, 93
Dogwood, Ala., 70
Dolomite, Ala., 31
Drummond Coal Company, 101

Ellen, Henry, 17
Evictions: (1894), 20; (1904), 31;
    (1908), 33

Fair Labor Standards Act, 91
Feldman, Glenn, 8
Fink, Gary, 5
Flynt, Wayne, 94
Fuller, Charles (President of District 20),
    118, 120–22, 124

Gorgas, Ala., 87
Graves, Governor Bibb, 77, 80, 84
Greenback Labor Party, 7, 14–17
Guffey-Snyder Bill, 77
Gutman, Herbert, 5

Hagler, Carey, 94
Hargrove, George (President of District
    20), 62
Hayes, Frank, 77
Hill, Herbert, 5
Honey, Michael, 5
Horse Creek, Ala., 30

International Union of Operating Engi-
    neers, 101, 103
Interracialism, 16–18; organizational divi-
    sions, 27–28; sexual side, 29, 34; soli-
    darity, 60; 1930s, 80–81; working to-
    gether, 92–94

Jasper, Ala., 58, 70
Jim Crow, 27–28, 42
Jim Walter Resources, 102, 116, 125
Job satisfaction, 90
Jones, Governor Thomas G., 20, 22
Jones, Walter (Organizer District 20), 71–
    72

Kelley, Robin, 5
Kelly, Brian, 7
Kennamer, J. R. (President of District
    20), 3, 36
Kilby, Governor Thomas, 58–59, 61, 80
Knights of Labor, 14–17
Ku Klux Klan, 42, 58, 80, 91

Labor Advocate, 4
Labor subcontractor, 26
Letwin, Daniel, 6
Lewis, John L., 68, 74, 77–79, 106
Lewis, Ronald, 113
Littlefield, Sam (President of District
    20), 108, 118

Littleton, Ala., 30
Living conditions, 12; camp life, 64–65; housing, 68, 89; sanitation, 46; segregation, 15–16

Maylene, Ala., 58
McKiven, Henry, 5
Mechanization, 98–99, 102–3, 113
Militia (1908), 3, 36
Miller, Arnold (President of United Mine Workers Union), 106–8, 112, 115–16, 125
Miller, Governor Benjamin, 73–75, 80
Mine, Mill and Smelter Workers Union, 76, 91
Mine Safety and Health Act, 105
Mineral Springs, Ala., 30
Miners for Democracy, 116
Mitch, William (President of District 20), 70, 73–74, 76–79
Mitchell, George, 81–82

National Guard, 22; (1908), 33; (1933), 73, 74–77; (1977), 123
National Industrial Recovery Act, 69–70, 77
National Labor Relations Board, 79
National Recovery Administration, 72
New Deal, 7
New South, 11, 40, 43
Nixon, Richard, 107
Norrell, Robert, 5, 113

Oates, Governor William C., 22
Operators, coal, 38–39; recruitment of blacks, 43–45; tight control, 48; racial strategy, 58–59; 1970s, 118

Park, Thomas Duke, 2
Parrish, Ala., 87
Paternalism, 53, 55–56, 64
Patterson, Governor John, 99
Pensions, 101
Perry, Charles, 99

Planters, 40–42, 45
Powderly, Ala., 15
Pratt City, Ala., 17, 20–22, 25, 87–88
Pratt Coal Company, 30
Pratt Consolidated, 51, 53

Race, 4–5, 12; mines segregated, 65; miners segregated and sharing, 66–67
Race baiting, 59; newspapers, 61
Reed, Mel, 5
Rogers, William, 5
Roosevelt, Franklin Delano, 8, 69, 72, 77–80, 84, 90, 100

Safety, 68, 83; accidents, 100, 105–6; black lung, 87–88, 95, 104; explosions, 85–86; rock falls, 86–87
Savage Creek, Ala., 85
Sayreton, Ala., 31
Scrip (clacker), 1, 6, 88. See also Commissary
Seymour, Ala., 58
Shortcamp, Ala., 87
Sipsey, Ala., 43, 55
Sorsby, Joe (Vice-President District 20), 60
South Africa, 108, 112–13
Southern Company, 108, 112
Southern Metal Trades Association, 57
Southern Research Institute, 96
State surveillance, 120. See also Wooten, Billy
State troopers, 119; special operations team, 121, 123
Steel Workers Organizing Committee (SWOC), 77
Stewart, John (President of District 20), 125
Strikebreakers: African-Americans, 18, 20; killed, 22; 1904 strike, 31; 1908 strike, 33–34
Striker violence, 73; 1949 strike, 94; 1977–1978 strike, 119, 122–23, 127
Strikes: (1890), 17; (1894), 19–23;

(1897), 24; (1903), 30; (1904), 31;
(1908), 32–33; (1933–1934), 73–75;
(1935), 77; (1974), 108–9
Strip-mining, 103–4, 113
Sumpter, Ala., 58, 65
Survey, 38, 45

Taft, Philip, 5, 53
Taft-Hartley Act, 125–28
Tennessee Coal and Iron Company
(TCI), 17, 20, 22, 24, 32, 44, 46–
48, 51–52, 59–60, 63, 78–79, 85
Tennessee Valley Authority (TVA), 95,
126
Townley, Ala., 70
Trevellick, Ala., 15
Turner Town, Ala., 70

United Mine Workers of Alabama, 19
United Mine Workers Journal, 23, 33, 37,
54, 62
United States Bureau of Mines, 105. *See
also* Safety
United States Labor Department, 59
U.S. Steel, 47, 88, 101
United Steelworkers of America, 91

Wages, 25, 56; (1933), 72, 74; (1935),
78; (1949), 94
Wallace, Governor George, 119–23, 126–
27
Walter Resources. *See* Jim Walter Re-
sources
Ward, Robert, 5
Warrior, Ala., 17–18
Washington, Booker T., 58, 100
Welfare capitalism, 47, 49–52, 55, 57
Whipping boss (shack rouster), 2, 53–54
Women: attitudes to black neighbors, 93;
miners, 113–14
Women's auxiliary, 34
Woodrum, Robert, 9
Wooten, Billy, 120–21
Working conditions, 12–13, 23, 26. *See
also* Safety
Workmen's Chronicle, 59
World War I, 56
World War II, 90–91
Wylam, Ala., 58, 61

Yablonski, Joseph A. "Jock," 106

Zieger, Robert, 5, 90